Manufacturing the Enemy

By the same author

Voices From the Other Side;
An Oral History of Terrorism Against Cuba

Cuba Under Siege

Manufacturing the Enemy

The Media War Against Cuba

Keith Bolender

PLUTO PRESS

To Rose and Reg
Wish you were here

First published 2019 by Pluto Press
345 Archway Road, London N6 5AA

www.plutobooks.com

British Library Cataloguing in Publication Data
A catalogue record for this book is available from the British Library

ISBN 978 0 7453 4028 9 Hardback
ISBN 978 0 7453 4026 5 Paperback
ISBN 978 1 7868 0568 3 PDF eBook
ISBN 978 1 7868 0570 6 Kindle eBook
ISBN 978 1 7868 0569 0 EPUB eBook

This book is printed on paper suitable for recycling and made from fully managed and sustained forest sources. Logging, pulping and manufacturing processes are expected to conform to the environmental standards of the country of origin.

Typeset by Stanford DTP Services, Northampton, England

Simultaneously printed in the United Kingdom and United States of America

Contents

Acknowledgments

A project such as this requires the assistance and support of a great many people. I would like to recognize those who have played an important part in the completion of this work. John Kirk for his immediate and consistent support, Noam Chomsky, Heriberto Nicolas, Karen Lee Wald, Raul Verrier, Fernando González, Yamil and Sandra and everyone at ICAP have provided invaluable information and assistance. As well as everyone else in Cuba, who have offered their encouragement and expertise. A special thanks to all the Cuban Five for their time. I'd like also to particularly thank Pluto Press for their interest and support, once again, of my work. Thanks to David Castle for his enthusiasm and Thérèse Wassily Saba for her editorial expertise and improvements. To friends and family, a special appreciation. And of course without the patience and encouragement of Magalita, this could not be possible.

Introduction

When Fidel Castro and his idealistic band of revolutionaries emerged triumphant in the early days of 1959, the United States soon determined that this nationalist movement could not be tolerated. American hegemony over Cuba, which they had maintained over the previous 60 years, was being threatened, and as Fidel Castro began implementing his new social/economic order, policies for regime change were implemented.

A variety of methods were unleashed to destroy the revolution. Isolation, restrictions preventing American citizens from traveling to Cuba, hundreds of acts of terrorism against civilian and commercial targets, an economic blockade with extra-territorial application, assassination attempts against Castro and other leadership figures, even an exile-led invasion were all utilized. In one form or the other, aspects of this siege against Cuba continue to this day.[1]

One of the longest-standing expressions of this antagonism derives from an institution usually recognized as separate from the state in a modern liberal democracy—that of an independent press. In fact, the mass media has enthusiastically endorsed the government's counter-revolutionary objectives to end Cuba's socialist experiment and force the country to return into America's embrace. The media's role has been foremost to propagandize the revolution in the most negative forms, resulting in the normalization of the demonization of the Cuban revolution and its supporters. Media has led the inexorable march toward creating a critical narrative that does not stand up to honest scrutiny.

Misinformation has been responsible for the preponderance of negative myths about Cuba. When myth replaces history, facts become immaterial to rational discussion. It is the means by which the worst charges against revolutionary society are believed and any attempt at authentic examination is denied. Corporate media's single-mindedness has been well served.

After an initial honeymoon period when the press was inclined to portray Castro and the revolutionaries in a relatively sympathetic form, in contrast to the universally loathed dictatorship of Fulgencio Batista, the tone turned dark. America had expected reform from Castro; instead, he gave them revolution. Once Fidel Castro started making good on his promises—which inevitably confronted American imperial interests—there was little doubt how public opinion would be shifted. Less than a year after the triumph and ever since, the most influential national media outlets have attempted to frame the Cuban Revolution as an unmitigated failure, a social evil that had done nothing positive for the people. Every mistake has been amplified, every misstep condemned as proof of the inadequacies of the movement. Every success diminished or ignored, every gain criticized in a self-constructed comparison that continually holds Cuba up to a higher standard few other nations are subjected to.

According to the rhetorical trappings the mainstream media has utilized for the past 50 years, little benefit has emerged from the revolution, while all shortfalls are solely the responsibility of the system—rarely putting into context the impact America's non-stop strategy of regime change has had on the island government's well-documented shortcomings. A self-imposed censorship has been applied so as not to disseminate essential information regarding this unrelenting hostility against Cuba, nor to provide background to America's historic imperial designs. Remarkably, the lack of self-awareness of this reality often reaches top government spokespeople, including President Donald Trump's press secretary Sarah Huckabee Sanders, who claimed in 2018 that the United States does not, "get to dictate how other countries operate."[2] It might be worthwhile to let the Cubans in on that revelation.

Media developed its Cuba posture in obedience to Washington's designation of the revolution as illegitimate. Once the ruling elites came out in bipartisan voice declaring Fidel Castro an enemy, the press went about slanting its coverage in conformity with foreign policy objectives. Destabilization, subversion and economic warfare have been the tools of regime change policy used by the US government; the media has willingly helped forge them. There was no effort to examine the revolution as a popular expression of true Cuban nationalism. The only explanation provided was one that alleged Fidel Castro was a master manipulator who had duped the Cuban people down the path to anti-Americanism, and then worse, communism. Consequently, politicians and media refused to understand the historical roots for revolution, as they could not admit it was United States' hegemony over Cuba that formed much of its basis. The dictator Batista might have been the lightning rod, but the storm against neo-colonialism had been brewing long before. Fidel Castro was the tempest that swept it all away.

Taking up the anti-American label became standard coverage as relations between the two former friends worsened. When the revolution moved into the Soviet Union sphere,[3] all the press needed was to put the word 'communist' in front of Cuba and everyone recognized the adverse implications. There was no longer any question as to the media's coverage of the island nation. It didn't matter what was being reported—from politics, tourism, health care or sports—if it was about Cuba, then editorial boardrooms across America would set parameters establishing how much positive and negative treatment would be standardized—and in the clear majority it was deleterious. Articles regarding new tourist facilities would invariably include denigrating observations of the lack of amenities. Cuba's international success in sports would turn to athletes 'defecting'; universal health care would inform at length the deficiencies in infrastructure; attempts at creating housing disparaged by emphasizing the lack of resources.[4] Little credited, much discredited.

A favorite ploy of the media is to offer expert opinions on how to fix the serious economic problems Cuba faces, while consistently ignoring America's debilitating economic embargo. A number of national outlets reported on the Brookings Institute's comprehensive 2018 study on Cuba's economy and the measures needed to improve it; the report not once mentioned the impact of US restrictions.[5] Brookings is one of a handful of influential think-tanks that both state and media elite defer to when either developing foreign policies or reporting in support of them. If the embargo (referred to as a "blockade" in Cuba for its extra-territorial economic, financial and commercial application) is mentioned, it is often to offer dubious justifications as to why it should remain, as in the 2014 editorial by the *Washington Post*.[6] And when reporting on Cuba's political structure, there is no effort to disguise the contempt the media holds with what is invariably described as a "non-democratic" system because it does not conform to capitalist imposed definitions.[7]

This bias has been apparent since the earliest days of the revolution. Following Fidel Castro's nationalization of farmland and industrial property, condemnation was based on the supposed lack of compensation. Conveniently ignored in the press was that the Cuban government offered payment, a proposal that was refused on the orders of the US government.[8] Thanks to the media's calculated withholding of the facts, to this day the perception is that the property was confiscated illegally, that Cuba owes billions in reparations.[9] Fidel Castro's move into the Soviet Union sphere in the 1960s can be considered a consequence of the regime change policies that included the embargo and America's strong-arming other nations not to do business with Cuba.[10] None of this has ever been covered in any depth. There was virtually no news of Havana's constant complaints to Washington to prevent the illegal overflights of Florida-based Brothers to the Rescue (BTTR) during the rafter crises of 1996. When Cuba took action and shot down two small aircrafts after more than a dozen incursions over national airspace, the only reporting would lead one to believe it was an unprovoked attack based on a single incident.[11] A consumer of mainstream media would also be hard pressed to discover that the head of Brothers to the Rescue, José Basulto, has a long history of terrorist acts against Cuban civilian targets.[12] After five Cuban intelligence agents were sent to infiltrate BTTR and other anti-revolutionary groups based in South Florida to try and prevent future acts of terrorism, the only reaction from the press was condemning the Cuban Five as spies deserving of their unjustly long sentences. As an outcome of the case, it was revealed that a number of high profile journalists from the *Miami Herald* and the Spanish-language version *Nuevo Herold* were paid by the US government to write damaging reports leading up to the trial, while at the same time conducting anti-Cuban propaganda on Miami-based Radio Televisión Martí.[13] According to Florida-based media critic Álvaro

Fernández, this breech of journalistic ethics helped ensure the Five would have no chance at a fair trial in Miami.

> They were doing stories for Radio and TV Marti[14] at the same time they were writing for the Herald on the same subject. Any American journalist worth his weight knows you've crossed a line if you are being paid by the government to write stories with a particular slant.[15]

Under the Office of Cuba Broadcasting (OCB), Radio Televisión Martí has cost US taxpayers millions since the 1980s, when the Reagan administration permitted the distribution of propaganda into Cuba. The anti-revolutionary media outlets have previously faced charges of misappropriation of funds and mismanagement.[16] It also seems that Radio Televisión Martí does not limit its propaganda solely against Cuba. A report by *Mother Jones* indicated that a negative video segment in May 2018 against liberal George Soros was produced by the US-funded network. Soros, described in the report as a "multimillionaire Jew" and "the architect of the financial collapse of 2008" was portrayed as a threat to Latin American democracy.[17] Other examples of when media and state directly converge include the now defunct magazine *Encounter*, an internationally influential publication that consistently supported US foreign policy dictates during the coups in Iran 1953, Guatemala in 1954 and Chile in 1971. The magazine, which folded in 1991, turned out to be a US and British intelligence asset, with the CIA directly subsidizing the editorial staff. It was one of many CIA-financed media outlets designed to advance US interests to an unsuspecting readership.[18]

The national media in the majority acceded to the *Miami Herald*'s analysis of the Cuban Five, one example of the paper's influence on the national press when it comes to Cuba. According to Fernández, whose blog *Progreso Weekly/Progreso Seminal* examines the paper's one-sided Cuban coverage, "So much of mainstream media look to the Herald as the outlet that provides the best, most 'expert' coverage on Cuba. And the Herald has always been anti-Castro." If the press was doing its job, Fernández noted, it would expose the violent background of anti-revolutionaries like Basulto, and report on the necessity of the country to protect itself from Cuban-American terrorists, including those responsible for the bombing of Cubana Airlines in 1976 that killed 73 passengers. This unknown history of terrorism that has claimed more than 3,000 civilian deaths in Cuba remains in a deep informational black hole.[19]

The consistency in which coverage of Cuba has contained so many negative qualifiers, while ostensibly providing non-judgmental reporting, indicates a conscious decision on the part of journalists and editors to ensure the consumer is exposed to a distorted perspective of the subject material regardless of the facts. Or as Warren Hinkle, a columnist for the *San Francisco Examiner* (a Hearst syndicate paper), once commented: "It's a journalist axiom that if it's anti-Cuba, it has to be true."[20]

Truth has little role to play in Cuban coverage. But one example occurred when a fact-free article was rapidly turned into accepted evidence in 2015 with a report on Cuban military in Syria. Both *Fox News* and *Daily Beast* claimed hundreds of Cuban military personnel were assisting Bashar al-Assad in the country's civil war. The report was substantial in details and expert opinion. The only thing lacking was evidence.[21] That didn't stop the lie from spreading across both traditional and social media, even reaching into the presidential election campaign when GOP candidate Ted Cruz echoed the claim to millions on *Meet the Press*:

> There're a couple hundred Cubans right now with a major Cuban general fighting in the Syrian civil war. You've got Iran. You've got General Suleimani in bed with the Russians. So you now got Russia, Cuba and Iran all arm in arm.[22]

Cruz's statement was shockingly revealing—and entirely untrue.

Sourcing the article revealed how the facts could be so far removed from reality. *Fox News* simply used an ideologically driven professor from the counter-revolutionary Institute for Cuban and Cuban-American Studies at the University of Miami who wrote a page-long study based on hearsay, and one anonymous US official supposedly confirming the misinformation. As far as any journalistic investigation went, none was apparently needed in accordance with Hinkle's dictum.

Matt Peppe at *Common Dreams* exposed the complete lack of media integrity in his piece: "The Imaginary Cuban Troops in Syria." Peppe revealed:

> The source at the Miami Institute indicated that, an Arab military officer at the Damascus airport reportedly witnessed two Russian planes arrive there with Cuban military personnel on board. When the officer questioned the Cubans, they told him they were there to assist Assad because they are experts at operating Russian tanks. It is unclear what nationality the "Arab" officer was. Perhaps said Arab determined the people aboard the Russian plane were Cubans because he saw them smoking cigars and drinking mojitos. The Cuban soldiers then volunteered—supposedly—they were "there to assist Assad" because of their expertise manning Russian tanks. However improbable this may seem to an unbiased observer, the source from the Miami Institute said that: "it doesn't surprise me."[23]

Peppe's account further exposed how flimsy the story was:

> And what about this anonymous "US official" who "confirmed" the report? They provide no photos, no video, no keyhole satellites, little specifics and little additional details beyond that which was fed to them in the Institute's report. Put simply: There's no indication that their "intelligence" was anything other than the report itself.[24]

Neither *Fox News* nor the other outlets ever rescinded or corrected this complete fabrication. The propaganda ranked right up there with former US ambassador to the United Nations John Bolton's spurious, baseless claim that the Cuban government was developing biological weapons,[25] prior to the invasion of Iraq and when the American population was still hyper-sensitive from 9/11.

There are hundreds of instances of how the press renounces basic journalistic practices when covering Cuba. When does a pattern demonstrate bias? It is most often a legal question but applicable to the topic of this work. The media has consistently published assumptions and misinformation regarding Cuba that reveals an overwhelmingly negative viewpoint. There has been little challenge to those suppositions, and this abrogation represents the media's greatest influence. Consumers have scant opportunity to contradict the Cuban narrative as there is almost no other viewpoint provided. Media's symbiotic relationship with the consumer is built on trust, a condition taken full advantage of, to the point of abuse, by the press that apparently has no intention of altering its perceptions of Cuba—regardless of the facts.

Information published is at all times based on a decision-making process—and, in the case of covering the island nation, there is no formula other than ensuring all adverse aspects are highlighted. The default position is to give priority to news that shows the country's social/economic make-up in the most disadvantageous light. It doesn't exclude the possibility of affirmative or fair reporting on Cuba, but within those articles, no matter how innocuous the subject, are found modifiers that attempt to diminish any of the positive characteristics of the topic. Additionally, standard techniques that contain anti-revolutionary markers along with actual misinformation are consistently included. Internationally renowned author and political activist Noam Chomsky described the media's attitude toward Cuba succinctly, "you can cut the hostility with a knife."[26]

A report on Cuba opening its first wholesale food outlet for former state-run restaurants converted to cooperatives was covered by *Fox News* in March 2018. The headline smirked: "Watch Out, Costco: First Bulk Store Opens in Communist Cuba."

Within the content of the article, a Cuban shopper was quoted, "The place is pretty, the service is good, but it's still the same price as retail. In truth, it doesn't resolve our problems," Carrazana said. "I hope this is like a seed for a wholesale market where we entrepreneurs can buy at a different price."[27] The reader would have no opportunity to verify the statement regarding pricing. If able to, it would be discovered it was not true.

Among the products sold by the wholesale market Mercabal are different varieties of beans, cigars, soft drinks, beers, as well as sugar, salt, jams, chicken, hamburgers and sausages, at a discounted price of 20 percent from the retail price as applied. Chicken is discounted by 30 percent.[28] Havana resident Maria Garcia confirmed the discounted pricing for wholesale merchants, who have to prove ownership of a private restaurant to purchase from the outlet. "I was there, saw the pricing and anyone who says they are the same as retail is not telling the truth."[29]

As the reader in the Fox article was only provided with information from a source who was either unaware of the actual pricing and structure of the new wholesale outlet, or was intentionally concealing accurate information that was not verified by the reporter, the only logical conclusion that could be reached was that the wholesale market was a waste of time and yet another example of the ineptitude of the country's bureaucracy. The headline itself, by including the descriptive "Communist" in front of Cuba would ensure the consumer would undoubtedly internalize all the derogatory implications associated with the designation even before getting to the article. There is no label other than "Communist" that creates such deeply rooted negative connotations within the American psyche. On the same page, *Fox News* ran a story regarding Saudi Arabia, but there was no headline labeling the country as an "Islamic Fundamentalist Medieval Monarchy."[30] The intent of the inclusion of a qualifier in one and the omission in the other is to lead the reader into predisposed value judgments on the subject matter. It is how the press utilizes the trust inherent in its relationship with the consumer in order to manipulate facts and create unchallengeable misrepresentations and falsehoods.

Journalist and media expert on Cuba Karen Lee Wald commented:

> The media never fails to remind everyone that Cuba is supposedly still communist, and that just puts all the critical aspects of that term out there. The media doesn't put "capitalist" in front of England on headlines about that country, but Cuba is an official enemy, so it has to be mentioned always. It's a way to slant the news against Cuba no matter the subject.[31]

Those descriptions establish the parameters to internalize positive or negative assessments based on preconditioned standards. Saudi Arabia's new monarch Muhammad bin Salman is described as a "benevolent autocrat,"[32] while Venezuelan's democratically elected president Nicolás Maduro is labeled a "dictator."[33] One is an ally of the USA, the other is not—with the media reinforcing the government's foreign policy designations.

Mainstream media has a long history of establishing who receives the dictator term and who doesn't. Egyptian leader General Abdel Fattah el-Sisi, who came to power in a 2003 coup, recently announced his intention to rule until 2034. A *New York Times* article commented that this would "further entrench his authoritarian rule" while recognizing he had jailed thousands of opponents and taken over the courts. The article, however, was completely absent of any description of this US ally as a dictator.[34]

When characterizations emanate from the so-called liberal media, it has an even greater effect. As Wald stresses that while Fox's ideological perspective is easy to disseminate, it is the supposed "liberal" media such as *The New Yorker* that can create a greater negative impression on those the USA has designated anti-American, such as Cuba. The reader is more readily willing to believe the misinformation as it tends to include more aspects of the truth from a source with a reputation for balance and left-leaning sympathies, she says. "It's like walking through a field of beautiful wildflowers not knowing where the landmines are."[35]

A textbook example occurred with Nicolas Kristof's column in the *New York Times* addressing Cuba's enviable health care program in comparison to the United States. While being overall balanced and often positive, including legitimate critique of the deficiencies in the system, Kristof couldn't resist opening the article with unrelated misrepresentations and criticism.

The first two paragraphs set the tone:

> Claudia Fernández, 29, is an accountant whose stomach bulges with her first child, a girl, who is due in April.
>
> Fernández lives in a cramped apartment on a potholed street and can't afford a car. She also gets by without a meaningful vote or the right to speak freely about politics. Yet the paradox of Cuba is this: Her baby appears more likely to survive than if she were born in the United States.[36]

What her living arrangement, the road condition or electoral choice has to do with health care is not explained because it is meaningless, except to be in compliance with establishing a negative narrative of Cuba before reporting anything constructive. Kristof's economic description could apply to many parts of America and most developing nations. His political criticism is pointless; Fernández has the unrestricted right to participate in the electoral process in Cuba; as do US citizens under their system. If they choose not to, it's also their right, the vote is meaningful if utilized. But the implication is that Cuba's political system is of no value unless altered to American rules—even if those rules include a structure where the presidential candidate with the least amount of votes wins the election (the definition of "getting by without a meaningful vote"). No one stops her from speaking freely about politics, unless she's being paid by the USA to promote regime change. In many aspects, Cubans are more involved in political dialogue; the nation-wide referendum on the new constitution is but one illustration.[37] So a positive article about health care was strewn with the landmines of distortion and bias. It goes without saying that the column made no mention of the American embargo's effect on the challenges Cuba faces with shortages of supplies and medicines. To do so would have introduced a contextual element to those historic denigrations that remain a foundational element in mainstream media's subjective coverage of Cuba.

Wald also points to the writings of Jon Lee Anderson, whose bio on Che Guevara and in many of his other Cuban articles,

> are supposed to be objective but the lies and innuendos are so cleverly intermixed with good, true points that it is impossible for those who don't know a lot about what's going on to see them, and for those who do see what's wrong to refute all of them.[38]

She adds that Anderson, considered to be a moderate when it comes to covering Cuba,

> has access to millions of readers, and none of us have a possibility of reaching even a fraction of that number to unspin the spin. And the spin is still there. But the lies and innuendos are so

cleverly intermixed with good, true points,[39] that it's difficult to separate fact from fiction.

The *Washington Times* remains the most stringent proponent of right-wing ideology, while *Fox News* is basically the media arm of the Republican Party. The two are consistently negative in their coverage of Cuba. But even the most recognized of the left-leaning national newspapers, including the *New York Times, Los Angeles Times, Washington Post* and *Chicago Tribune* reliably show an anti-Cuba partiality, as do the television networks that claim to represent the middle ground in the political spectrum—*MSNBC, CBS* and *CNN*. All reveal the same disregard, with varying degrees, toward recognizing America's historical imperial designs on Cuba and the realities of revolutionary society. Then it becomes no coincidence that the *Wall Street Journal* and the *New York Times*, the nation's two most pre-eminent newspapers representing the range of left and right viewpoints, carry the same adverse message about the island nation.

The result is that while the coverage may on the surface seem to be impartial, closer examination exposes the integral anti-Cuban spin that has predominated in press coverage throughout the revolutionary period; in fact, it existed well before Fidel Castro came on the scene.

In all the various forms, the mainstream media's unrelentingly deleterious coverage of Cuba has developed the one-sided narrative that has unfairly burdened all attempts at reconciliation between the two adversaries. The coverage has been exceptionally effective at shaping a warped version of revolutionary Cuba. Combined with the US-imposed travel restrictions still complicating the average American's ability to visit the island, the media has created a well-entrenched adverse perception that is difficult to challenge and even harder to overcome—except when an honest look at the facts is presented without preconceptions.

Questioning those preconceived ideas is a difficult task as long as the mainstream media remains the gatekeeper of information. This remains so, despite the modern fragmentation of how an individual receives the news through various social media and internet sites that can provide alternative perspectives. Some are not necessarily any less disingenuous but at least offer the ability to track down information that affords different and more nuanced points of view as well as background than the establishment press has neither the time nor inclination to offer. Regardless, corporate media retains an inordinate amount of weight when formulating opinions and value judgments, particularly in matters of foreign affairs. The average American consumer of news relies disproportionately on the major television networks and newspapers for information on those countries that the US government has designated friends or enemies, with less inclination to contest those classifications. As a result, the mass media has a freer hand to construct positive or negative narratives that most often fall in compliance with American government foreign policies, thereby becoming the handmaidens to the requirements of the ruling class.

When it comes to Cuba, it's the perfect convergence of propaganda—US strategy has been counter-revolutionary since the beginning, the press has supported that policy based on political and economic ideology, and the public has little chance to challenge those perceptions as travel restrictions prohibiting most Americans from visiting Cuba have been put in place for decades. The average US citizen has few opportunities, even if so inclined, to see first-hand if the media's anti-revolutionary coverage is based on any actuality of what is happening in the country. In the rare occasions when restrictions are eased, as when President Obama permitted individuals to travel to Cuba with few bureaucratic obstacles as part of his opening in 2014, that specific regulation was partially shuttered by President Trump three years later.[40] While the current president did not completely roll back the permission to travel, the island nation remains unduly complicated for US citizens to visit due to the regulations. Trump's ending of one of the legal categories permitting individual travel has had a harmful effect on the emerging private sectors of the Cuban economy, at the same time reducing the opportunity for face-to-face exchanges so important for examining the various myths and misperceptions of the revolution.[41] Part of the rationale for the president's roll-back, other than the craven surrender to Florida's hard-right Cuban-American community, was the fallout from the dubious "sonic attack" controversy. Since 2017, United States officials have claimed that several of their Havana embassy officials, including many CIA agents posing as diplomats, have suffered from health problems after being subjected to irritating noise levels. No assertion has ever been made that Cuba authorities have been responsible, and no tourists were affected. Regardless, the incident led Trump to reduce embassy staff by half and issue warnings against travel to Cuba.[42] The "sonic attacks" theory—now debunked as fake news—was initially promoted as an established fact by the mass media.[43]

As a consequence of the travel restrictions, the media has demonstrated little restraint in its consistently one-sided coverage of the island, secure in the knowledge it is in tacit alignment with US foreign policy goals, all the while providing analysis to a trusting consumer overwhelmingly unfamiliar with revolutionary Cuba. Add in the lack of information regarding Cuba's historic struggle for self-determination long before Castro's revolution,[44] and the result is that the media is able to offer up and have believed the most insidious distortions imaginable in what has to be considered one of the worst examples of the abrogation of acceptable journalistic standards. It makes the failings made while covering the lead up to the invasion of Iraq pale by comparison.

The media has consistently decided how Cuba should be treated: through the systematic dehumanization of the revolutionary leaders; the routine exaggeration of the country's military capabilities and international influence to spread revolution; and the disingenuous falsification of the attitudes of most Cubans living on the island. In addition, the press has long applied double standards to Cuba when comparing the inadequacies and difficulties facing any developing nation, unfailingly blaming the socialist nature of Cuba as the culprit in all economic problems; while conveniently denying the deficiencies capitalist third world countries face to similar if not greater degrees.

The biased coverage does not come by happenstance. Journalists and editors make a conscious decision regarding who to interview and what facts to include, thereby determining tone and intent of the information. Self-designated experts in American traditional and social media, academia and political spheres consistently discuss what Cuba will look like post-Castro—even though there is now no Castro in charge.[45] The vast majority of these opinions are presented from the standpoint of political transition and reconstruction of the economy—code words for regime change. Millions of US taxpayer dollars have been spent on such anti-revolutionary organizations as the Cuban American National Foundation, study groups Cuban Transition Project, US–CUBA Business Council and the development of government policies such as the Commission for Assistance to a Free Cuba, which goes so far as to dictate whom the Cubans can elect if the embargo is to be lifted.[46] Websites such as *Havana Times* promote a disingenuous perspective as a supporter of the Cuban people as long as they are most often anti-government, while consistently using regime change terminology and calling for the re-imposition of US-style capitalism. The media overwhelmingly utilizes these "experts" as primary source material, creating a foundational bias that is internalized as the accepted baseline for how the readership should negatively perceive the country. On rare occasions, in these speculations can be found the voices of those Cubans who support their government, who want change through national measures and not foreign impositions. Their opinion is neither sought nor valued in America's continued strategy of re-imposing hegemony.

North American political experts on Cuba invariable are preferred from the list of right-wing Cuban-American politicians such as Marco Rubio, who has never been to the island. Besides Rubio, the go to sources since the 1980s have been predominately anti-revolutionary politicians or their enablers in the academic and government circles, including agencies such as the Cuban American National Foundation. Florida-based Mario Diaz-Balart, Carlos Curbelo and Ileana Ros-Lehtinen round out the Cuban-American members of Congress who are consistently interviewed to promote the corporate media's well-established anti-Cuba agenda. Their quotes are rarely balanced with an opposing viewpoint. When it comes to mainstream media, those in power decide what information is fed through the portals and which are deemed inappropriate. That's why those Cuban-American "experts" are given priority. Anti-revolutionary information is presented to the public as acceptable material, while those pieces that may put the country in more contextual realities are often ignored.[47]

When Cuban nationals are interviewed, invariably they are "dissidents" or those within recognized anti-Castro viewpoints. Any who support the revolution and its social structure are rarely provided an opportunity to have their voice heard. Cuban coverage has predictably resulted in a narrow, ill-informed view of revolutionary society. Media chooses who to interview, whose story has importance and who will be ignored.

In their seminal work on media, *Manufacturing Consent*, Edward S. Herman and Noam Chomsky addressed the idea of how the press selects interviews, who become worthy and unworthy victims. The idea was expressed when a Polish priest murdered behind the Iron Curtain during the Cold War earned substantially more coverage than priests shot in Latin America by American-backed dictatorships. The Polish priest was the worthy victim, the Latin American priests unworthy.[48]

Cuban dissidents and anti-revolutionaries get coverage and credibility; those in support of Cuba are dupes of the regime according to the press: the worthy and unworthy. This makes it easy for the embargo, the history of terrorism and all other forms of American aggression against Cuba to be under-reported or completely ignored. Finding examples of the US mass media examining, let alone acknowledging, the impact of the embargo and other forms of hostility and the impact they have had are as rare as snowfall in Havana.

Corporate media is then able to manipulate the truth, not by what it tells but by what it doesn't. While not speaking directly about Cuba, US Senator Bernie Sanders addressed the condition in an article in *Our Revolution*:

> Media is not just about what is covered and how. It is about what is not covered. And those decisions, of what is and is not covered, are not made in the heavens. They are made by human beings who often have major conflicts of interest. As a general rule of thumb, the more important the issue is to large numbers of working people, the less interesting it is to corporate media.[49]

Cuba's well-documented and self-admitted mistakes in building a new society have been well reported in the media and are known to the general public. The facts regarding the country's social and economic accomplishments less so, thanks in large part to what news the media decides to disseminate, and which information it decides to withhold. Even seemingly innocuous articles, including those that have information beneficial to the United States consumer, often are disregarded or downplayed. In late March 2018, Cuba announced an agreement with an American company to produce and market the medication Herberprot-p. The Cuban developed drug has been used successfully to treat diabetic foot ulcers, a condition more than a million Americans suffer from. The Herberprot-p story garnered a considerable amount of coverage in Cuba and Latin America, and some low-level media notice in the United States. There was nothing in mainstream media.[50]

* * *

It is the intent of this work to demonstrate that Cuba's revolution and its socialist society had no chance of receiving anything close to fair treatment by the US corporate media. Using specific examples from the early days of the revolution up to the most current coverage to establish the one-sided perspective, the project will additionally determine that this history of unbalanced reporting (going back to the nineteenth century) is a reflection of the mass media's guiding purpose within United States society. America is the shining example of unfettered capitalism, and the for-profit establishment media is a vital component to promote, defend and justify the system. They are integral to it, survive because of it, and compromised by the bottom line, to the detriment of journalistic standards. The vast majority of its advertisers are corporations who by definition represent US-style capitalism and greatly influence the press in its promotion of American foreign policy goals. This multi-billion-dollar media industry, of which 90 percent is controlled by just six corporations,[51] has a reactive negativism to any ideology that is determined to be anti-capitalism—whether it is or not.[52] The basic tenant of journalism integrity—fairness—is often thrown to the wayside as media's primary goal now is the shareholder's wealth, not what is in the best interest of the consumer or society. Media critic website *Project Censored* succinctly described the relationship: "Corporate media have become a monolithic power structure that serves the interests of empire, war, and capitalism."[53]

It is then but an easy matter to template socialist Cuba as deserving of nothing more than constant fabrication and propaganda. Cuba's social/economic system was targeted not only for its anti-American stance, but also because policy makers and media required the revolution to fail in large part to ensure it did not become a role model for other developing nations to emulate. Defying US imperialism could not go unpunished.[54]

President Donald Trump calls the media the "enemy of the people," his rhetoric is based on self-serving interests he deems are being challenged by the press. While his target is wrong, the aim has some merit. The media often reflects the opposite of what the majority support, in favor of corporate objectives.

As Paul Street wrote in *Truthdig*:

> The dominant U.S. commercial and corporate media are a means of mass consent-manufacturing indoctrination, diversion and dumbing down on behalf of the nation's intertwined corporate, financial, imperial and professional-class "elites." Merging the dystopian visions of Aldous Huxley, George Orwell, Ray Bradbury, Neal Postman and Phillip K. Dick, they are a bastion of power-serving propaganda and deadening twaddle that work across hundreds of broadcast channels and through countless print and internet outlets to keep the U.S. citizenry allegiant and subordinated to big capital, the professional and managerial "elite" and the U.S. imperial state.[55]

A reliable social axiom states that other news outlets in countries deemed to be anti-American are "state controlled" or "government run." Corporate media standardizes this concept at the same time as refusing to acknowledge its own complicity in support of Washington's foreign policy objectives, regardless of public opinion.

Historic examples abound demonstrating this compliance. The theoretical separation between state and media was relinquished dramatically during the lead-up to President George Bush Jr.'s invasion of Iraq. The mass media from both the left and right with few exceptions became nothing more than lapdogs rather than watchdogs, unquestionably parroting the dubious rationales leadership presented to the public to justify the unprovoked attack on a sovereign nation.[56] Despite the majority of public opinion objecting to the war, the media became stenographers faithfully prostrating itself to the informational disbursement requirements of the government in order to promote the invasion. Possibly the most infamous failure of the media came when the propaganda reports of Iraqi soldiers pulling Kuwaiti babies from incubators and killing them was swallowed whole by the press, publishing the false claims without any fact-checking. The reporting helped sway public opinion to initially support President Bush Jr.'s illegal invasion. Only recently has the press attempted to claim otherwise.[57]

Concerning foreign policy, the media has shown a readiness to fall in line with state objectives, notwithstanding the ideological editorial perspectives of ownership. That's why the left-leaning *New York Times*[58] was as much a supporter for the invasion of Iraq as the conservative *Washington Times*. When it comes to protecting America's international interests, the media and the state are usually as one. Additionally, much of mainstream media went along with Washington's euphemistic use of the term "enhanced interrogation" during the Iraqi conflict.[59] To call it what it was, torture, would have disputed the precepts of American exceptionalism promoted so rigorously in the press.

American media has often been as subservient to state requirements, through the guise of private ownership beholden to the power elites, as the government-controlled press in "un-American" countries it criticizes. Mass media ownership is in the hands of the corporate establishment. These elites are capitalist, reactionary and in obedience with America's imperialist foreign interests. The ideal of a free press is increasingly harder to accept when ownership is continually reduced to a handful of conglomerates all in lockstep with most government policies, particularly when it comes to foreign relations;[60] even to the point of the American press' acquiescence to government requests to suppress stories for the sake of ill-defined national security concerns. Former *New York Times* reporter James Risen is a notable instance when his articles on the CIA's activities in Iran and NSA domestic spying were squashed or delayed by his bosses at the *New York Times*, on demand from the government. His account is a fascinating insight into just how un-free the press is.[61]

As the media has become a multibillion-dollar industry, a frenzy of mergers has wiped out hundreds of competitors. The shrinking of media ownership diversity in deference to corporate control continues unabated. With it comes the diminishing of journalistic integrity and a narrowing of those who would offer varying viewpoints.[62] Jeff Cohen, media critic and founder of Fairness and Accuracy in Reporting (*FAIR*), has called the current effort to end net neutrality by corporate media ownership, "the greatest threat to the free press."[63]

Media critic Edward S. Herman, who passed away in 2017, focused much of his work on media manipulation and propaganda.

> The mainstream media are elite institutions. The ownership of the media is concentrated in the hands of very wealthy individuals. The media system is really a powerful set of structures. Most people don't have a choice. They don't have a spectrum of available choices that they can look at and say, "Oh, I like this or that." So, you have a very limited, constrained set of options, to begin with. So, that's a bias that's built into the structure of the system.[64]

The result is a type of self-imposed censorship where articles deemed outside the norm are ignored. If a reporter wants to write about corruption in the military or atrocities abroad, he or she will have a harder time with career advancement and those stories will usually not be picked up by other media. There is a consistency where editors and news directors of all or most of the major media companies agree upon what information will reach their audience. In virtually all cases regarding foreign relations, this little mini-oligarchy of media overlords provides news that is closely in sync with the official pronouncements of the US government. Coverage that does not conform to standard anti-Cuban information rarely sees the light of day. Squashing articles written by journalists who have strayed from the media/state concession of a topic is one of the five filters Noam Chomsky and Edward Herman describe in *Manufacturing Consent*. Cuba fits neatly into all the filters, including the most powerful one when the press creates a common enemy to stoke fear in order to rally consensus among the population.[65]

It is of no disclosure that these ultra-capitalist media owners conform to the political ruling class and its foreign policy objectives. Media then becomes state controlled by the conjunction of the financial aims of private ownership and the political goals of leadership. Under US rules of proprietorship, the media's voluntary compliance to incontestably disseminate government propaganda becomes more effective than overt state-run news organizations. The perception is that privately operated media equates to independence and a democratic barrier to state authoritarianism. In fact, when mainstream media ownership finds itself under the control of the uber-rich reactionary corporate elements of society, you don't need government pressure to ensure compliance, it comes willingly.

"It is much more difficult to see a propaganda system at work where the media are private and formal censorship is absent," Herman noted.[66]

Mainstream media's power to propagandize was no more evident than in the role it played in putting Donald Trump in the White House, with reporters just now engaging in a humbling retrospective.[67] The focus on Hillary Clinton's emails just prior to the election is but one aspect of how media moved the needle in favor of The Donald.[68] Middle East expert Juan Cole observed that *CNN* provided Trump with a national audience "every night at 7:30 pm throughout the summer and fall of 2016 and just let him talk, or whatever he does, for an hour without even a semblance of journalistic analysis. Supposedly left-leaning *MSNBC* did the same thing."[69] Furthermore, it was reported that certain mainstream television commenters like Sean Hannity were advising Trump with regard to policy and how to handle media and to this day remain nothing more than cheerleaders for the leader.[70] One of the most influential media conglomerates made clear its intention to promote the pro-Trump agenda when in April 2018 the Sinclair Broadcast Group directed its 200 television stations to condemn "fake news" in support of the president's attack on the critical press he receives.[71] Chris Hedges refers to this situation as media's role in establishing "inverted totalitarianism."[72]

Usually, when covering election campaigns or certain other national issues, it is easy to identify the ideological divide of the top newspapers, television and radio outlets. The consumer understands the media's left or right stance when it comes to health care, taxes, immigration and other topics that affect domestic matters. Switch to foreign affairs, and it is remarkable how consistently the national media covers the issues, regardless of national ideological bent. America's empire is based on military might and economic predominance. It is expressed in protecting interests, not friendship, and results in the regime change philosophy for those nations deemed to be against what benefits the United States. Since World War II, America has been involved at various levels in the overthrow of governments, including democratically elected ones in Iran, Guatemala, Chile, Congo, Haiti, Dominican Republic, Nicaragua, Honduras and a host of others. The normal basis for these interferences has been American opposition to national liberation movements that object to Washington's corporate domination of the host country's resources. Cuba's revolution is one of the few movements that succeeded in ousting US hegemony and keeping it out—but at a great cost.

When the USA determines the necessity of meddling in other countries, the media has most often come along for the ride, providing cover for all the dirty tricks and illegal subversion carried out in the name of promoting American values. Current examples include coverage of the disaster in Yemen, told with certain elements of truth, but conveniently ignoring America's active role. The Yemen calamity includes the added component of disregarding Saudi Arabia's part in all this—if the war is even mentioned.[73] Outlets one would expect to take a more critical eye on the Yemen story have abrogated that right, as media watchdog organization FAIR noted in a 2018 report. The group recounted that *MSNBC*—designated as part of the liberal media—ran only one segment that focused on the USA's role in Yemen in 2017; and zero in the second half of the year. As of April 2018, *MSNBC* had not run a single article on Yemen, the report continued, much less on the USA's role in it. The US-supported, Saudi-led bombing campaign has caused upward of 1 million cholera cases and killed over 10,000 civilians.[74]

Whether supporting American allies—no matter how distasteful—or denigrating those perceived to be anti-American—no matter how undeserving—the mass media can be counted on to adhere to the official agenda of the state. The media continually excused, or ignored, the excesses of the worst dictatorships in Latin America from the 1950s to the 1980s because they were allies of the US government. The current countries in that category are such human rights abusers as Saudi Arabia, Pakistan and Egypt. On the other side, the USA hit list includes Venezuela, Iran and Syria.[75] Cuba, of course, has never left the anti-American ledger.

However, it is not just Cuba. With rare exception, the mass media does not challenge the state's designations of allies and enemies nor defy foreign policy aims. Saudi Arabia's medieval social restrictions have been recognized, but invariably contextualized with positive comments on how the country is "progressing."[76] Women's rights in the kingdom represent a perfect example of how media controls perception through selection. When in 2017 the Saudi government intimated women would be given the right to drive, the *New York Times*, *CBS News* and other mass media were nothing but effusive in its extensive coverage and editorials. As were they when the law finally went into effect a year later, the media treating it like the Saudis had accomplished a major human rights breakthrough instead of establishing a trivial standard every other country in the world had accepted during the past century.[77] However, following the arrest of some of the country's most influential feminists, the same media provided a few minor articles, but not one editorial condemning the incarcerations.[78] The media forgives much of the abuses while always reminding the consumer of the importance of Saudi alliance. Forgiveness reaches all the way to rarely mentioning the embarrassing fact of how many Saudis were 9/11 terrorists.[79] Only when the journalist Jamal Khashoggi was murdered in 2018 did an ideological split in media coverage temporarily emerge.[80]

China's record on human rights is considered far worse than Cuba's, despite not suffering under an embargo or regime change strategies. The country has arrested hundreds of lawyers and activists, many who are never heard from, including Wang Quanzhang who was detained in 2015.[81]

The difference is what Alternet media critic Adam Johnson described as the "North Korea Law of Journalism," which states that journalistic standards "are inversely proportional to a country's enemy status." As a result, the more antagonistic the USA is to a country, the more lackadaisical journalists can be with the truth while reporting on said state.[82]

American foreign policy has long been determined by picking the good and bad guys, then justifying imperial interventionism superseding national sovereignty, not on publicly promoted humanitarian grounds, but on conditions determined by economic interests. Corporate media then willingly provides the informational paradigm in order to convince the public of the state's noble intentions. No better examples can be found than America's efforts at regime change in Cuba, and more currently its support for an illegal coup in Venezuela. Demonstrating how corporate media operates hand in hand with government foreign policy objectives, the accepted informational model is that a legally elected president (Nicolás Maduro) is a fraud; while the United States has the right to decide that an unelected unknown (Juan Guaidó) is now leader. The actual basis for the coup—oil and race—is left unsaid.[83]

Under Hugo Chávez and now Nicolás Maduro, the American media is relentless in its approbation, citing the nation's socialist make-up as the root of all problems. The majority of the reporting has focused on the legitimacy of the violent opposition, coinciding with the apparent undemocratic aspects of the current leadership. The substantial social gains are glossed over, the fact that Venezuelan elections are more democratic than those in the USA, and that millions are better off now as a result of the redistribution of resources, are simply ignored. America's hostility, including its support for the army-led coup against Chávez in 2002, receive similar scant attention.[84] The short-lived coup revealed the *New York Times*' stark corporate bias when the lead paragraph in its editorial in support was filled with a string of preposterous falsehoods: "With yesterday's resignation of President Hugo Chávez, Venezuelan democracy is no longer threatened by a would-be dictator. Mr. Chávez, a ruinous demagogue, stepped down after the military intervened and handed power to a respected business leader, Pedro Carmona."[85] No mention that Carmona was a right-wing extremist with close ties to US business interests, who promised a roll-back of all of the social justice programs instituted by Chávez. Also of rare acknowledgment in the media is the American financing of the opposition. Venezuela has become the number one target for the press, often surpassing the vitriol usually reserved for Cuba.[86] Old anti-Cuba favorites, such as Marco Rubio, have now become Venezuelan experts. *CNN* provided him a column to spout his anti-Maduro views, with no alternative perspective allowed.[87]

An article on the exceptional cases of Venezuelan parents giving up children[88] receives prominent play with the angle that this is a common event, while reporting on American efforts to provide illegal funding and material aid to promote violent opposition groups in Venezuela are relegated to low-level coverage.[89] Coverage of Venezuela since Chávez was elected has consistently backed regime change.[90] *Foreign Policy* magazine took the remarkably brazen step of publicly advocating just that possibility with its 2018 article "It's Time for a Coup in Venezuela."[91] Promoting the ending of democracy with the imposition of military rule harkened back to the dark ages of US imperialism in Latin America. It is distressingly reminiscent of the media's treatment of Chilean president Salvador Allende in the 1970s. In both cases, the media instinctively taking the side of the wealthy, well-armed and US-supported opposition against a populist revolution committed to helping the poor. The result of Allende's overthrow was years of right-wing military dictatorship and thousands killed. In the infrequent occasions when the mass media does provide accurate information about Venezuela, it is usually an individual columnist with direct first-hand knowledge who proves false the overarching critical narrative.[92] Unfortunately, the impact of such articles, as in the case of the *Toronto Star* column challenging Canada's anti-Venezuelan stance, do little to stem the onslaught of media misinformation.

In early 2019, American economic action against Venezuela included imposing sanctions on oil sales to the USA and withholding funds to the Maduro government by blocking international bank accounts. This is taken from the anti-Cuban playbook by making the economy so bad that the people will rise up and toss out their own government. All this is in agreement with US strategy to re-install a capitalist friendly regime that will hand back oil production and revenues to private companies—a policy supported by the media including the supposedly liberal media *MSNBC*.[93] The one-sided treatment focused almost exclusively on covering anti-Maduro protestors.[94]

Sometimes the propaganda systems intersect against the two nations as when the *New York Times* published a 2019 report claiming Cuba's medical program in Venezuela was used as a political weapon to help President Nicolás Maduro hold onto power.[95] The article "riddled with factual inaccuracies, omissions and misrepresentations,"[96] quoted a series of unnamed sources who purported that Cuban doctors working in Venezuela would confirm a patient's political leanings before providing treatment. Readers were then presented with a series of factual errors regarding Venezuela's electoral process and the preposterous assertion that Cubans were allowed to illegally vote under a system that even Jimmy Carter described as one of the most fraud-proof in the word.[97]

America's vilification of both Venezuela and Cuba elicited media support through the *New York Times'* utilization of dubious allegations from unnamed sources in a blatant testimony to journalistic maleficence.

Media shouts against a pair of designated anti-American countries contrast sharply to the silent press coverage of Honduras. After a US supported right-wing coup in 2009, followed by actual disputed elections in 2017, the country has devolved into the highest murder rates in Latin America. Thousands have fled the violence and economic dislocation, yet no mainstream media has called for the ouster of president Juan Orlando Hernández, a stanch pro-American neoliberalist. There's been no call, as there has been scant attention. So while the general public is well informed about the problems in Venezuela, few would know of the even worse difficulties in Honduras. Media as the gatekeepers of information remain the key element in establishing perceptions in conjunction with foreign policy requirements.[98]

In early 2018, violent protests against the Nicaragua government's social security reforms resulted in mainstream media predominantly supporting the anti-Sandinista side. This was in agreement with state aims of regime change. According to editor and author Max Blumenthal, much of that biased coverage was from a journalist who had no experience and who filed reports littered with falsehoods. In his analysis, Blumenthal noted:

> The *Guardian*, *The Washington Post*, the *BBC* and *NPR* have assigned an American anthropologist with no previous journalistic experience to cover the crisis in Nicaragua. The novice reporter, named Carl David Goette-Luciak, has published pieces littered with falsehoods that reinforce the opposition's narrative promoting regime change while relying almost entirely on anti-Sandinista sources. An investigation for *MintPress* reveals that Goette-Luciak has forged intimate ties to the opposition, and has essentially functioned as its publicist under journalistic cover. Having claimed to work in the past as an anthropologist and "human rights defender," Goette-Luciak operated side-by-side with activists from a U.S.-backed opposition party known as the Sandinista Renovation Movement, or MRS … U.S. government-funded organizations have supplied the MRS with millions of dollars' worth of election assistance, and continue to fund its activists by funding their NGO's and social media training.[99]

Nicaragua has long been a target for American regime change desires, and Blumenthal reveals the media's role in supporting state objectives:

> Media outlets like the *Guardian*, *NPR* and *The Washington Post* feign objectivity before their readers, presenting themselves as arbiters of truth in an era of fake news. However, in countries where Washington is pushing regime change, these same outlets have dispatched a corps of writers to embed with U.S.-backed opposition elements, provide them with publicity, and sell their goals back to the American public. Goette-Luciak is one of the clearest embodiments of the disturbing trend.[100]

Corporate media help set the terms of discussion regarding the issues they cover by pointing toward specific sets of questions and ignoring others. When news outlets highlight particular points of contention, they encourage audiences to see these as the central aspects of the story and discourage consideration of other facets of the topic. So critical coverage of Cuba's nationalization of agricultural property under the Land Reform Act in 1960 had no contextual reporting of the compensation offers, historical precedent or even the United States doing the exact same thing during their revolution.[101]

Coverage of the Cuban dissident arrests in 2003 lacked information regarding their accepting funds and aid from the USA in violation of international laws of diplomacy, nor was there any recognition of Cuba's right to arrest nationals working in support of America's hostile policies. Rarely allowed into the media debate is the notion that the Cubans have the right to chart their own course free of US interference, or any accounting of the harm the American embargo and regime change tactics still inflict. These are viewpoints that exist on the far fringes of respectable analysis, appearing in limited forms amid the deluge of opinion pieces and articles written about the shortcomings, failures and critics of the Cuban government that has been the mainstay of media coverage for the past 60 years.

Even in those rare instances that the media appeared to have something positive to say about Cuba, it often turned out to be a different tack in compliance with customary state objectives. An editorial in the influential *Washington Post*, "Embargo Must Go"—purported to call for the end of the economic punishment, not so much for the harm it does to the Cuban people, but as a way to expedite the collapse of the Castro regime through the flooding of American tourism and capitalist ideals.[102] An all too common rationale, one that ignores the reality that the average Cuba is well aware of both the positive and negative trappings of American consumerism. However, it was at least recognition of the injustice of the embargo, even if it was disingenuous as to why it should end. More positively, other topics in the past 20 years such as the Cuban Five, Elián González and Alan Gross did see a partial shift in the press, albeit in the minority, where context and the Cuban side was permitted in partial measures. It established the ability of some media to report specific issues on their merits even while maintaining underlying anti-Cuban misinformation.[103]

This modification gained further traction when presidents Barack Obama and Raúl Castro announced a move toward normal relations in 2014. American corporate media fell in line with the change in state attitude with a series of articles that gave increased framework and space to Cuban issues, often taking a relatively positive approach. Beneath it however, was the consistency in the narrative that Cuba had to change its system before the USA would establish full relations. It was yet another example of the media reflecting the alteration in Washington's strategy with Cuba—this time using the carrot instead of the stick to induce regime change.

* * *

For more than a century, there have been countless instances of media manipulating the American public in compliance with state intentions. Historically, Cuba was one of the first, during the Spanish–American War of 1895 (Cuba's Second War of Independence) that saw the two main papers of the day fighting over who would print the mostly fictitious yet sensational scoops to sway public opinion in favor of entering the conflict.[104]

During World War I, media outrage over the sinking of the RMS *Lusitania* helped influence sentiment toward America's entry in 1917. Throughout the Cold War, the unquestioned reporting that the Soviets had a larger nuclear weapon and military capability helped keep the unreasonably fear of a communist takeover a self-created national security concern. The media's false narrative that the Reagan administration's over-spending on the military led to the demise of the Soviet Union remains one of the great political myths.[105]

A classic misdirection helped embroil the USA in the Vietnam War following the media's unquestioning acceptance of the government's version to what happened in the Gulf of Tonkin.[106] The war remains one of the low points in subservience, with the majority of corporate media supporting foreign policy goals for most of the duration of the conflict. At one point, the *Washington Post* going so far as to call the Vietnam War a "just cause," this from an ostensible liberal media.[107] The only credible news came from the war correspondents, and their coverage led various Republicans to blame the media for being partially responsible for America's defeat. The US government made sure that level of press freedom didn't happen again, and so for the Afghanistan and Iraq invasion, rules were imposed where all credentialed reporters had to be "imbedded" with military units. The media voluntarily handed over its independence with few objections. The self-censored reporting, biased in support of US government perspectives, came as no surprise.[108]

Mass media was derelict in its coverage of the Vietnam conflict in most aspects, none more so than ignoring the historical fact it was a struggle for Vietnamese national independence. To do so would have defied the well-developed description that the USA was not an invader but a defender of South Vietnam against the godless communist horde.[109] To its credit, some important outlets did confront the truth about the war with the publishing of the "Pentagon Papers." This was, however, after years of supporting the conflict and only when public sentiment turned overwhelmingly against it.[110] It is in sharp contrast to today's apparent priorities, when whistleblower Chelsea Manning went to the *New York Times* and *Washington Post* with proof of US war crimes in Iraq and Afghanistan, the papers refused to respond, then tried to denigrate the information. It was only after Manning's attempts to attract mainstream media's attention failed that she went to WikiLeaks with the explosive report.[111]

Nicaragua in the 1980s came under media coverage in obedience of state goals when the murderous Contras were chosen as worthy "freedom fighters" against the unworthy socialist regime of Daniel Noriega.[112] The Contras were fighting to maintain American hegemony, Noriega's movement was for self-determination. All Central America during that decade was delineated between right-wing dictatorships portrayed as staunch US allies and those in opposition either communist dupes or international revolutionaries.

During the Iran–Contra scandal, much of the coverage mitigated the evidence of the US government's illegal activities or tried to justify it in context to Cold War Realpolitik.[113] The scandal provided another illustration of how corporate media is beholden to government foreign policy goals when it uniformly criticized independent journalist Gary Webb for his reporting on the Central Intelligence Agency's complicity in smuggling tons of cocaine for sale into the USA to fund the Contra rebels in Nicaragua.[114]

Nicaragua continues to be in the media's cross-hairs, the latest example occurring when the government of Daniel Ortega has been accused by mainstream media of horrific human rights violations during a series of street protests that began in early 2018. A report on the abuses cited three main media organizations for its facts: *Confidencial*, *100% Noticias* and *La Prensa*. The three are enemies of the Ortega government; and all are funded by the United States through official entities like the National Democratic Institute (NDI) and the National Endowment for Democracy (NED). The NED has been characterized by retired US Congressman, Ron Paul, as:

> an organization that uses US tax money to actually subvert democracy, by showering funding on favored political parties or movements overseas. It underwrites color-coded "people's revolutions" overseas that look more like pages out of Lenin's writings on stealing power than genuine indigenous democratic movements.[115]

Historically the media's coverage of Cuba has been able to easily traverse the widest range of narratives based on shifting state necessities. When Cuba was fighting against Spanish colonialism, it was the media that created an image of a helpless native unable to gain independence due to incompetence, immaturity or ignorance. America had to step in. When it did, the press then informed the public the Cubans were happy, subservient and indebted to the USA for achieving what they could not. The years of American hegemony were nothing more than a time when US interests were able to show the unsophisticated locals the right path to government. When the revolutionaries told the Americans to leave, it was the media that led the outrage—comforting the reader that the USA had done nothing wrong, that Fidel Castro and his lot were mentally unhinged, ingrates that turned against their benefactors with no justification. And then worst of all—they became communists. The media has a long history of developing the biases and misinformation that has stained the relationship between these two countries for more than 100 years.

When it comes to Cuba, it is of little difficulty to see the hypocrisy in how the press treats the island nation, an "official enemy" as against how coverage is handled toward an ally, even one as unsavory as Saudi Arabia. Cuba's supposed human rights violations (based on the lack of multi-party elections and the other trappings of a strictly defined Western Liberal social/economic system) are constantly criticized. The actual human rights that Cuba advances as a developing nation, including education, health care and housing, are begrudgingly recognized and rarely allowed to be mentioned unless in conjunction with social limits. Tangible human rights violators like Saudi Arabia are treated with kid gloves, despite the medieval attitudes toward women and capital punishment, as well as its religious rigidity against Christians and Jews.[116] Culture plays a strong part in the patriarchal structure of Saudi society, but the media usually downplays the ultra-reactionary practices with the pretext that the country "has to find its own path at its own pace" toward modernity.[117]

That consideration is seldom provided to Cuba, neither is the recognition of the social pressures the revolution has felt since its earliest days as a consequence of America's non-stop aggression and strategy of regime change. Cuban leadership considers itself to be under siege, necessitating measures to protect its citizens that the press condemns as human right constraints. Policies that in much the same way reflected civil right restrictions that were put into place and accepted by American society following 9/11. The mass media did its job well in justifying measures such as the Patriot Act, but giving the same consideration to others who have faced far more incidents of terrorism is not appropriate. Nor is describing Cuba's economic deficiencies allowed in other terms than the fault of the system, with no recognition of the debilitating US embargo the country still suffers under. This is but one demonstration of the media's ability to arbitrarily decide what information is legitimate and what is meaningless. There is not just an economic embargo against the island, but an informational blockade that can be considered as damaging to Cuban society and its efforts to develop.

Cuba presents a perfect example of the media setting the parameters of perceptions. Those opinions have been consistently critical, offering little space for nuance, balance or objectivity. Regime change promotion comes from foreign policy dictates, but the responsibility for convincing the American audience that Cuba should be forced to abandon its social/economic make-up falls to the mainstream media. Reporting in favor of overthrowing a sovereign nation's form of government does not countenance the possibility that the United States might not have the right to intervene in the internal affairs of others. It is just a conventional fact that the revolutionary society is not worthy of legitimacy and the US government is merely trying to "free" the Cuban people. This historical fantasy has been reflected faithfully with little variation for the past 60 years by the national media.

Cuba is the standard bearer for media manipulation, stretching back since before the beginning of revolution. Coverage of Cuba in the United States has been consistently biased, often rejecting the basic journalistic tenet of balance and fairness, all in service to imperial objectives. Similar substandard practices can also be encountered in media throughout other Western democracies. It has been an unrecognized conspiracy to denigrate the Cuban Revolution and its attempts to establish social justice programs through an economic system deemed anathema to corporate controlled media. The press, with its command over public opinion, has succeeded in presenting the revolution as a failure. Not surprisingly, as the media, no less a capitalist institution as the stock market, could barely allow the revolution's socialist values and efforts at egalitarianism to be presented as any sort of positive model for other developing nations to follow. The media has done its job extremely well in presenting anything but a one-sided perspective, based on the control of information—what is used and what is left out.

It is a concept that has been recognized and expressed by both humorists and journalists. Mark Twain is sometimes credited with saying: "If you don't read the newspaper, you are uninformed. If you read the newspaper, you are misinformed."[118] Or as progressive journalist Erwin Knoll observed, "Everything you read in the newspapers is absolutely true except for the rare story of which you happen to have firsthand knowledge."[119]

The media then is all about trust. It is the greatest value. It is guarded closely and self-promoted constantly. With that social contract secured, the press can then go about constructing a specific narrative secure in the knowledge it will be for the most part accepted. When Americans read something in corporate media, they tend to have confidence in the information. And the media's entire existence depends on that belief. Even in these days of fake news and splintering social media outlets, most Americans trust the mainstream media they consume to provide them with accurate information, according to a 2017 study by the American Press Institute.[120]

Depending on political perspective, the consumer may watch *Fox News* with full confidence, but have a low opinion of the accuracy of *CNN*. The reverse is true, according to the report. A September 2018 poll by Gallup reinforced the idea that while overall trust in the media has decreased in the past decade, it is mostly based on the consumer not believing in the media that presents opposing information to his own opinions in a specific issue.[121] Media trust is becoming more and more partisan.

However, when it comes to Cuba, it doesn't matter what the individual reads or watches or listens to—anti-revolutionary reporting and the lack of balanced information is consistent regardless of the perceived ideological bent of the specific media. The outcome is predictable—the overwhelming majority of Americans have a negative opinion about Fidel Castro and the revolution.[122] Media's relentless one-sided coverage combined with the travel restrictions make such a consequence completely predictable.

A revealing yet not unique example of how media utilizes trust to present a distorted perspective under the guise of expertise occurred after Fidel Castro's death in 2016. A flurry of articles in Western media was consistent in the condemnation of the Cuban leader and his legacy, ignoring or diminishing the revolution's accomplishments and the honest outpouring of grief felt by millions in Cuba and around the world.[123]

One was noteworthy for its seemingly strong command of facts to support a critical perspective on Cuban society under the revolution. A closer examination reveals something quite different. The November 2016 column by Mark Milke appeared in the *Toronto Globe and Mail*, containing little historic perspective on Cuba, and less understanding of the true basis for the revolution. Nevertheless, his writing implied knowledge of the subject matter, interjecting opinion with selective facts that have a basis of truth but distort the actual reality of the topic. It created an anti-revolutionary bias accepted by the average reader who has been provided no context or background information to balance the author's one-sided perspective, complicating the separation of truth from fiction. In the column, he wrote:

> One could blame Cuba's economic and social decline partly on the American embargo on trade with Cuba. I would, but then I support free enterprise. But Cuban communism, like other varieties, always disdained capitalism and with it international trade; all the American embargo did was reveal how self-sufficient socialism was a mirage.[124]

In actuality, the United States instituted the extra-territorial aspects of the embargo in the early months after the triumph of the revolution, long before Fidel Castro declared it socialist. The embargo prohibited American enterprises from doing business with Cuba after refusing to accept Havana's offers to compensation for nationalized property. The revolutionary government was more than willing to trade with the United States, and continues to push for normal economic relations. Additionally, the USA then placed effective pressure on other countries in the Americas to stop commercial relations, with only Mexico and Canada refusing.[125] Even European nations such as Britain were forced to pull back from trading with the island, cancelling an order to sell military aircraft to Cuba in the early 1960s.[126] Havana never disdained trade with the capitalist countries of the world, or with anyone, the only condition that it would be conducted under new laws protecting national interests. In fact, Cuba chartered a path of international non-alignment in the first few years, making it clear it would conduct business with any country regardless of ideology. This was based on Cuban nationalism, not international communism—a concept consistently misrepresented in the mainstream media. It was the United States that made it impossible for Cuba to trade with American companies, and then with most of the rest of the capitalist world. With little other option, Fidel Castro moved toward the Socialist Bloc for economic and military security as much as for ideological conformity. The column continued with some dubious historical evidence:

> Some background: Before Mr. Castro came to power in 1959, Cubans suffered from a grasping, corrupt dictator and the U.S. mafia was involved in the island's casinos, to name two issues. However, Cuba was not an economic straggler and it already "topped the charts" on multiple social indicators.[127]

The background has a grain of truth but falls far short. The dictator—Fulgencio Batista—was fully supported by the United States in its continued hegemonic control over the island. And the mafia, under the acknowledgment of the USA and backing of Batista, ran much more than the casinos. They had influence in directing Batista on national policies and were moving toward dominating the island economy in far more areas than just gambling.[128]

The most disingenuous part of the column occurred when Milke moved into the realm of social programs. He used general comparisons to other countries to try and prove Cuba was doing just fine before the revolution.

> Consider education. Jorge Salazar-Carrillo and Andro Nodarse-Leon, the authors of *Cuba: From Economic Take-Off to Collapse under Castro*, note that in 1954, Cuba spent 4.1 per cent of its GDP on education. That proportion was higher than any Western European country and just above that of the United States (4 per cent). That translated into a comparatively high literacy rate in the 1950s and high female participation.[129]

The above information has little meaning as there is no comparative to post-revolutionary education programs and no context to the differences between rural and urban indices. One of the most consistent anti-revolutionary propaganda is the attempt to demonstrate how far advanced Cuba was economically and socially before Fidel Castro took over and supposedly ruined everything. The media and anti-Cuba experts point to areas such as education and health care to try to substantiate the country's failures under the revolution.

What is missed is comparative data. The benefits from the country's social programs were in the vast majority enjoyed by those living in Havana and Cuba's other urban areas. In the countryside, they were virtually non-existent before the revolution. Fidel Castro's movement was aimed at changing that dynamic, to try and provide those in the rural regions with similar community assistances. To erase the urban centric attitude of a government official who stated: "Havana is Cuba, the rest is landscape."[130]

Milke's observations are hollow at best, unless taken in comparison to how pre-revolutionary urban Cubans lived as opposed to their rural neighbors. He went on to comment:

> Or ponder Cuban health care. Cuba in 1957 already had more doctors per 1,000 people than did Norway, Sweden and Great Britain. In 1958, according to even one recent regime-friendly academic paper, Cuba "ranked in the first, second or third place in Latin America with respect to its healthcare indicators. Circa the 1950s, that success included long life-expectancy rates, and the lowest infant-mortality rates in Latin America."[131]

Those facts are again skewed entirely in favor of Havana citizens who enjoyed a longer life and fewer infant mortalities, while the rest of the country lived under appalling conditions. Leaving that information out simply misdirects the reader to believe in a Cuba that did not exist before the revolution.

The column was based on how the revolution has failed Cuba, but without using pre- and post-revolution data for the whole country, it is impossible to determine the truth. Simply rattling off evaluations with other nations in the 1950s without specifics is an artificial construct that has little relative significance.

Comparisons between pre-revolutionary Havana and the rest of the country:

Sixty per cent of physicians, 62 per cent of dentists, and 80 per cent of all hospital beds were located in Havana in 1956–57. There was only one hospital in rural Cuba. Four out of five workers in the countryside received medical attention only if they paid for it; as a result most had no access to health care. Infant mortality averaged 60 per 1,000 but that figure was reduced by more than half in Havana. In 1958 there were approximately 6,000 doctors in Cuba for a population of seven million. An estimated 50 per cent left in the first year after the revolution following the new government's order that doctors had to be redistributed throughout the country. To replace the loss Cuba built three new training schools by 1962. By 2006 there were 70,000 doctors for a population of 11 million, almost all with one or two specialties. In 2010 infant mortality had fallen to six per 1,000, on par with American statistics. Life expectancy in 1959 was 59 years; in 2006 it was 75. In all of Cuba, the number of hospitals has risen from 57 before the revolution to 170 today, plus 250 polyclinics (health centers), previously unknown; beds available in hospitals and clinics have doubled, from 21,000 to 42,000, from 3.3 per 1,000 inhabitants to 5.4.[132]

Those living in the countryside suffered from 1,000 calorie daily deficit and were 16 percent under average height and weight. Normal life expectancy was five years less in rural Cuba. Before the revolution, 23.6 percent of the Cuban population was illiterate. In rural areas, over half the population could not read or write and 61 percent of the children did not go to school. To address this problem, Castro asked young students in the cities to travel to the countryside and teach the people to read and write. Known as the Literacy Campaign, the 12-month program started in early 1960 and involved hundreds of thousands of students. By its end, Cuba had a literacy rate of 99 percent of the population.[133]

Employment in rural Cuba during the nine months when there was no sugar to harvest, known as the dead time, was 20 percent, underemployment averaged 13.8 percent annually. Thirty percent of the lowest income population earned only 4 percent of Cuba's total income. Social security covered just 53 percent of the population. Although Cuba ranked ahead of most other countries in Latin America purely in average GDP, thanks to the skewing of the economics in Havana, a third of the population lived in poverty. Most Cubans living in the countryside in 1957 had no running water (85 percent), no toilet (54 percent), no electricity (93 percent), nor a refrigerator (96 percent). In contrast, the proportion of urban Cubans with electricity was at 87 percent; with a refrigerator at 40 percent; with running water at 82 percent and with a toilet at 93 percent. Access to water, electricity and proper housing is now averaging at 80 percent, including the most remote regions of the country.[134]

Disparities in cultural and social facilities were extensive. Havana had 60 theatres in 1958, while there were only 125 in the rest of Cuba. While Havana was the first place in Latin America to have a television broadcast, more than 90 percent of the rural population had never seen a television before 1960.[135]

Economically, those who lived in the country faced practices dating back to medieval times. Many of the major sugar mills, including the vast United Fruit Company operation in Boca De Samá worked on the truck system, where the laborers would be paid in script that could only be used to purchase food and goods at the company store. Prices, which were usually much higher than elsewhere, were set by the company. The system permitted the *campensinos* to gain credits during the eight to nine months when they were not working the cane, in order to survive. It also allowed the company to keep the workers constantly in debt and poverty.[136]

Wage levels have been put forward by the anti-Castro adherents as proof Cubans were actually well off before the revolutionaries arrived. Statistically, the island appeared to be in fine company in 1958 when comparing income levels to advanced nations, coming in eighth in the world for industrial workers and seventh for agricultural laborers—ahead of most European countries and behind the United States, Canada, Sweden, Switzerland, New Zealand and Norway. The predominance of Havana's economy and status as an expensive city helped produce averages that misrepresented overall conditions.[137]

Cuban intellectual Manuel Yepe described what life was actually like prior to the revolution.

> The truth is that the background for the crimes of the tyranny, and the insurrectional arms struggle against it, was very different from the idyllic image that, 50 years after the fact, some people try to paint for the Cuba of the '50s. In reality, hundreds of children sought sustenance through begging, cleaning car windshields and shining shoes or selling newspapers in the streets and city squares or in the country where poverty was extreme. Many of the elderly and handicapped lived on charity. Long lines of men waited for work. And there was the widespread anguish of thousands of women looking for employment as domestics or prostitutes in brothels or working the streets. There was a proliferation of bars and gambling dens for the poor where the humble population was cheated of every last penny in the hope of changing their grim everyday reality.[138]

A 1957 report by the Catholic University Association revealed the extreme disparages that existed between the have and the have-nots,

> Havana is living in extraordinary prosperity while rural areas, especially wage workers, are living in unbelievable stagnant, miserable, and desperate conditions. We firmly hope that, in a few years, Cuban will not be the property of a few, but the true homeland of all Cubans.[139]

When considering the data in context to rural and urban Cuba before and after the revolution, the reader most likely would have accepted a completely different conclusion than the one Milke expounded. Instead, the consumer is left with a misguided opinion of the "failures" when in fact the truth is the opposite. His writings have contributed to the mound of anti-Cuban propaganda so difficult to overcome.

The consequences are entirely anticipated, that of the general public coming to perceive Cuba as an altogether undesirable place, their leaders unworthy and the revolution a colossal mistake that has left nothing but a hardship on its citizenship. While the reality is far removed from the storyline, the media's focus on Cuba's shortcomings lends itself to the exposure of a grain of truth being expanded into a set of irrevocable facts that become difficult to refute. Cuba's struggle to maintain levels of basic medicines in hospitals and pharmacies is turned into an indictment against current efforts at universal health care, ridiculed as a failed social experiment that no developing country could afford, as the *Washington Examiner* condemned.[140] Criticizing an ideal that Cuba never claimed and then ignoring the damage that the US embargo continues to impose on the ability to purchase medicines is one example of the lack of journalistic standard consistently applied to the revolutionary government.

The media has done its job effectively in denigrating the complex problems of a developing nation that decided by revolutionary means to establish true self-determination while trying to survive under the hostility of the world's greatest power. Combine that with US laws making it complicated for Americans to see for themselves the good, the bad and the indifferent in Cuba, the media's role becomes even more influential in shaping public opinion. That opinion has been consistently harmful. Cuba is the prime example of the convergence of media coverage into one, almost universal, negative treatment of this misunderstood and misrepresented island and its social system—a system that the media intentionally obfuscates and misinforms in compliance with the myths most Americans hold about socialism.

James Barrood is the CEO of the New Jersey Tech Council, one of the nation's largest tech trade associations. In 2015, the Council led a trade mission to Cuba. Upon his return, Barrood wrote a column for his local paper addressing the standard misconceptions regarding Cuba—all promoted for the past half-century by the mainstream media—and the enlightenment experienced when he arrived there.

> Our group was made up of business leaders from many industries including mobile software/apps, biotech, IT staffing, renewable energy, construction, engineering, banking and others. Whatever our preconceptions about the island were, they were mostly turned upside down. Before my first trip, I was told to expect little more than a communist dictatorship filled with

> unhappy and poor people. I can only speak for what I observed: that is not what I saw in the many meetings I held, or in the many areas of Cuba I visited. Rather, I found one of the most literate, healthy, educated, cultured, proud, warm and happy societies on the planet.[141]

He finished the article by addressing the ubiquitous media-driven misinformation:

> We must forget our preconceptions that Cuba is a third-world, backward, poor island of 11 million people. It is not. Rather, in many ways, it is a modern miracle. I encourage you to visit, not as a cigar or rum aficionado nor a beach bum, but as a passionate student who wants to engage a people and culture, and simply learn.[142]

Currently, one of the most insidious accusations the press has presented as fact is the claim the Cuban government was intentionally withholding food from the population to divert it to tourist facilities. That misrepresentation of food shortages in Cuba came from the *New York Times*.[143] It is a classic case of how the media constructs Cuban coverage by taking a kernel of truth and extrapolating it, with no evidence, into something sinister. The 2016 article in the *New York Times* focused on the important issue of food shortages in Cuba, the rising costs associated and inferred that it is rooted in the burgeoning demands of the tourist industry. A few locals are interviewed complaining and the main source of the theory came from an American university professor who has studied the island economy. Few Cuban officials were interviewed, little counterpoint offered and no proof that the government was intentionally diverting food to the hotels. The increased number of tourists coming to Cuba has put additional pressure on food production, but there is no government policy to take produce from the local markets to feed tourists. In fact, Havana often imposes price controls to ensure food for citizens in response to higher demands from the tourist industry. There was also no recognition that many hotels bring in their own food sources to ensure quality and quantity, and that certain agricultural cooperatives were selling part of their surplus product directly to tourist facilities.[144] The reader is left with the impression that the Cubans must live under a terrible system. The press has accomplished its goal.

* * *

The national media is currently under attack, led by President Trump, for being purveyors of "fake news." This is based not on the veracity of reporting, but on perception of bias. Facts are perverted by partiality. Is this the case with Cuba? Has the media reported fairly on the deficiencies of Cuban revolutionary society or is it real fake news where predisposed negative judgments dominate Cuban coverage since the revolution, and even since the United States gazed covetously at their southern island neighbor more than 200 years ago.

The work will examine how America's most influential newspapers, radio and television have consistently treated the Cuban Revolution, from the early days after the triumph, through the Bay of Pigs invasion and the Cuban Missile Crisis, to Cuba's move to the Eastern Block of nations in the 1970s to the end of the Soviet Union in 1989. Including how the media has handled the Cuba issue of the past decade up to President Obama's opening with Cuba, Fidel Castro's death, and the current roll-back under the Trump administration.

One of the most important illustrations of how conditions change but Cuba coverage remains consistent occurred following the fall of the Soviet Union almost 30 years ago. The media didn't miss a beat, dropping the Cuba as 'communist nation' coverage in favor for a quick turn toward supposed human rights issues. The dissolution of the Soviet Union also saw the press, with utmost confidence, predict the end of the socialist experiment in Cuba based on the fallacy of the population rising up and throwing off their own government. Any major social change in Cuba is cause for the press to speculate with unfounded certainly that the end of the revolution is near. The media continues to report on the veracity of that flawed expectation, while routinely using the same anti-revolutionary 'experts' to continue to spout the identical misinformation. People like Cuban-American Republican Marco

Rubio maintain the fiction that there is no popular support in Cuba for the government, insisting that the newly legislated hostility under the Trump administration is aimed at the revolutionary leadership and not the people.[145] The media diligently report it with little investigation as to its truth; yet, Rubio is still one of the select few the press considers as a trustworthy expert on the realities of the island nation. It is because the corporate media has always failed to understand, intentionally, the populous foundation of the Cuban Revolution. Those supporters remain active in grass-roots organizations and continue to be the strength of Cuban society to this day. A society that has never been as top down as the media has portrayed it—to acknowledge it would lend legitimacy to the revolution.

Media supposedly offering a balanced coverage of Cuba will use phraseology that accepts the practices of American imperialism. Even while criticizing President Trump's roll-back of Obama's openings with Cuba, the media can miss the point. "Not only does this ignore the reality that attempts to strong-arm Cuba's government into reforms have failed for over 50 years."[146] Instead of challenging the assumption that the USA has the right to try and force any country into "reforms," the report's focus is on the failure of these attempts. The implication is US imposed "reforms" would be acceptable if successful, all the while euphemistically referring to "strong-arm attempts" instead of listing what that really is—embargo, terrorism, propaganda and unrelenting approbation against a system it has arbitrarily deemed suitable for regime change.

An attempt to obfuscate and mitigate, combined with an intentional withholding of information are consistent methods of how the mass media has covered Cuba. It is what Palestinian poet Mourid Barghouti describes as "Secondly." As Barghouti explained in his memoir *I Saw Ramallah*:

> It is easy to blur the truth with a simple linguistic trick: start your story from "Secondly," and the arrows of the [Indigenous peoples] are the original criminals and the guns of the white men are entirely the victim … It is enough to start the story with "Secondly," for my grandmother, Umm Ata, to become

> the criminal and Ariel Sharon her victim. The Palestinian rock throwers are the wrongdoers while Israeli occupation and criminal treatment is ignored.[147]

Secondary coverage came sharply into view in the case of the Palestinian child slapping the face of an Israeli soldier—ignoring the cause of the slap to instead concentrate on the response.[148]

Cuba has long been victimized by the coverage of secondary. From the number of illegal incursions Brothers to the Rescue made before Havana acted, to the arrests of dissidents proven to have accepted illegal material and financial aid from the US government for anti-government purposes,[149] the media finds it far easier to cover the consequences and ignore the background. It permits the reporting that all inadequacies or seemingly irrational acts are the fault of a malevolent regime. When the dissidents were arrested or the planes shot down, the news was exclusive to unconditionally condemning the government with no recognition of what happened previously to trigger those actions—the coverage of secondary.

When US contractor Alan Gross was detained for bringing in illegal military grade, high-tech communication equipment, the mainstream media simply denounced the arrest as proof of Cuba's anti-American rigidity. Little was said of Gross knowing he was aware what he was doing was illegal, lied about it being for Havana's Jewish community, and then admitted he was being paid by USAID, the agency with a long history of interference in Cuban internal affairs.[150] The media, with a few noticeable exceptions, tried to diminish the crime by dutifully, and incorrectly, reporting that Gross was just conveying "cellphones" into Cuba, and that the arrest was completely arbitrary.[151]

Gross is but one example of America's long history of hostility against this small country being unreported or misrepresented. Terrorists like Luis Posada Carriles are described as "freedom fighters," the regime change policies are aimed at the Castro government and not the people. America's aggression against Cuba is simply misunderstood or done with such noble intent that if it does go wrong—as in the case of Alan Gross—it's either from an honest mistake or the intransigence of the Cuban side.

One of the favorite media tropes against Cuba is the refrain that Cubans are fleeing the island in large numbers because of the revolutionary government's shortcomings. The implication to an innocent reader is that this also results from failures of the Cuban government. While comparative emigration data are hard to find,[152] at first blush, it's not clear that Cubans leave in notably larger rates than any other of President Trump's "shithole countries" allegedly sending busloads of murderers across the Rio Grande. They're definitely not fleeing "breathtaking homicidal violence"[153] found elsewhere in Latin America. Cuba remains one of the safest places to visit in the Americas.

Sometimes, however, the mainstream media does allow honest information regarding Cuba—most often coming from outside the United States.

An article in *La Monde Diplomatique* provided a rare insight into what the Cuban Revolution really meant:

> It may be that the heroes of the Sierra Maestra would find the question of orthodoxy versus reform irrelevant. Journalist Fernando Ravsberg points out that "Soviet-style socialism was never a political aim in Cuba: it was seen as a means of saving the revolution, whose first goal was national independence. Under those conditions, the struggle goes on, with or without socialism."[154]

This perception into the actualities of the revolutionary movement and its nationalist priorities does not conform to the American media's fictional historiography regarding Cuba, and therefore has no place within the information conduit. It reflects what George Orwell was referring to when he wrote: "Who controls the past controls the future; who controls the present controls the past." In a very Orwellian way, the American mass media has controlled the information regarding Cuba's past and present, and attempts to dominate its future, all to ensure the average US citizen knows only the worst of the nation's social structure. It is a deliberate attempt to demonize a people, a society and a history. Much of the rational for such vilification is because Cuba's system has been in conflict with America's world order for the past 60 years, and as such is condemned as unworthy.

The media is supposed to shine a light on truth and challenge propaganda, if it is really free. When it comes to Cuba, the light has been switched off for decades, darkness is the norm and only a few slivers of sunshine are allowed to penetrate the blackness of ignorance.

News speak, alternative facts, fake news—all these terms are indicative of the pressures the media faces in this day of instantaneous response through social media and the plethora of opinions on the net. Dictionary.com named "misinformation" as the word of the year for 2018.[155] It becomes more problematic to distinguish what is true and what is propaganda, even within the halls of mainstream media. It's not what the media reports, but what it stresses. The emphasis on Cuba is an inexorable string of spin, shallow perceptions combined with an intentional denial of historical context. It is of absolutely no revelation that the outcome has been an adverse, distorted attitude held by the majority of Americans. Until the media reports honestly on Cuba, that perception will remain.

Media's control of information provides unrestrained power to shape the message. Where there is but one track—destructive—in covering Cuba, the message is abundantly clear. It becomes axiomatic that the revolution is to be seen as a social constraint on advancement, that the majority of individual Cubans long to overthrow their leaders but are prevented by history's most insidious police state, and that American hostility is aimed solely at government officials and in support of the people. In fact, the exact opposite is much closer to the truth, and it is a truth intentionally denied all in service of the mass media's capitalist masters in adherence with the state's international agenda.

There is no hidden truth to be revealed—quite the opposite. The media's treatment of Cuba is predictable. There could be no other certainty to consider within the capitalist mass media institution. How Cuba is treated is based on an internal, established actuality, unstated for the most part, but obvious in its intent and outcome. The mainstream media submits subconsciously, to the extent of internalization, the information filters it uses when it comes to Cuba. Those filters create acceptable establishment attitudes that overwhelmingly slant coverage in favor of counter-revolutionary perspectives and against Cuban socialist society and its leadership.

What this work hopes to accomplish is to demonstrate how consistent this truth is, how effective it has been, how it has warped the perceptions of American citizens and harden the reflective intransigence of the Cuban ruling class, and to examine the detrimental consequences that have befallen both sides of the Florida Straits as a result.

Cuba has been justifiably criticized for the failings, excesses and shortcomings in the construction of a revolutionary social/economic system. The media has the absolute legitimacy to criticize; but it does not have the right to present a consistently partisan viewpoint with little regard to context, background or balance. The media's emphasis on the negative, and the withholding of the facts necessary for the consumer to fully understand the news, has led to the misinformation so prevalent regarding Cuba's revolution.

While the press represents the face of misinformation, there is a long if usually unstated history of the government's role as the puppet master manipulating an acquiescent media. In a rare acknowledgment, then CIA director William Casey commented in 1981: "We'll know our disinformation program is complete when everything the American public believes is false." While not specifically remarking on Cuba, Casey's reveal is without question most applicable to the island nation.[156]

Media propaganda against Cuban reality did not start with the revolution. It has long employed critical messaging while covering the island's uneven route to national independence. Undoubtedly the most damaging experience occurred during the Spanish–American War (known in Cuba as the Second War of Independence) from 1895 to 1899. Two famous newspapers battled for supremacy as to which one would best shape public misinformation. The *New York Journal* owned by William Randolph Hearst and his competitor Joseph Pulitzer's *New York World* deliberately urged their country into war in large part based on their jingoistic exploitation of the conflict, the most memorable incident being the hyper-aggressive fabrications following the explosion of the battleship USS *Maine* in Havana harbor. The papers' battle for higher circulation figures was constructed on a series of "startling fictions and bogus dispatches" regarding the war, Cuba, the competency of its people and their right for true sovereignty.[157] So began the formation of the American media's administration of truth between the small island nation and the superpower to the north.

1
Media Control of Cuban History

The American battleship USS *Maine* was considered out of date by the time her long-delayed commission took place in 1895. Still, the ship retained such serviceable importance that she was sent to Cuba three years later, ostensibly to protect US citizens during the ongoing conflict between nationalist revolutionaries and the Spanish empire. It was to be an impressive show of force by the emerging military might of the United States.

Cuba's history, its relationship with the United States and the mainstream media's management of the dialogue between the two countries has been forever defined by what happened next.

The USS *Maine* entered Havana harbor quietly on the night of February 15, 1898. The silence, however, was appallingly disrupted when an explosion ripped the ship apart, tearing out her hull and killing more than 200 on board. The following morning twisted parts of the superstructure could be seen protruding above the water, with the majority of the USS *Maine* resting on the bottom of the harbor where it remains to this day.[1] A monument to the victims was erected in 1925 on the Malecón seafront boulevard in Havana, eventually providing two extremely distinct historical interpretations.

Without waiting for a formal inquiry, American officials and the press deemed the sinking to have been the result of a mine laid by the Spanish navy. Future president Theodore Roosevelt (who led his Rough Riders up the famous charge of San Juan Hill during the war's final battle at Santiago de Cuba on July 1, 1898) had no hesitation in drawing an immediate conclusion just one day after the explosion: "The *Maine* was sunk by an act of dirty treachery on the part of the Spaniards."[2] His comments, widely reported, left no doubt as to who was responsible and what response was demanded.

That's when the most influential newspapers of the day created a narrative that continues to complicate the contentious relationship between the United States and its island neighbor. At the time of the explosion, both William Randolph Heart's *New York Journal* and the *New York World* owned by Joseph Pulitzer were the recognized frontrunners of a yellow press that had little compunction in reporting the most outrageous claims in pursuit of increasing readership. When it came to foreign affairs, however, the two papers were often on the same page in support of the United States' newly developing imperial muscles. It was the beginning of media's reflection of the state's international objectives.

Cuba had long been coveted by Washington and the press was usually supportive of this imperial policy. Leading up to the USS *Maine* explosion, tensions were running high between the United States and Spain over Cuba. An intercepted letter from the Spanish minister in Washington created a media furor that helped whip up war fever. The letter apparently contained unflattering references to President William McKinley and immediately Hearst's papers exaggerated the incident, with the *New York Journal* running the incendiary headline, "WORST INSULT TO THE UNITED STATES IN ITS HISTORY."[3] This came on top of several years of stories in which the *New York Journal* writers whipped up chauvinist support for war with Spain.

The USS *Maine* incident provided the perfect opportunity for the *New York Journal* and the *New York World* to sanction Washington's decades-long strategy of attempting to establish jurisdiction over Cuba. The papers rallied public sentiment for America's entry into the conflict under the guise of avenging the sinking. "Remember the *Maine!*"[4] became the rallying cry of the press—it remains a jingoistic marker to be referenced against real or imaged threats to American interests. The media war drums became directly complicit in helping the government achieve the goal of turning Cuba into a protectorate, in direct opposition to the local population's desire for true self-determination.

Immediately after the explosion of the USS *Maine*, the press moved to ensure there was no doubt as to what had to be done. The *Evening Journal* blasted in front page headlines just days after the tragedy: "Crisis at Hand, Cabinet in Session, Growing Belief in

Spanish Treachery."[5] Followed shortly after by the demand: "WAR SURE. *Maine* destroyed by Spanish This Proved Absolutely by Discovery of the Torpedo Hole."[6]

The *New York Journal* offered the enormous sum of $50,000 for the capture of those responsible for the USS *Maine* explosion, noting: "The physical facts, even in advance of the investigation, indicate that the *Maine* was blown up by a submarine mine."[7] The only response, the editorial board concluded, was for America to enter the war, defeat the Spanish and liberate the Cubans. The final objective, to place the island under American dominion, was left unstated.

While the papers vied for who best would create war fever, fierce competitive aspects often imposed itself hypocritically on the coverage of the rival. In response to the *New York Journal*'s speculation of the cause of the explosion, the *New York World* indignantly chastised their competitor's reporting as "reckless war scares" and "manufactured news." This despite the *New York World*'s own inflammatory coverage calling for war and boasting it was the first paper in the country to print the news, including purely speculative indications that it was a mine or torpedo that had sunk the USS *Maine*.[8]

The press, however, soon shouted with one voice demanding war. From the headlines of an April 1898 edition of the *New York Tribune*: "War Almost Inevitable, Sentiment in Washington." Predictions soon followed, "Hostilities Not Far Off, War Likely Within a Week."[9]

The predictions were correct; the media's unceasing calls in lockstep with the political objectives made war inevitable. Despite Spain acceding to all US demands, in April 1898, the marines came in and within six weeks, the war was over. The press had stirred up the population, synchronously providing the US government cover to impose its manifest destiny on the island of Cuba. The conflict was a triumph for American imperialism and its self-created delusions of benign intervention. It was a disaster for Cuban nationalism.

That connection was recognized by only a few astute observers. "Whipped up by unscrupulous journalists the public hastily held Spain responsible for the vengeful destruction of an American warship," wrote Samuel Flagg Bemis.[10] "Public sentiment had been worked up by the sensational press, frequently called the 'yellow press.' It had manipulated the real news, spread unfounded reports, putting all before their readers with scare headlines," observed James Ford Rhodes.[11] It was, "doubtful … that the war would have developed without the agency of the most vicious and cynical behavior of a part of the American press that our nation had yet seen," Roger Burlingame noted.[12] The public would have to wait more than 100 years before similar instances were revealed through the coverage of the Iraq War.

The incident that sparked America's entry into Cuba's struggle against Spanish colonialism was not to be forgotten. For almost 50 years, *Maine* Day was celebrated in Havana on February 15 as an expression of the unselfish act of the Americans and the eternal gratitude of the Cubans—according to the victors. In 1929, the *New York Times* reported on the everlasting friendship between the two countries during one celebration: "Cuban armed forces marched side by side with the 120 United States Marines in an impressive parade in observance of the thirty-first anniversary of the sinking of the United States battleship *Maine*."[13]

After the revolution, the inscription on the USS *Maine* monument was altered to reveal the nationalistic Cuban perspective: "To the victims of the *Maine* who were sacrificed by the imperialist voracity and their desire to gain control of the island of Cuba. February 1898—February 1961"[14] Cuba's government to this day considers the sinking as the avenue utilized to establish more than half a century of foreign hegemony.

By the time of the USS *Maine* incident, the fighting between Cuban nationalists and their Spanish overloads had been raging for three years. On the island, the struggle remains known as the Second War of Independence—the first attempt ten years earlier in 1866 having proved unsuccessful. History teaches its American students the conflict is recognized as the Spanish–American War, nomenclature consistently referred to by media to ensure the denial of the presence and contribution of the Cubans. United States officials refused the rebels participation in the peace conference in Paris, thereby establishing their non-existence in the conflict and making the public's acceptance of American dominion over Cuba considerably less complicated. The media played a significant role in establishing the historical fiction that the rebels were mere bystanders and consequently unworthy and unprepared for self-government.

For the Cubans, their final struggle to gain independence after 400 years of Spanish colonialism started in 1895. It was a desperate clash, with the Spanish adopting a scorched earth policy in order to deny the rebels vital resources. Infamously, the war introduced the horrors of concentration camps when the colonial power forced thousands of civilians into urban enclosures where they slowly starved. Leading the revolutionary movement was the country's historic icon, José Martí. The poet turned soldier paved the ideological way for independence, while warning the Cubans to be careful not to remove one colonial power in favor of another.[15] Martí lost his life early in the war, since becoming the recognized national hero by both sides of Fidel Castro's revolutionary divide.

When the Americans entered the war in 1898, it was widely acknowledged that the Cuban rebels were on the verge of victory. American officials were desperately looking for an incident to justify entry in the conflict in order to circumvent that from occurring. The USS *Maine* provided the spark, but it was the prior years of biased press coverage that established the groundwork for the public to accept the political necessity to interfere and take jurisdiction of the island. The media of the period was unrelenting in keeping Spanish atrocities in the forefront, at the same time providing "evidence" the Cuban rebels were incapable of achieving liberation on their own. Only through the efforts of the United States would the Cubans be free. In concurrence with that description, the press endorsed the chronicle that the locals were child-like, uneducated, ill-mannered and certainly unqualified intellectually, politically and culturally to run their own country. It would be Uncle Sam who would impart on these uncivilized rebels the proper path toward self-determination, under American guidance and definition. This would be achieved benevolently, reluctantly, but it would be attained under the strict supervision of America's parental authority over the Cuban child. For the nationalists, it was the culmination of Martí's worst fear—exchanging one colonial master for another.

One of the media's favorite techniques to elicit public support for intervention was to utilize the suffering of Cuban women and children, implying the United States had to come to their rescue due to the impotency of the rebels to protect the weakest elements of the population.

The *New York World* shouted: "The injustice, rapine, the murder of helpless women and children" taking place "in an island lying at our doors." The paper so then demanded, "an enlightened nation which has assumed the guardianship of human liberty in this hemisphere ought not to permit."[16]

Other rationales included the divine right of intervention, the theme of the *Philadelphia Inquirer*'s plea for military action: "At our very doors the most atrocious crimes in the name of Spain have been committed. Have we no duty to perform before God. We will not shirk our duty."[17] Noble deeds superseded normal etiquettes: "One may not enter his neighbor's garden without consent," the *Cleveland Plain Dealer* editorialized: "But if he saw a child being ill-treated by a tramp, he would throw ceremony to the wind and rush to the rescue of the child without asking permission."[18]

Readers were provided with various reasons to justify why Cuban men were either incapable or incompetent to protect their women, children and country. Sometimes the implication was not so subtle, with various articles denigrating Cuban manhood—particularly when compared to the superior example of the American male. "The Cuban is lacking chiefly in the qualities that are conspicuous in American men—virility, initiative, will power, tenacity, reverences for women and conscience," wrote Howard Grose.[19]

Worse yet, Cuban men couldn't even win the fight for independence. To contemplate giving self-governance to these unworthy rebels would not only be misguided but absolutely intolerable. So said the *Philadelphia Manufacturer* in 1898:

> They are helpless, idle, of defective morals and unfitted by nature and experience for discharging the obligations of citizenship in a great and free republic. Their lack of manly force and

> self-respect is demonstrated by the supineness with which they have so long submitted to Spanish oppression, and even their attempts at rebellion have been so pitifully ineffective that they have risen little above the dignity of farce. To clothe such men with the responsibilities of directing self-government would be to summon them to the performance of functions for which they have not the smallest capacity.[20]

Or as minister Washington Gladden was reported in the *New York World* saying: "A people incapable of freeing itself is incapable of governing itself."[21] The *Chicago Tribune* explained, in 1899, the nature of a Cuban man:

> The natural child of Spanish tyranny is a sort of banditti government, consisting of a cruel personal domination, smothered unrest and open revolt ... The result is a (Cuba) nation with little science, less progress, no invention, and uninterrupted backwardness and widespread poverty.[22]

With women and children exposed to untold brutality and the Cuban men of no use to save them, to have neither the intellectual capacity nor social skills to take on the mantel of self-determination, the press accentuated the narrative that there was no option other than for the United States to enter the fight for the salvation of the innocent and the civilization of the ignorant.

American media had established legitimacy for intervention into Cuba's war of independence by publishing a series of articles on the invented inadequacies of the rebels, all the while offering no opportunity for the average Cuban to challenge those negative preconceptions. The public accepted the narrative of incompetency, relying on the press to report accurately on the war situation. Instead, readership was subjected to a barrage of propaganda and misinformation, this time on the basis that the Cubans had accomplished little in their struggle for freedom and were incapable of protecting the most vulnerable members of society. What the press intentionally failed to acknowledge was that Washington's foreign policy relied on the perception of failure, in order to fulfill the goal of exercising control of the island. It went unrecognized and unstated because the press was in full compliance with that aim. General opinion at the time was expressing reluctance at America's imperial expansion; the politicians needed to alter that view and the press readily provided inflammatory, selected analysis in compliance.

The coverage of Cuba's Second War of Independence was demonstrably biased and slanted in support of American foreign policy goals. However, media deference to government objectives regarding Cuba began well before 1898, stretching back to when US politicians started to look covetously upon the island after the declaration of the Monroe Doctrine in 1823.[23] The Doctrine, named after President James Monroe, determined that the Americas were the political and economic playground of the United States and no European power should interfere.

The most infamous example of that imperial desire came from Secretary of State John Quincy Adams, who in that same year promised Cuba would fall into America's hands through the unalterable laws of nature:

> There are laws of political as well as of physical gravitation; and if an apple, severed by the tempest from its native tree, cannot choose but fall to the ground, Cuba, forcibly disjoined from its own unnatural connexion with Spain, and incapable of self-support, can gravitate only towards the North American union, which, by the same law of nature, cannot cast her off from its bosom.[24]

It wasn't long before the newspapers took up the analogy, with journalist Alexander Jones switching the fruit: "At present the pear is ripe neither for the Cubans nor ourselves." And then James Ford Rhodes switched it to a plum: "The plum was ready to drop into America's mouth."[25]

Possessing Cuba developed into a natural, ordained right that would occur through patience or fortune. Just as the magazine *Puck* related through an 1897 cartoon of Uncle Sam waiting for the fruit of Cuba to drop into his basket, with the headline: "Patient Waiters Are Not Losers." Under ran the caption, with Uncle Sam saying as he looked up at the Cuban fruit: "I ain't in a hurry; it'll drop in my basket when it gets ripe."[26] In his hamper was the previous harvest representing California, Texas, Alaska and Louisiana. For Cuba to become part of the United States was simply a matter of time.

In a 1906 interview with the *Minneapolis Journal*, Indiana senator Albert Beveridge stated that having Cuba fall into America's imperial basket was an obvious reality:

> That Cuba should be American is the highest example of manifest destiny in history. Geography makes her American—she is geographically part of Florida. Her position in the Gulf makes her America. No island so small ever maintained a separate existence near a country so great and a government so powerful.[27]

There seems to be no reporting on whether the average Cuban citizen subscribed to that perception.

Author and Cuban expert Louis Pérez Jr.[28] commented that historically the press was an important element in establishing American foreign policy intent over the island:

> Cuba has been an obsession for the United States since the time of Jefferson. It has always been said that, because of the economy, the investments, but it really has to do with the concept of national security of the U.S. For Americans, since the nineteenth century, since they took possession of Louisiana and Florida, Cuba was presented as its southern border, the egress and entry to the Gulf of Mexico. From that moment on, it was a strategic point for them and it entered into the American mindset that Cuba was going to be their possession.[29]

Pérez went back even further, describing how Cuba has been rooted in America's imagination almost since the time Columbus "discovered' in 1492 what he described as the most beautiful island he had ever seen. The island's beauty soon evolved into one of the Spanish government's most prized possession in the New World. The United States became determined to take hold of it.

* * *

Washington utilized the explosion of the battleship USS *Maine* and subsequent media coverage as the catalyst that brought America into the Cuban war for independence, resulting in the concept that the liberation of the island and the management of a proper civilization could only transpire through ownership. It was the completion of a long sought-after foreign policy goal, one fully backed by the mainstream media.

The war ended when US forces defeated the Spanish in Santiago de Cuba, six weeks after entering. The storyline was then established as to who won and who would enjoy the spoils of victory. The *New York Times* reported: "The Cubans who have made a pretense of fighting with us have proved worthless in the field. It would be a tragedy, a crime, to deliver the island into their hands."[30] After the battle, *New York Times*' correspondent Stanhope Sams was direct in his disdain for the locals:

> There is no Cuba. There are no Cuban people. There are not freemen here to whom we could deliver this marvelous island. We have fought for a spectral republic ... If we are to save Cuba, we must hold it. If we leave it to the Cubans, we give it over to a reign of terror.[31]

Coverage effectively constructed a storyline where the Cubans had no military influence despite three years fighting and bringing the Spanish to the verge of defeat. In reality, it was precisely because the Cubans had been so successful in weakening the Spanish forces that the Americans were able to come in and end the conflict in just six weeks. It was the rebels who harassed the enemy constantly, reducing their forces and allowing the marines to land at Santiago unopposed. Cuba's contribution was vital.[32]

Those facts were rarely acknowledged within the media. Instead, the account maintained that American efforts alone won the war, the Cubans were of no substance militarily and, by extrapolation, were unworthy to govern. The public then readily believed the United States had to exert domination over these ill-equipped locals. Justification was constructed as a consequence of the blood and capital expended to save these unfit Cubans; ownership was expected as the result of their effort. It was the press that established and maintained the fiction that because it was American might that saved Cuba, it was American right to own it. On the third anniversary of the Spanish defeat, the *St Louis Democrat* expressed the prevalent sentiment when it reminded readers, "it was the Americans who emancipated Cuba."[33]

Thanks to the newspapers of the day, the public came to appreciate how authority over Cuba was not only required, but was also an ethical imperative and a noble endeavor. *New York Tribune* publisher Whitelaw Reid made the case when he wrote:

> Are we not … bound in honor and morals to see to it that the government which replaces Spanish rule is better? Are we not morally culpable and disgraced before the civilized world if we leave it as bad, or worse?[34]

No right-thinking person would disagree that the United States was enforcing jurisdiction over Cuba not only for the sake of the locals, but also for the good moral standing of the imposing force. And when no Cuban voice was allowed to speak, the media had accomplished the political goal most effectively.

When the press did notice the Cubans, it was usually in the continuation to portray them as children, unable to protect their own country, with no experience or aptitude for governance. The media's descriptions that US efforts alone were responsible for Cuban "freedom" became accepted dogma. Those biased portrayals helped the USA enforce control and remained in use to defend continued authority. It was a deceit the media sustained throughout the more than half-century hegemony, until Fidel Castro established a Cuban truth that the press has unrelentingly attacked ever since.

The war ended with Spain losing its last colonies in the New World. Besides Cuba, the United States took the Philippines, Puerto Rico and the Pacific island of Guam. With it, the USA entered onto the international stage as a great power.

Once the conflict was over, a three-year military occupation was imposed on Cuba, with governor Leonard Wood permitting

American businessmen to snap up the best parts of agriculture, transportation and industry, while the locals faced various restrictions in the reconstruction of their own country. With Cuba now under effective US domination, the media had no compunction in reinforcing the negative perceptions of the rebel Cuban leadership and its inability to govern. Now saved from the Spanish, the Cubans had to be saved from themselves.

The unfortunate Cubans had badly misunderstood US intentions, naively believing once the Spanish were defeated, the Americans would leave. In that they were sorely mistaken, and it was the mainstream media that informed the rabble in no uncertain terms what the new reality would look like.

Often editorial cartoons depicted a fatherly American figure either cleaning up a soiled black Cuban child or cradling an infant in his protective arms—all to promote the concept of a country unable to take care of itself. If an adult was represented, it was usually a Cuban women being taught to drive a car or ride a bike as metaphor for slowly learning the skills of self-government.[35] The teacher, of course, would determine the readiness.

One of the most effective imagery used by the press in support of American hegemony was the return to the allegory of the Cuban as child, a device so effectively employed to justify US entry into the conflict. Now the media reported the Cubans were nowhere close to the social maturity needed for government, providing justification for US domination, offering no other viewpoint than what benefitted American business and political interests.

Newspapers and magazines in all the major cities described the island population as misbehaving toddlers, infants lacking any intellectual capacity or ill-mannered adolescents in need of America's firm hand and parentage.[36] To this day that conceit can be found in US media reports on the current relationship between the two countries.

The *New York Times* made clear in a January 3, 1899 article: "We are guardians, self-appointed to the Cuba people. Our honorable duty to our wards demands that we faithfully care for their estate until they are of age and discretion to take care of it themselves."[37] This was printed two days after the American flag was planted on the island, the Spanish colonial power at an end and the US military occupation underway. Cuba was at last under United States governance, and the media expected it to stay that way.

Connecticut Senator Orville Platt, who soon became infamous for creating the legislative control over the island, was covered in the press in 1901: "In many respects they are like children. They are passionately devoted to the sentiment of liberty, freedom and independence but as yet have little real idea of the responsibilities, duties and practical results of republican government."[38] Platt would demonstrate, just a few months later, the lessons the Cubans would have to learn under American tutelage.

Besides the child imagery, education and race also played a role in the justification of domination. The *New York Times* concurred with the political perspective that Cuba's substantial black population would have a negative influence on the abilities of the whites to govern. The paper warned of an, "irresponsible government of half-breeds. The negroes, too, who in varying degrees of mixture, constitute nearly one half of the population are another uncertain element."[39] The consequences would be dire, the *New York Times* warned:

> If we are to save Cuba we must hold it. If we leave it to the Cubans, we give it over to a reign of terror—to the machete and the torch, to insurrection and assassination. It would be a tragedy, a crime, to deliver the island into their hands.[40]

When those illusions were too subtle, some newspapers went for the more direct approach. The *Hartford Post* disgracefully denigrated the revolutionaries in an editorial that stated: "President McKinley was right when with all his power he successfully resisted the demand of Congress and of a large section of people that these cowardly, good for nothing insurgents be recognized as an independent government."[41]

Anyone in Cuba who dared object to the new colonial arrangement were described by the *Washington Post*, "as a handful of professional agitators, whom in all probability, we shall have to hang or exile if we want to set up civilized institutions in Cuba."[42] Following a violent uprising in 1906 against American occupation, the *Chicago Tribune* posited the ultimate solution:

> If it were physically possible and not abhorrent to the principals of civilization it would be desirable to submerge the island of Cuba until most of the population had disappeared and then resurrect it. Then the island would be washed clean and it would be a decent and attractive place for Americans to settle.[43]

While the *Chicago Tribune*'s reaction was extreme, the mainstream media consistently championed the conceit that the Cubans were simply not ready for self-government, logically inferring the USA had no choice but to impose its civilizing benefits. Denigrating Cuban capabilities is a biased narrative that maintains itself in the corporate press to this day.

With Cuba still under US military occupation, the *Washington Evening Star*, in 1901, commented:

> It would seem that the present generation in Cuba is unfitted for self-government. The next generation, trained in a different school and provided with different ideals of government, could very likely meet the necessary obligations of government with success. The people need a strong hand over them.[44]

And the *Chicago Tribune* couldn't put it any clearer when it editorialized: "We are obliged to protect Cuba from itself."[45]

Readership was left with but one conclusion—the USA was going to stay in Cuba for its own good, for the advancement of the unworthy citizenry. No consideration was given to the achievements or aspirations of the locals. It could not, if the press was to fulfill its duty to state objectives. During the military occupation from 1898 to 1901, the real strategy of imposing jurisdiction over the island for the benefit of American political and economic interests would not be reported in any depth—the media deemed those facts would be inconvenient to the ownership narrative—until it became necessary for the press to crank up the propaganda machine one more time.

Dominion once concluded, the political establishment in Washington had to go about setting up the legislative cover for long-term hegemony. It came in the form of the Platt Amendment, introduced and named after Senator Orville Platt—the man who so condescendingly perceived the Cubans as unworthy children. With the law in place, it was now up to the press to make sure the American public understood the Platt Amendment was of absolute necessity, regardless of the hesitation or objection of the Cuban people. The Amendment was introduced as an appendix to the American-designed Cuban constitution of 1901 and ratified as part of the permanent treaty of 1903, remaining as law until 1934. The Amendment put in writing American domination of Cuba's social/economic system as well as controlling the country's foreign policies. Some of the most onerous aspects of Platt to Cuban sovereignty included: the right to intervene in Cuba's internal affairs including during peaceful protests; denial of setting foreign policy; and giving the USA a naval base which happens to still exist at Guantanamo Bay. The Amendment also set up conditions to arrange political and economic systems for American interests primarily: prohibiting the transfer of land to any power other than the United States; mandating that Cuba would contract no foreign debt without guarantees that the interest could be served from ordinary revenues; encouraging American investment at favorable conditions; and promoting the colonization of Cuban land.[46] Connected with the Amendment were treaties that ratified a tariff pact giving Cuban sugar preference in US markets and protection to selected products sold into Cuba. America dictated the price they would pay for the island's vital cash crop, sugar. It was the development of the one-sided integration of the island's economy to the northern power.

By 1905, more than $50 million worth of property was in American hands, primarily sugar, tobacco and construction. Cheap immigration labor was introduced, forcing wages down and restricting local workers opportunities in production and manufacturing. Those Spaniards who had stayed maintained dominance over small businesses, limiting further native participation in the emerging capitalist-based economy. Direct American investment controlled 80 percent of all sugar mills, the banks, the electric and telephone company, and all oil refineries.[47] US speculators bought up hundreds of thousands of prime acreage, leading to approximately 75 percent of all arable land being under foreign command by 1958—predominately American. What was left for the nationals was civil service and local government participation, often leading to corruption and manipulation as the only means to advance politically and socially.[48]

The Amendment was not without a sense of irony. One clause prohibited Cuba from negotiating treaties with any country other than the United States, "which will impair or to impair the independence of Cuba" or "permit any foreign power or powers to obtain ... lodgment in or control over any portion" of Cuba. While Cuban nationals bridled at the restrictions to self-determination, America simultaneously told the unappreciative islanders they now had independence, at the same time as refusing them the right to conduct the basic prerogatives of state. On the few occasions the Cubans made an attempt to exercise autonomy, as occurred when the American-installed Tomás Estrada Palma government contemplated a trade agreement with England in 1902, the indignant reaction from the United States was swift and revealing. Officials expressing outrage were given wide press coverage, as Special Envoy to Cuba, Tasker Bliss thundered:

> It would be an extraordinary spectacle, if Cuba geographically a part of our own country and exercising the powers of an independent nation solely as the result of the expenditure of our blood and our capital, should conclude a treaty of friendship and commerce with England and not with us.[49]

Although the Platt Amendment met with ferocious opposition from Cuban politicians and the public, the legislation was passed by just one vote. Final acceptance was the result of blackmail; with the US side telling the "free" Cubans that they would have to accept the Amendment as a condition for ending military occupation. The Amendment was a stark example of US duplicity: on one hand claiming to be providing independence, while at the same time stripping the locals of all essential characteristics of sovereignty.

Understanding the hypocrisy of the legislation, US politicians realized the need to sway public opinion. Convincing the Cuban side was no longer required, as the Amendment permitted the United States to intervene militarily in order to quell any local unrest—a condition put to use on many occasions. The press, having done such an admirable job of portraying the Cubans as needing American guidance to attain independence, then went about convincing its readership independence could only be realized through the Platt Amendment. And it was the return of an old favorite—Cuba as child—that helped accomplish that goal.

Editorial cartoons were particularly effective in conveying the idea that the Cubans were children who had to accept the Platt Amendment for their own good. To take the medicine, whether they liked it or not.

A 1901 *New York World* drawing portrayed a Cuban delegation as a group of five boys waiting for an American official to give them a spoonful from the Platt Amendment medicine bowl, to swallow it without complaint. The caption reads: "Now, then, open your mouths and shut your eyes. And you'll all get something that will make you wise."[50] Two months later, the *New York World* was more direct, with a depiction of an American businessman looking over the fence at two politicians forcing the Platt Amendment down the throat of a struggling Cuban child.[51]

Whether Cubans liked it or not, Platt was the guideline for America's legal jurisdiction over the island. As far as the press was concerned, it was what the Cubans had always longed for. The *New York Tribune* triumphed that the Amendment was: "The promise the US made is fulfilled … Free Cuba is an accomplished fact."[52]

In those rare instances when the truth of the Amendment's real purpose was spoken, it was far removed from public awareness. In a moment of private candor, Military Governor Leonard Wood knew exactly what the United States had accomplished under its rules. "There is, of course, little or no independence left in Cuba under the Platt Amendment. It is quite apparent that she is absolutely in our hands."[53] He also had no doubt as to when that situation would change: "The US must always control the destines of Cuba."[54]

If any ungrateful Cubans were thinking about protesting the Amendment, the press was ready to come to its defense. Those who would object to US intentions were scolded by the *Philadelphia Inquirer*, claiming they were "military adventurers and scheming politicians," who represented "the most ignorant and radical classes of the Cuban population." Besides, it was apparently obvious that the Amendment was there to "safeguard the independence of the republic of Cuba." And "no Cuban can have any reasonable occasion to object."[55]

When, in 1906, the locals dared to protest violently against the restrictions imposed under the Amendment, the *Chicago Tribune* made sure its readers understood that America's legal right to put down these churlish, immature demonstrators was a noble, self-sacrificing endeavor:

> The United States reserved the right to intervene in the affairs of Cuba whenever necessary to preserve public order and insure the protection of life and property … That is where we stand now. We are the parent, Cuba is the child; and the child is about due for a good spanking.[56]

After the protests, it was the *Washington Post* agreeing with President Theodore Roosevelt that the Cubans, "must cease their family quarrel or he will be compelled to apply the rod to them."[57] The *New York Times* refined the analysis in an editorial the same year: "Our Cuban neighbors are in truth very much like children. They are above the age of spanking, yet they manifestly stand in need of correction."[58]

With Cuba not even having the liberty to protest without a foreign power interfering, the country was now fully under US domination. During this time, the American press preserved the fiction of Cuban freedom and self-determination and made sure readers were not to forget who was responsible for it all. Platt was simply, the *New York Tribune* boasted, "the promise of the US made is fulfilled … Free Cuba is an accomplished fact."[59]

In the years that followed, American interests were integrated into all aspects of Cuban society, including the press. Newspapers set up in the new republic were often financed and directed by American concerns. Not surprisingly, this media maintained Washington's version of recent history. The *Havana Post*, the largest English language paper in Cuba under US ownership, reacted with great indignation when the more independently minded newspaper *El Heraldo de Cuba* criticized US imperial policy in Mexico in 1916:

> One would think that after the Americans set Cuba free and guaranteed her sovereignty … that there would never be heard anything but kindly phrases for the great and good friend of the north, but such is not the case for it is a startling fact that practically all newspapers are in active sympathy with Mexico … Has Mexico guaranteed to the world that the sovereignty of Cuba shall never be impaired, as the United States has? No?[60]

The *Havana Post* report came with great exasperation and very little sense of irony. Foreign domination was so complete that even the local media accepted and internalized the rationalizations for integration.

During the decades of hegemony, the media became an important component in constructing a false historiography within the psyche of the American public, one that stated it was the United States that unselfishly rescued Cuba and provided freedom from their Spanish overlords—and that the Cubans should be eternally appreciative of the great social/economic benefits US benevolence brought. "The Americans capacity for self-deception was exceeded only by their insistence that the Cubans, too, subscribed to the deception—and should be grateful." So wrote Louis A. Pérez Jr. in his seminal work on American perceptions of Cuba.[61]

Along with the view that Cubans should be eternally appreciative, the press and the politicians of the 1940s and 1950s maintained the perspective that the locals were still not mature enough for the Americans to relinquish control. Following protests in 1947, the newspapers widely quoted US diplomat Ellis Briggs that: "It is time that Cuba grow up."[62] To bestow adulthood on the citizens would have denied the claim the Cubans were unfit for true self-government. The end of that deceit came when the revolutionaries took over in 1959, Fidel Castro plainly stating: "I believe that this country has the same rights of other countries to govern itself."[63] With the child card no longer possible to play, the media switched from criticisms of competency to biased anti-revolutionary condemnations. It is a standard of misinformation still much in use to this day.

By the late 1940s, American domination over the island nation was running smoothly, eliciting little need for the media's usual remonstrations. When the press did give the country any attention, it was invariably focused on Havana and the wonderful playground it was offering American vacationers, gamblers and those looking for more. Havana became the Paris of the Caribbean, or the Paris of Latin America or the Paris of the Americas, according to the press.

"A winter playground," so described journalist Gary Schumacher, while in 1953 the *Saturday Evening Post* called Havana, "One of the last of the world's sinful cities."[64] Other media turned the capital of Cuba into a Disneyland for adults, "play land of the Americas," "a veritable fairyland," "a land of enchantment," a "paradise on earth."[65]

And while tourists flocked to the island for fun and sun, the media were always there to remind vacationers of how this was made possible.

"Not until the United States came to the aid of these people were they released from their bondage," travel writer Marian George wrote in 1930. Adding disingenuously that before the USA came along, Cuba "had no government, there were no schools outside of a few of the largest towns, the country was full of beggars, the towns were unclean and there were swarms of hungry, homeless destitute people everywhere."[66]

Fellow travel writer C.H. Forbes-Lindsay invoked the classic imagery of inadequacy when he explained, "the Cuban has neither the force nor the executive ability to carry out his designs. For a full century, he has conspired to throw off the galling yoke of Spain, and he would never had done it but for the intervention of the United States."[67] For the more direct approach, Henry Wack editorialized, in 1931: "But for the liberation of our Cuban neighbors by the US ... Havana would still be the dump it was in the last century."[68]

After a ten-day vacation to Cuba, Wilkes-Barre mayor Daniel Hart brought together archetypal historical revisionism and metaphor when he gushed to the American-owned *Havana Post*:

> I am more than proud that America played its part in giving to Cuba and her people the freedom long prayed for. Cuba loves America and Americans. There isn't anything they will not do for our country. Cuba is our child. I wish her to be the loveable child she is.[69]

Not surprisingly, the average tourist developed an inflated sense of entitlement when visiting these welcoming locals, expecting unrestrained and eternal gratitude for the bestowment of freedom and civilization. That predominate sentiment of superiority was infrequently challenged, although on rare occasion it was recognized. The *Havana Post* commented acidly in a 1916 editorial that these stateside visitors, "think because they are Americans, the Cubans should take off their hats when they pass by or get down on their knees and weep tears of gratitude at every opportunity."[70]

Fidel Castro shattered the conceit of eternal indebtedness, the shock still reverberating to this day in America's conscious and in the media's anti-revolutionary narratives. The charismatic leader burst into the attention of mainstream press in the mid-1950s with the coverage initially describing him as a romantic, almost comic book action character. There was little depth to the reporting, journalists having an easier time superficially labeling the man and not the message. From the start, Fidel Castro's critical opinions of America hegemony came from a Cuban perspective, as did his examinations of the profound social ills the nation was facing. The press ignored the deeper meaning of his reproachful statements against the United States and assumed he was simply working toward ending the Batista dictatorship—nothing more. His underlying commitment to true Cuban liberation regardless of the consequences it would have to the relationship with the northern neighbor was not understood. It could not have been, as it was the press who invented the fiction of an obligation for perpetual friendship through the obedient gratitude of a people forever in debt to the USA for its "freedom." No Cuban would intentionally want it otherwise, the press had constantly reported. When Fidel Castro revealed an alternative truth and put Cuban interests above any foreign power, the media in its total incomprehension turned against him with unrestrained fury.[71]

Before Fidel Castro was denounced as traitorously anti-American, journalists had been turning him into a one-dimensional, quixotic figure with little regard to how the United States' domination of Cuba was driving the underlying rationale for the revolution—or how it could negatively affect the relationship between the two countries. A prime example was when Fidel

Castro visited New York in April 1959, the media treated him like a rock star, following and photographing his every move, reveling in the image of guerilla fighter defeating a brutal dictator. His interviews were mostly fluff pieces, including one conducted by *Meet the Press* or at the meeting with the American Society of Newspaper Editors.[72]

Few reporters recognized the future damage these disingenuous descriptions were doing. One who did acknowledge the potential consequences was Herbert Matthews of the *New York Times*, who complained the North American press were romanticizing Castro as:

> If he were a knight in shining armor who had come to Havana on a white horse and who was going to make democracy bring social justice but otherwise let things go on as before. In reality, Americans were welcoming a figure who did not exist, expecting what could not and would not happen, then blaming Fidel Castro for their own blindness and ignorance.[73]

Matthews became famous for being the first journalist to track down Fidel Castro in the mountains in 1957, sending balanced, truthful and sympathetic reports of the revolutionaries and their struggle against Batista. Matthew's access to the Cuban leader, and subsequent biography, led many of his colleagues to criticize him for being duped by Fidel Castro following the revolution's alignment with the Soviet Union. It ruined his career, as he was forever after stigmatized for his journalist integrity—something of rare concern when covering Cuba.

When the relationship between Cuba and the USA deteriorated in the first year of the revolution, Castro's expressions of anger, ingratitude and anti-Americanism worsened. The press was no longer describing him as a romantic figure.[74] For such a long time the press had shaped, sustained and believed in a historical fiction they created, and expected Fidel Castro to follow right along. When the Cuban Revolution pushed back on that historiography, in strong anti-American terminology, there was nothing from the press but disbelief turning to mistrust, then contempt.

It wasn't only the press that misread Fidel Castro's definition of true Cuban independence. Washington's expectation was as self-delusional as the media's—that Fidel Castro would simply become the latest Cuban leader to acquiesce to the continuation of US jurisdiction over the country. A 1958 report from the Senate Foreign Relations Committee, prepared by Vermont Senator George Aiken, was startling in its misreading of the situation to the point of near desperation:

> Happily for the United States, if there should be a change in the government of all Cuba it is difficult to conceive of the possibility that any new regime would be unfriendly to the United States. The Cubans know and cherish the fact that we assisted them to attain independence.[75]

Former US Ambassador to Cuba Earl E.T. Smith recalled the prevailing opinion among Washington officials in late 1958, "that they would be able to control Castro." When that fallacy fell apart a few months later, political demands for punishment against these ungrateful Cubans was taken up enthusiastically by the press.[76] What the media and the politicians missed, intentionally or through blind ignorance, was Fidel Castro's demand for a Cuban definition of nationalism. He commanded overwhelming public national support, and that combination would soon collide with America's historical mythology resulting in unfortunate and long-lasting consequences. It became yet another example of state and media converging to present a united front on Cuban foreign policy, in this case with tragic consequences.

The *New York Times* reporter Matthews again seemed to be a lone voice when he tried to warn his readers that the upcoming storm was being blown by anti-American sentiment. "It is disturbing to find that the opposition, which contains some of the best elements in Cuban life, is today bitterly or sadly anti-United States," he wrote in early 1957.[77]

When the reality was fulfilled in revolution, the media still could not bring itself to examine why it had transpired. It was less complicated to develop a new anti-Castro narrative, than it was to examine if there were legitimate justifications for the revolution's denunciations of American neo-colonialism. Making it personal meant not having to scrutinize the real issues.

By the end of 1960, the coverage was focused on personality—that Fidel Castro was crazy, he was a Svengali, or worse, a communist. It was far easier to tell the public that this new Cuban leader was evil, that his followers were being deceived down the path to communism, that they were under the spell of Fidelismo, and that the USA had absolutely no role, or blame, in what was happening. This was now the American government's position, with then Vice-President Richard Nixon comments widely reported after meeting Fidel Castro: "He is either incredibly naive about communism or under communist discipline. My guess is the former."[78]

* * *

That the average American had no idea what was going on in revolutionary Cuba and why, in large part as a result of misinformed press coverage, came as no surprise to the few reporters who were covering things on the ground. "We do not have any comprehension of the way they feel or to a considerable extent what is happening there," Matthews reported in early 1960.[79] When the revolution destroyed the decades-old media narrative of a benign Cuba accepting American over-lordship, the press reacted like a scorned lover. The *New York Times* wondered in early 1960, "how to explain the inexplicable" and determined: "What is happening in Cuba is a mystery."[80] No longer a sympathetic figure, now Castro is "an enigma … to the diplomats and journalists who have dealt with him," wrote correspondent Irving Pflaum in 1960.[81] Soon he would become evil incarnate.

The media became mystified because it had refused to acknowledge any other informational frame of reference. Cuba was to be eternally grateful to the USA for its freedom and independence; American hegemony was benign and progressive. The press created those images on its pages, as well as in the public's mind, which had no basis in fact. It led to reactions of disbelief, misunderstanding and anger at the loss of a reality that had not existed—thanks to the media's success in narrating fiction and expectations instead of reporting the truth.

The final blow to American credulity came when the Cubans moved into the Soviet Union sphere after the disastrous Bay of Pigs invasion in 1961. The decision by the Castro government to embrace Soviet orthodoxy was a result of ideology, economy and security, influenced by America's now stated desire to destroy the revolution, fully supported by the mainstream media. For the American public, however, it was the ultimate shock to a relationship first betrayed, now completely shattered.

Years later, America's most trusted news broadcaster Walter Cronkite synthesized all the myths of pre-revolutionary Cuba and the disastrous impact of Fidel Castro:

> The rise of Fidel Castro in Cuba, his successful revolution against Batista...was a terrible shock to the American people. This brought communism practically to our shore. Cuba was a resort land for Americans ... and it was just a part of America, we kind of considered it part of the United States—of course, it is part of America—we considered it part of the United States practically, just a wonderful little country over there that was of no danger to anybody. The country was a little colony. Suddenly, revolution and it became communist and allied with the Soviet Union ... An ally of the Soviet Union off our shores—it was frightening.[82]

From friendly neighbor to frightening foe—concepts developed, promoted and sustained by the media's historically deceptive coverage of the island nation. It was a reflection going back to the Spanish-American War, commented on by American Clarke Musgrave, who fought with the Cubans in 1895 and had little sympathy for the newspapers reporting invented fantasies as facts:

> Some of the very writers who in Havana had misled the public with faked stories of victorious insurgent armies sweeping the island now found material at the expense of the Cubans in the expose of the phantasms created by their own imaginations.[83]

His comments retain validity in the subsequent period leading up to and after the Cuban Revolution. When Fidel Castro made clear the new rules of the game, the media did not take kindly to having its images shattered. Instead, it went on a rampage of misinformation and outright falsehoods about the Cuban Revolution that persists to this day. The press had established, in the public's mind, the incompetency of the Cubans for self-determination after 1899, justifying American hegemony and continued domination of a people it didn't understand or appreciate. Current mainstream media's coverage of Cuba retains remarkable similarities—focusing on the shortcomings and inadequacies of the government and the citizens who support it, with no context to regime change polices that contribute to the difficulties. The clear implication is the Castro government has been incapable to the point of incompetence—a self-invented chronicle of the supposed failings of Cuban independence and its leadership that has its historical antecedents stretching back more than a century.

It wasn't long after the revolution triumphed that the media put those misinformed narrative concepts into full force.

2
The Media versus the Revolution

Months after the triumph of the Cuban Revolution, political elites and mainstream media still could not grasp the new reality. Decades of domination assimilated the arrogant fiction of ownership, of the United States deciding Cuba's fate. The media had no hesitation in replicating the prevailing imperial attitude that Castro's misguided perceptions of national independence were conditional on American design.

"We should decide whether or not we wish to have the Cuban revolution succeed," proclaimed Assistant Secretary of State J.C. Hill in September 1959.[1] In early 1960, Robert Kennedy then made it clear what that decision would be. The overthrow of the Castro regime, he said: "Is the top priority of the US government, all else is secondary, no time, money, effort or manpower is to be spared."[2]

While politicians expressed policy, the press was tasked to manufacture acceptable public opinion in support of regime change. The method utilized was to demonstrate how malevolent, brutal and unstable Castro and his followers were becoming as they turned the revolution inexorably against American hegemony. In conjunction, media promoted the perception that such animosity was completely undeserving, and in fact incomprehensible as to why these rebels would so malign their benefactors. The *Saturday Evening Post* reflected the common sentiment that what was taking place in Cuba was, "a mystery to the outsider."[3]

With few American newsmen on the ground in the first months of the revolution, reporting turned from any semblance of fact-based coverage to strictly emotional or speculative commentary. An absurd angle the media tried to convince itself, and its readers, of was that Fidel Castro had actually betrayed the revolution he led. It was as if the press, and by extension the United States government, would determine the rules and definitions of what the revolution could, and couldn't do. It also provided moral justification for the increasing number of terrorist attacks against Cuban civilian targets. Presidential candidate John F. Kennedy's comments were given front page coverage in the *New York Times*: "Castro and his gang have betrayed the ideals of the Cuban revolution and the hopes of the Cuban people."[4]

When Kennedy became president, his opinion surprisingly matured from the superficial concept of betrayal, to a more honest and deeper understanding of the revolution's necessity. Speaking to French journalist Jean Daniel, on his way to meet Castro in 1963, the US president articulated:

> I believe that there is no country in the world, including all the African regions, including any and all the countries under colonial domination, where economic colonization, humiliation and exploitation were worse than in Cuba, in part owning to my country's policies during the Batista regime ...To some extent it is as though Batista was the incarnation of a number of sins on the part of the United States. Now we shall have to pay for those sins.[5]

That revelation did not, however, prevent Kennedy from publicly support every effort at regime change, including economic embargo and acts of terrorism.

Historian Van Gosse suggested the misguided concept of betrayal was a reaction from those in the media who completely misread and romanticized the revolution, hoping it would somehow conform to American expectations—something Fidel Castro clearly stated it would never do.

> The reporters, editors and publishers who wrote or condoned pro-Castro coverage earlier did genuinely feel betrayed by Castro in power. It was as if North Americans discovered that Fidel really did mean what he said about a great cleansing national revolution.[6]

Betrayal was in fact not to the revolution, but as part of the fictional relationship the media had created where the Cubans were expected to be eternally grateful to their benevolent protector. *TIME* magazine's indignation showed in 1960 when it described Cuba no longer as a paradise, but an irate and "truculent neighbor."[7] Even before that, *TIME* was working hard on establishing the anti-revolutionary narrative with an extensive front cover report less than a month after the triumph. Their January 26, 1959 article titled "Cuba Democracy or Dictatorship?" focused on the government's execution of the worst elements of the Batista regime, legally tried and convicted under overwhelming popular support. *TIME* condemned the trials while downplaying the brutality of the US-backed Batista regime. Acknowledging the need for change, the article criticized the extremes Fidel Castro was implementing in one of the first attempts to convince American readership that US hegemony needed to be tweaked, not eliminated. "He is full of soaring vaguely leftist hopes for Cuba's future but has no clear program."[8] That dissembling demonstrated the writer had never heard Fidel Castro express exactly what the revolution was about and wanted to achieve, or simply desired to create the foundation for America's ersatz bewilderment as to why the Cubans were acting so aggrieved. Revealingly, there was not one word that Cuba under American control produced the horrors of Batista's regime or the need for revolution to establish true independence. The revolutionaries, *TIME* reported, were turning into a bunch of bloodthirsty radicals with the sniff of communism about them.

Revolutionary anger was as unfathomable as the lack of gratitude. No more were the Cubans humble or subservient, these people were displaying a demand for respect and recognition of their historical grievances. When the country moved fully into the Soviet sphere for economic and political security following the Bay of Pigs in 1961, the media easily manipulated the flow of information now curtailed under the travel conditions imposed on US citizens by their government. From describing pre-revolutionary Cuba as a tourist playground, it was a quick turn to now define the nation as an armed camp, a repressive state and a colony for the Soviets. The press could get away with those descriptions as the newly emplaced travel restrictions permitted almost no challenges to the fallacies. Few in the media were reporting first hand from Cuba, instead they relied almost exclusively on the predisposed accounts of the anti-revolutionary exiles, who were more than happy to provide the most damaging details possible of what was happening in their homeland.

Historical revisionism became the media's clarion call. "The War for Cuba's Freedom" the *Roanoke World News* exclaimed, "True to the principal that it did not covet territory, the United States gave full freedom to the Cuban people within 2 years—as soon as they could be prepared for it."[9] The article promoted the accepted idea that it was the USA that solely determined the conditions of "freedom" based on the inadequacies of Cuban abilities—as well as the intellectual dishonesty of ignoring American neo-colonialism.

That unrecognized one-sided relationship expressed itself in the notion of Cuban gratitude, or lack thereof. It was a topic some in the media used as justification to criticize the Cubans and the revolution. "The history of this island since its liberation from Spain, does not record many examples of Cuban gratitude for contributions made by the United States in lives blood and dollars," griped the *New York Times*' correspondent Ruby Hart Phillips in 1961.[10]

Fidel Castro and the revolutionaries simply shrugged and declared that self-determination would be resolved by the Cubans—no longer by the American press, politicians or public.

As the relationship devolved deeper into hostility, the media for the most part maintained its self-imposed ignorance as to the roots, proclaiming that things should carry on as normal once the Batista dictatorship was removed. The idea that Cuba had no legitimate complaint against the country that had provided them with "liberty" remained a newspaper standard.

"Castro has rejected friendship with the country that liberated Cuba in 1898" the *Charleston News and Courier* criticized in early 1960. "What is Castro doing to us, the country that liberated Cuba in 1898," grumbled the *Bangor Daily News*.[11]

It was the rare report that recognized the Cuban perspective, when Herbert Matthews acknowledged, "Dr. Fidel Castro is the greatest hero that their history has known."[12] It was that type of reality-based journalism from a Cuban angle that eventually led to Matthews being ostracized by his media colleagues as being a dupe of Castro and a communist sympathizer.[13] His narrative of a positive Fidel Castro fully supported by the Cuban people could not be allowed to stand.[14]

With no rational account offered to explain the origins of revolution—a deliberate censorship refusing to acknowledge Cuban nationalism as its cause—the media found it simpler to denigrate the revolutionaries and the masses of misguided followers. Classic metaphors were brought out, portraying Castro as a spoiled child, or as mentally unstable. Those who supported him were the worst sort—ungrateful, uneducated and easily manipulated by Castro's incomprehensible anti-American exhortations. The reader could accept Fidel Castro's mental instability and his supporters' churlishness as a palatable motivation for why the Cubans were rejecting American hegemony. Delving into the historical injustices, desire for true self-determination and the roots of Batista's dictatorship would shed too much light on American culpability. It was far easier to deflect onto something uncomplicated—that it was a continuing character defect of the ill-mannered Cubans who were not intellectually capable to resist Fidel Castro's mind-controlling manipulations. The Americans were certainly not to blame. And so the press went to work.

The *New York Times* reporter Tad Szulc described Fidel Castro as "an over grown boy,"[15] while correspondent Edwin Tetlow wrote, "I do not believe that Fidel Castro ever grew up fully, I have never known him to display that kind of emotional stability we attribute to the mature adult." Even more denigrating, Tetlow blandly stated that maybe Fidel Castro, "was just being Cuban."[16]

The editorial cartoonists added their impression of Castro's supposed immaturity when he was depicted as a spoiled child in a playpen, with the caption reading, "Spare the rod and spoil the child." This was published in the *Charleston News and Courier* on January 1, 1960[17]—the one-year anniversary of the triumph. It was apparent what slant the mainstream media would take to ensure the public would appreciate just how ungrateful and vindictive these Cubans were, having the temerity to challenge America's one-sided historiography of the past 50 years.

Even Fidel Castro acknowledged media attempts to frame the conversation against the revolution, invoking the very same images of a child to explain the Cuban side of its history under US rule:

They deprived the Cuban people of the prerogative to govern themselves. They deprived the Cuban people of their sovereignty; they treated the Cuban people like little children to whom they said: "We give you permission to do just this, and if you do more we will punish you." The Platt Amendment was imposed and we either behaved ourselves—behaved ourselves in the manner convenient to the foreign country—or we would lose our sovereignty.[18]

While that conversation was widely reported in Cuban revolutionary papers, this native perspective rarely made it to media in the United States. To do so would have challenged the long-held beliefs so carefully constructed over the decades. It would have given the American reader an insight that simply would not be permitted or be approved of by the political elite.

Not that the anti-American feelings were completely ignored. The lone voice of the *New York Times* reporter Herbert Matthews recounted in an article how Fidel Castro expressed his treatment as a child in the United States as: "Bitterly resentful of the way he said Ambassador Philip Bonsal had talked to him and treated him from the beginning it was so humiliating."[19]

When revolutionary policy unfolded in spring 1959, the press no longer considered Fidel Castro a child—just crazy. Columnist George Sokolsky pondered about his "psychological peculiarities" just three months after the revolution triumphed, while author Nathaniel Weyl wrote that Fidel Castro was suffering from, "paranoid schizophrenia." US ambassador Bonsal was reported in the mainstream press as describing Fidel Castro as, "a highly emotional individual," suffering from, "definite mental unbalance at times."[20]

This media-created chronicle, one that survives to this day, was to establish the mental instability and immaturity of Fidel Castro, and by implication the revolution itself. It made Cuba's rejection of America altruism understandable—it was nothing the blameless United States had done, but simply the mass hysteria of an ill-educated rabble following an unhinged cult figure.

The concept of imposing control over an unstable Fidel Castro, as a parent would do to a disobedient child, continued well into the 1980s. Under President Ronald Reagan, the media promoted the idea that Cuba had to be taught a proper lesson, under such articles as *US News and World Report*, "Reagans Goal: Cutting Castro Down to Size."[21] Even as the press became more focused on Latin American politics in the 1980s, Cuba didn't escape attention, sometimes creating a false intersecting. The *Washington Post* and *New York Times* reported as fact the rumor that Fidel Castro had sent 500 Cuban military personnel to El Salvador—reports that turned out to be completely false.[22]

During the Reagan administration, the USA established one of the most expensive media propaganda tools against Cuba—the government-funded Radio Televisión Martí. Operated under the Office of Cuba Broadcasting (OCB), more than $800 million of US taxpayer's money has been spent on these programs that have often been beset with corruption.[23] Radio Televisión Martí is generally recognized as a waste of time and money, as the Cuban government has effectively blocked transmission. Regardless, the OCB continues to receive funding that helps support many in the anti-Cuba industry based in South Florida. One of the latest schemes was revealed in 2018 with the OCB admitting it was creating fake accounts on Facebook and other social media outlets to inspire dissent and to spread propaganda in Cuba.[24] Anti-Cuba media has entered the twenty-first century—same story, different platform.

* * *

While the personal attacks on Cuban leadership continued, the press activated its biased reporting on the government's new social/economic policies. It was the beginning of the long process to ensure that anything good was rarely covered, or if revolutionary accomplishments were noted, negative comparatives would be included to diminish the affirmative aspects of the developing socialist society.

One of the first opportunities for the press to attack came with the nationalization of property. It is a myth that haunts Cuban–American relations to this day.

Fidel Castro made clear that a prime objective of the revolution would be to return the land to those who worked it. The

Agrarian Reform Law nationalized close to 500,000 acres, mostly owned by large American companies including the exploitive United Fruit Company.[25] That, along with taking over the Cuban Telephone Company, a subsidiary of ITT, as well as other foreign industries, cemented America's intent to end the revolution. "With the signature of the Agrarian Reform Law, it seems clear that our original hope was a vain one; Castro's Government is not the kind worth saving," acknowledged a high-ranking US official.[26]

Media outrage was predicated on the distortion that the nationalization process was illegal due to the Cuban government's lack of compensation. The extended implication was the revolution itself lacked legitimacy, a self-created fiction still promoted by the press to provide cover for America's regime change strategies. The media focused on the kernel of truth found in the compensation issue yet ignored the husk of information that would have provided context as to why no reparation was paid. Not because the Cuban government didn't offer it—but as a result of Washington's rejection to accept or negotiate.

The revolutionary government proposed reparation payments based on a 20-year fixed-term bond at interest rates of 4.5 percent, more than one point higher than what was available in the United States at that time. The proposal was well within international standards and United Nations guidelines.[27] Cuba's calculation for compensation was furthermore based on the October 1958 property assessments, unadjusted for 30 years due to landowner pressure not to increase taxes. The United States demanded payment on an arbitrary value they put on the land at time of nationalization, regardless of what was reported on the tax rolls. Fidel Castro's response was that either the foreign companies had been cheating the Cuban people for years based on undervalued tax calculations, or were trying to defraud them now by inflating land prices. As there was no other hard evidence to go on, the Cuban side stuck with the values based on tax rolls.

The American position on nationalization demanded the immediate return of property or full compensation to be paid in cash based on their inflated values. It was a situation impossible to meet following the $500 million stolen from the treasury when Batista fled, a fact that some in the mainstream US media did report on accurately.[28] Nor was it an international legal requirement to pay in full a price that one side arbitrarily sets. Fidel Castro's offer in the early 1960s to set up a committee to resolve the differences and arrange payment schedules was rejected by the USA. The Cuban government brought up the matter again in 2001, with Washington refusing to consider negotiations. Following Obama's opening in 2014, the topic has been discussed during the various bilateral meetings but still with no resolution.

When it became apparent that the American side had no intention of negotiation, the revolutionary government accelerated nationalizing property (regardless of what foreign entity owned it) with little regard to reparations. However, by the 1980s, compensation for nationalized properties belonging to all non-US countries had been settled.[29]

The refusal to accept or even negotiate compensation has rarely been reported by the mainstream media—while claims of the illegality of nationalization have long remained a propaganda tool.

In 1992, State Department spokesman Joe Snyder told the *Los Angeles Times*: "The Cuban government, in violation of international law, expropriated billions of dollars' worth of private property belonging to US individuals and has refused to make reasonable restitution." He then conveniently conflated the misinformation regarding the compensation matter with justification for America's economic punishment. "The US embargo … is therefore a legitimate response to the unreasonable and illegal behavior of the Cuban government."[30]

The matter has become so entrenched in the strategy of regime change that the 1996 Helms–Burton Act incorporated resolution of compensation as but one condition before the embargo and travel restrictions would be lifted.[31] America's blockade against Cuba was actually well considered before reparations became an unresolvable issue. The first step was scaling back and then eliminating the Cuban sugar quota, a proposal made two days after the Agrarian Reform Law went into effect on June 3, 1959, more than a year before the Americans decided to refuse to negotiate reparations.

Fabrication over the issue of compensation continues to be peddled in the press. A 2014 article in the *Boston Globe* re-introduced much of the fiction, claiming that Havana owes billions to the United States. The report restated the misinformation that, "the embargo was actually triggered by something concrete: an enormous pile of American assets that Castro seized in the process of nationalizing the Cuban economy." [32] Deeper in the article was a comment that American corporations were reluctant to openly pursue the claims for public relations reasons.

> The embargo has taken on more and more political meaning, and Cuba has become more destitute. The corporations that have these claims are very sensitive to bad press ... So they decide to keep a low profile and work quietly behind the scenes where possible.[33]

What the article failed to mention, other than anything about the offers of compensation, was that American entities affected by the nationalization have long ago written off the losses from their corporate taxes, permitted by the US government. The vast majority consider the matter settled and have no intention of pursing any further financial aspects.[34] Regardless, the Cuban side has consistently expressed interest in discussing the remaining outstanding claims with the intent to coming to a mutually agreeable resolution. And for the past 20 years, Havana has pursued a legal claim against the US government for billions in lost revenues as a result of the embargo.

CNN covered one of the most outrageous compensation claims in a 2016 account when it told the story of the family of Meyer Lansky who wanted Cuba to pay up for his casino. Lansky was part of the Mafia controlled gambling industry in pre-revolutionary Cuba, all supported by the Batista dictatorship.[35] The report noted: "'I think it owes us,' Gary Rapport grandson of the notorious Mafia criminal Lansky said of the Cuban government. 'We are the heirs of the estate of Meyer Lansky—they owed Meyer Lansky.'" *CNN* did point out that there's little chance of any payment as Lansky never put in a claim with the US government for the seized property.[36]

With the press consistently providing biased coverage of the nationalization issue, the next few years after the triumph of the revolution solidified media partiality and culpability. Two incidents focused the one-sided narrative. The first was during the April 1961 illegal invasion of the country by a group of ex-Batista supporters, trained and supported by the United States; the second followed a year later, with a crisis that brought the world to the brink of nuclear war—exacerbated by a press committed to confrontation and rumor mongering.

Three months prior to the April 1961 Bay of Pigs invasion, the Eisenhower administration decided to break diplomatic ties with Cuba. A *New York Times* editorial claimed the president had no choice, but warned of, "all the problems that come with a lack of diplomatic relationship ... the lack of knowledge and information through loss of contact, the increased tensions."[37]

The same editorial then exposed what would be a consistent construct of the media—creating parameters to arbitrarily establish value judgments with no acknowledgment of how American regime change policies impact those standards:

> Castro is carrying out a social revolution in Cuba and it has always been his contention that it is a Cuban, not a Communist revolution. Its success or failure in practical terms will depend on whether it fulfills the normal aims of a social revolution—redistribution of wealth, diversification of the sugar economy, industrialization, raising the general standards of living, building new schools, hospitals, roads and the like. A Cuba that was a distant appendage of the Sino-Soviet bloc or that was in a state of conflict with the United States for any length of time would fail to achieve these revolutionary aims.[38]

The *New York Times* intentionally misconstrued the revolution's foundation. It was not just a social movement, but a cultural and national upheaval that was meant to end foreign control of Cuba's historiography, in conjunction with instituting true self-determination. Cuba's actual accomplishment of those post-revolutionary social goals listed by the *New York Times* has been impressive, particularly as they have been realized, despite America's hostility including economic warfare and regime change policies.[39] Part of the credit was due to the economic and political support the Soviet Union provided. Those achievements can be compared very favorably to the far fewer social justice programs instituted while the country was under American hegemony.

With scant surprise, the *New York Times* has published no editorials examining the influence US actions have had in creating the conditions where Cuba without hesitation moved into the Soviet sphere.[40] Not just for political alignment and national security but also to ensure those social goals were irreversible. Proof of that commitment is found following the Soviet Union's collapse in 1989, where despite the loss of Moscow's significant financial support, the Castro government maintained such social benefits as free health care, education and subsidized housing. This was sustained during the worst years of Cuba's Special Period, when economic output dropped by an estimated 35 percent.

Intentional media manipulation became easily revealed during its coverage of the Bay of Pigs invasion. Prior to the attack, the *New York Times* editorial lectured the revolutionaries on how they should behave, the paper arrogantly dismissed suspicions of an impending assault. In its January 3, 1961 edition, the paper practically ridiculed Cuba for its well-justified fear. "It is incredible to us that the Cubans can believe we are about to invade their island," the *New York Times* remonstrated, adding that: "It is difficult for Americans to understand that others can honestly believe things about us that we know to be false."[41] The editorial was written when the *New York Times*, and many other major newspapers, were aware of the planning for the Bay of Pigs invasion. The attack just a few months later showed those "others" to be much more astute in assessing the truth. It has long been the function of the corporate press to denigrate Havana's legitimate worries and complaints, and to portray American hostility as either of no concern or completely non-existent.

The Bay of Pigs (known in Cuba as the battle at Playa Giron) remains an emotional connect with the anti-Castro militants and the preponderance of the mainstream media who saw it as a heroic attempt to liberate the island. The Cuban side considered the invaders as traitors who were trying to end the new government and return the country back to the control of American economic/political interests. The vast majority who made up the invasion force were anti-revolutionaries, who were promised positions of power under a re-installed US hegemony.

The invasion was intended to be a military operation that would catch the revolutionary government unawares. Great effort and expense was spent to clandestinely train the exiles in unknown military bases in Guatemala and South Florida. The problem with the covert plan was that the Cuban government knew about it from the inception—and the press was also well in on the secret with no compunction to keep it that way.

More than 20 years after the event, the *Washington Post* did an extensive retrospective of just how open the information was prior to the invasion, with the operation an easily accessible topic among the Cuba-American exile community in Miami.[42] It noted that just a few days before the invasion, the *New York Times* ran a front page story by Tad Szulc on the details, not wanting to be scooped by other newspapers planning to publish similar accounts. The April 7 article proclaimed under the headline "Anti Castro Units Trained to Fight at Florida Bases."[43]

The *New York Times* was not the only media outlet to run information on the assault, with the majority approving of the plan to retake Cuba. It was unrestrained press coverage revealing the details of the operation as one reason why the Bay of Pigs failed, the exiles maintained, along with John Kennedy's refusal to send in American planes. While the latter may have merit, the former charge does not hold up to historic scrutiny. In a 1966 speech, Clifton Daniel, then managing editor of the *New York Times*, disclosed that the Szulc story was toned down after Kennedy appealed to the editors on national security grounds. But shortly after the landing, when it proved to be a foreign policy disaster, Kennedy told editors of the *New York Times*: "If you had printed more about the operation, you would have saved us from a colossal mistake."[44] Even though publicly, it was perceived that Kennedy was blaming the nation's foremost newspaper for the failure.

Well before its April 7 article, the *New York Times* was publishing reports outlining the plans for the invasion. On January 10, 1961, correspondent Paul P. Kennedy reported from Guatemala that preparations were taking place for what some Guatemalans said would be "an offensive against the Cuban regime" that was "being planned and directed, and to a great extent being paid for, by the United States."[45] Another headline blared: "US Helps Trains an Anti-Castro Force at Secret Guatemala Air-Ground Base."[46]

The actual reporting during the battle was just as disastrous for the press as it was to the invaders. The *Wall Street Journal* led the lies with a story falsely claiming at least three landings in "a land, air and sea struggle." The *Miami Herald* spoke of battles raging "throughout" the island. The United Press International wire service remarkably tried to portray the predominantly reactionary elements of the exiles as, "revolutionaries ... appeared to have knocked back Fidel Castro's forces in the initial assault."[47] Not one of those reports carried a grain of truth, as the Cuban forces quickly repelled the invasion in a small area of the beach at Playa Giron, and more than 1,200 quickly surrendered. The revolutionary government was never in any real danger and the battle was over in less than three days.

The *Miami Herald*, which clearly wanted Castro gone, eagerly reported imaginary gains by the undermanned exile force, while offering no sources at all in its breathless accounts. Beneath a banner headline that read "Invaders Slug Into Interior," the *Miami Herald* reported on April 18, 1961, that the anti-Castro rebels, "were pushing into the interior of Cuba" after launching assaults, "at several key points" on the island. By the day the article ran, it was all over, except for media fantasies.

While somewhat more cautious than the colorful account in the *Miami Herald*, the *Wall Street Journal* of April 18, 1961 reported that at "least three widely scattered landings" had "brought an immediate state of emergency and brisk fighting inside Cuba and rapid repercussions around the globe." The *Wall Street Journal* noted that the "cut off of telephone and cable communications by the Castro government and conflicting battle reports made the tide of fighting difficult to assess," but then printed a complete fabrication: "The invaders seem bent on cutting Cuba in half, then wheeling westward to Havana, about 100 miles from their original beachhead."

The *Wall Street Journal* didn't hold back from publishing what it acknowledged were unverified reports that anti-Castro forces had captured the Isle of Pines and freed 10,000 political prisoners;

had taken Santiago de Cuba, the country's second-largest city, and seized Raúl Castro, Fidel's brother. "None of these reports were confirmed, however," the *Wall Street Journal* added[48]—doing its best to provide cover for legitimizing unfounded rumors through a valueless disclaimer that had no effect on the reader's level of believability. Everything in the report, however, was simply untrue.

Reporters afterwards faulted the government for providing incorrect information, trying to absolve themselves from any blame for the series of absolute falsehoods. Within weeks of the failed invasion, one of the leading journalists in America, James ("Scotty") Reston of the *New York Times*, charged in a column that US government officials and the CIA had fed reporters erroneous information about the assault on Cuba.

"When the landings started," Reston wrote, "American reporters in Miami were told that this was an 'invasion' of around 5,000 men—this for the purpose of creating the impression among the Cuban people that they should rise up to support a sizable invasion force."

"When the landing ... began to get in trouble, however," Reston added,

> officials here in Washington put out the story—this time to minimize the defeat in the minds of the American people—that there was no "invasion" at all, but merely a landing of some 200–400 men to deliver supplies to anti-Castro guerrillas already in Cuba. Both times the press was debased for the Government's purpose.[49]

It was an easy matter for the media to accept that debasement when for decades it had consistently sustained the position that America had the right to ownership of the island. Supporting the invasion in conjunction with state objectives was provided without compunction. Expecting the invasion to succeed simply was a reflection of the informational hubris created by the media. While the press tried to negate its responsibility in reporting the misinformation, the biggest delusion was the perception that the average Cuban would be thrilled to welcome back the worst elements of the Batista dictatorship to re-install American hegemony. As Fidel

Castro succinctly commented on the failure to understand that the Cubans would fight: "What could they have thought of us Cubans? Who would believe that a people would be so stupid to receive them with open arms?"[50]

Propaganda from the press helped create the historical illusion that Cubans were irresponsible, lazy, unfit for self-government and would be desperate for the United States to rescue them from the clutches of the revolutionaries. After the Bay of Pigs, there was no other option but to continue to misinform the public against Cuba—now saying the Bay of Pigs was a failure because of incompetence or government manipulation of information, not because the Cubans fought for their country against US imperialism. The press found it easier to abrogate self-reflection to promote a prejudiced narrative beholden to American political and capitalist elites.

A half-century after the failed invasion, old myths still held tight. In an extensive 2012 article by the *Miami Herald*, the first two paragraphs encapsulated the memory bias of the event:

> In the days before Christmas 50 years ago this weekend, 1,113 Bay of Pigs fighters captured by Fidel Castro's forces and imprisoned for 20 months were finally released to a heroes' welcome in Miami. The first planeload of POWs arrived at Homestead Air Force Base on Dec. 23, 1962. Gaunt and betrayed by the John F. Kennedy administration, members of the proud Brigade 2506 were bused to Miami's Dinner Key Auditorium, where waiting relatives engulfed them with hugs at a massive reunion that made front-page news. Five days later, JFK and his wife Jackie would be at the Orange Bowl to welcome them, too.[51]

The article's assumptions illuminate how media selects perspectives and creates self-perpetuating conventions based on accepted yet misinformed actualities. They are "fighters" instead of illegal invaders; they are "POWs" even though no state of war existed between Cuba and the USA; and the explanation of the failure lies solely with John F. Kennedy's betrayal. It is entirely unacceptable to mention Cuba's ability to easily repel the invasion as a condition of overwhelming public support for the revolution.

"These men invaded our country, they were traitors. In any other situation they would have been shot," Cuban historian and author Manuel Yepe said.

> But Fidel released those who were wounded, and negotiated the release of the rest. Compare that to the way the American's treat their prisoners who have been in Guantanamo Bay for years, with no charges, and no hope of leaving.[52]

One truth was reported accurately after the Bay of Pigs fiasco: Fidel Castro's announcement that Cuba was now officially socialist. The invasion helped convinced Havana of America's unrelenting attempts to end the revolution, which solidified the country's embrace of the Soviet Union for economic and military security in return for ideological alignment. Fidel Castro's declaration of the socialist nature of the revolution[53] enabled the mainstream media to swiftly shift from the debacle of its coverage of the Bay of Pigs to the horrors of having a communist outpost just 90 miles off the shores of America. It was a concept readership could readily accept and internalize. Biased reporting on Cuba was thereafter unquestioned, as the political designation that accompanied every article about Cuba permitted the "free" press unlimited range to denigrate, misinform and malign whatever was happening there. Because nothing in revolutionary society could be of value as it had sold out to the communists, the public was so informed. As a result, comments such as from Richard Nixon were widely reported and believed: "A dangerous threat to our peace and security, at our very doorstep," he decried, condemning Cuba as giving the Soviets, "squatters rights in our own backyard."[54]

With the revolution now within the Soviet sphere, Cuba became a mortal danger to America's body politic—a cancer that needed to be eradicated. It was the press that called for the political scalpel. Alex Graven wrote in the *New York Times*, demanding the removal of the "cancer of a Communist regime at our doorstep before it metastasis and invades Central and South America." The *New York Times* additionally editorialized that Cuba was a "point of infection by the Communist virus for the whole hemisphere."[55]

There was no further need to denigrate the personality of Fidel Castro or the revolutionaries; the press could now turn on the policies. The capitalist-controlled mainstream media had no requisite to examine root causes or even take a glance at American culpabilities—all that was necessary now was to frame the dialogue in ideological terminology. With that established, the press embraced its role to misinform and propagandize, to report half-truths and outright falsehoods, all in service to ensure no positive reporting emanated from Cuba's new social structure. As Havana closed in on itself as a response to American aggression and its strategy of isolating the island from international trade, the country then became off-limits to US citizens. Washington's travel restrictions prohibited all but a select few to see for themselves what was actually happening. The press became the sole conduit of information—and arbitrator of the revolution's value—judgment that has unfailingly been negative, cynical and distrustful.

* * *

Just over a year after the Bay of Pigs, the press refocus on Cuba took place in October 1962, when the missile crisis brought the world to the brink of nuclear war. What did explode was media outrage over the audacity of this small nation daring to ensure its survival, and the traditional arrogance that the United States was the sole arbitrator of whom is worthy to possess nuclear weapons.

Rightly or wrongly, the Cuban government was extremely concerned that the United States was planning a full military invasion in mid-1962, after the Bay of Pigs folly of using ill-trained exiles to retake the country. A proposal by the Joint Chief of Staff outlined a wide-ranging campaign of assassination, terrorism and support for an internal uprising that would lead to an invasion by the US military. Named Operation Mongoose, the plan was given scant mention in the press until 25 years later, when the *New York Times* revealed details in an article, "Papers Show 1962 Plan Against Castro."[56] The operation was only abandoned in January 1963, months after the missile crisis.

So while Cuba felt it had legitimate concerns of a second invasion, the press was more than content to selectively inform the public that Castro was now a bloodthirsty tyrant bent on the total destruction of the earth. Unlike the Bay of Pigs, details of a potential second invasion were never leaked by the press. Cuba's position that the missiles were defensive was weakened when they were discovered by US spy planes, a subversion Fidel Castro had consistently objected to. He admitted years later that the plan to place Soviet missiles in Cuba should have been announced publicly, "as it was our right to defend ourselves."[57]

In a 2013 article, *The Atlantic* reviewed the media's irresponsibility in exacerbating the danger of the event and its vital role in creating the false version of the crisis:

> On October 16, 1962, John F. Kennedy and his advisers were stunned to learn that the Soviet Union was, without provocation, installing nuclear-armed medium—and intermediate-range ballistic missiles in Cuba. With these offensive weapons, which represented a new and existential threat to America, Moscow significantly raised the ante in the nuclear rivalry between the superpowers—a gambit that forced the United States and the Soviet Union to the brink of nuclear Armageddon. On October 22, the president, with no other recourse, proclaimed in a televised address that his administration knew of the illegal missiles, and delivered an ultimatum insisting on their removal, announcing an American "quarantine" of Cuba to force compliance with his demands. While carefully avoiding provocative action and coolly calibrating each Soviet countermeasure, Kennedy and his lieutenants brooked no compromise; they held firm, despite Moscow's efforts to link a resolution to extrinsic issues and despite predictable Soviet blustering about American aggression and violation of international law. In the tense 13-day crisis, the Americans and Soviets went eyeball-to-eyeball. Thanks to the Kennedy administration's placid resolve and prudent crisis management … the Soviet leadership blinked: Moscow dismantled the missiles, and a cataclysm was averted.[58]

As *The Atlantic* pointed out, every sentence in the above description is misleading.[59] The actualities, that America had a far superior nuclear missiles arsenal, that Cuba genuinely felt threatened by another invasion, the placement of missiles was not illegal and the key component of the resolution was predicated on Kennedy agreeing to remove the missiles in Turkey was absent from media reports and kept that way until years later. The one illegal act, Kennedy's blockade of Cuba, was the incident that had the greatest potential for setting off a world war. The press continues to maintain the historical fiction of the incident, ignoring America's role in almost bringing an end to humanity.

Instead, press coverage was epitomized during an *NBC* report vilifying the Soviet Union for placing the missiles and threatening the lives of the American people, with no mention of US missiles doing that same thing to the Soviet population.[60]

At the height of the crisis, President Kennedy requested television time from all three of the broadcast networks (*ABC, CBS, NBC*) for 7pm on Monday, October 22. The president demanded that the Soviets remove all missiles from Cuba, adding that failure to comply could result in military action:

> I call upon Chairman Khrushchev to halt and eliminate this clandestine, reckless, and provocative threat to world peace and to stable relations between our two nations. I call upon him further to abandon this course of world domination and join in an historic effort to end the perilous arms race and transform the history of man.[61]

One of the country's most respected newspapers then took the president's threat and turned it into reality when it blasted a frightening front page headline the following day: "Kennedy Orders Invasion of Cuba," so declared the *Washington Post*, using a low-level bureaucrat as the source. The subhead declared the USA would be striking various targets and the Americans would find little resistance. Anyone reading the *Washington Post* that day would undoubtedly be prepared for World War III. Few would realize the report was completely false; at no time during his speech had Kennedy ordered an invasion.[62]

Media's depiction of possible invasion carried echoes of the historical narrative of Cuban inadequacies. The *Wall Street Journal* ran an article by Ed Cony predicting the island would be "soft picking" and that Havana "would be a plum worth picking."[63]

The missile crisis provided another example of the national press, regardless of its national political bent, maintaining a united foreign policy front in compliance with state requirements. Additionally, it was another watershed moment in how the media consistently covers Cuba, crystalizing the misinformation, lack of context and manipulation of evidence.[64] A more comprehensive and balanced examination of those dangerous October days was found in a 2012 *Guardian* article by Noam Chomsky, outlining the myths that have grown up since the incident and the role the media played in pushing the world to the brink.[65]

* * *

After the crisis passed, the United States publicly renounced further plans for an invasion, but not its support for terrorism. The attacks against civilian targets continued, moving from such state-sponsored programs as Operation Mongoose in the 1960s[66] into the hands of various Cuban-American anti-revolutionary organizations including Alpha 66 and Omega 7 in the following decades. These activities were part of a long history of terrorism against Cuba, which the government has claimed have cost more than 3,500 lives. The acts include attacks on students teaching farmers to read and write, biological warfare, bombings of department stores and tourist facilities. The most infamous was the October 1976 downing of Cubana Airlines 455, with all 72 on board. It remains the second worst act of air terrorism in the Americas after 9/11.[67] While most of the previous terrorism was ignored, the media did provide substantial coverage to the Cubana Airlines bombing—albeit with rare mention of the history of violence against Cuban civilians by those organizations based in the United States. The biggest failure of the press, however, was an honest description of the two recognized masterminds of the downing.

Orlando Bosch and Luis Posada Carriles were well known to US intelligence services, both connected to the CIA. The pair had a long history of terrorist acts against Cuban civilians, including the planning of the bombing of Cubana Airlines. Evidence indicated that Bosch and Carriles hired two Venezuelans to plant the explosives on the plane, which exploded minutes after take-off from the Barbados. Besides the Cubana incident, Bosch and Carriles were accused of various acts of terrorism going back to the early 1960s. Bosch was arrested in Florida in 1968 for firing a bazooka at a Polish freighter in Miami harbor. The freighter, on its way to Cuba, was one of more than 50 terrorist incidents linked to Bosch—the majority were against Cuban civilian targets.

Posada Carriles was a member of the Cuban American brigade at the Bay of Pigs in 1961, following that as a CIA agent in the 1960s and 1970s. In the mid-1970s, he was accused of various acts against Cuban officials outside the country, and during the 1980s was involved with the Contras in Nicaragua. He admitted in a series of articles with the *New York Times* to the bombings of Cuban hotels in 1997, resulting in the death of Italian tourist Fabio Di Celmo.[68] Posada was subsequently arrested in 2000 during an attempt to assassinate Fidel Castro at a conference in Panama. The intent was to eliminate the Cuban leader at the University of Panama where he was scheduled to speak. Authorities discovered more than 33 pounds of C-4 plastic explosives in the auditorium, which would have killed hundreds of Panamanian students along with Castro. In 2004, Posada was sentenced to prison for his part, but four months later then Panamanian President Mireya Moscoso issued a pardon. Both have subsequently passed away peacefully in Florida: Bosch in 2011 and Carriles in 2018.

Bosch and Carriles were well covered by the Florida press, consistently described as militants, freedom fighters or leaders in the anti-Castro movement. Bosch was even given a day in Miami honoring his efforts to fight Castro. The *Miami Herald* has been particularly kind to the two terrorists.

But it hasn't been just the *Miami Herald* that has treated the pair with an amount of sympathetic publicity most certainly undeserved. On live radio, on June 6, 2002, and again in the June 16 issue of the *Diario de las Americas*, Bosch reiterated his call for terrorism against Cuba. On August 21, 2001, he published a widely reported Declaration of Principles in which he considered terrorist actions against Cuba as legitimate. On December 5, 2002, the *Miami New Times* quoted Bosch as saying in reference to the Cubana Airlines bombing: "There were no innocents on that plane. They were all henchmen."[69] The plane was full of Cuban youth returning from a fencing tournament in Venezuela.

Carriles has been interviewed on numerous occasions, including in the *Miami Herald* supplement Tropic, in which he wrote a major piece in the November 1991 issue of the publication, making clear his continued support for violence against his former homeland. Even as late as 2005, when Carriles was arrested for illegal entry into the United States, the mainstream media was reticent to describe him as a terrorist, despite the heightened sensitivity to the topic following 9/11. The *New York Times* couldn't bring itself to accurately describe Carriles when covering his arrest, instead describing him as someone who, "spent 45 years fighting a violent losing battle to overthrow Fidel Castro."[70] No mention that his targets were civilians, not leadership. That standard of not labeling him as a terrorist was maintained even by journalist and author Ann Louise Bardach, a recognized expert on Cuba, who wrote in the *Washington Post* during the same incident that Carriles was "the fugitive militant, would-be assassin of Cuban leader Fidel Castro and prison escapee who is wanted by Venezuela for the 1976 shoot down of a Cuban airliner that killed 73 civilians."[71] In an article a week later, the *Washington Post* at least did allow the topic of terrorism to be mentioned, but still couldn't bring itself to be completely honest:

> Luis Posada Carriles, a CIA-trained Cuban exile *implicated* [emphasis added] in a series of terrorist incidents, applied for political asylum in the United States yesterday, prompting at least one congressman to assert that granting the request would undermine the nation's credibility in the war on terrorism.[72]

When Carriles died, both the *New York Times* and the *Miami Herald* continued to describe him as a "militant," whose only intent was to "bring down the Castro government" with no acknowledgment that his militancy caused the deaths of innocent civilians—the very definition of a terrorist. The *Miami Herald*'s obituary disingenuously indicated it was only Castro he was after:

> Luis Posada Carriles, the Cuban exile militant who left no bomb or bullet unturned in a fruitless four-decade-long series of attempts to kill Fidel Castro, died early Wednesday morning after a long battle with throat cancer. Probably the last of an aging cadre of Miami exiles who pursued Castro with a violent vengeance—at first with the not-so-silent support of the United States government, later in an increasingly lonely solo mission—Posada Carriles died peacefully in his sleep at Memorial Regional Hospital in Hollywood.[73]

The *New York Times*' lead paragraph maintained the fiction that he was some sort of freedom fighter: "Luis Posada Carriles, the anti-Castro militant and former C.I.A. operative who made headlines for decades for his failed attempts to topple the Cuban dictator, died on Wednesday in Miramar, Fla., He was 90."[74] Even when the article accurately described the definition of a terrorist, the paper couldn't bring itself to apply it to Posada:

> Mr. Posada spent nearly 60 years on a quixotic and often bloody mission to bring down Fidel Castro by any means possible. He was accused of using bombs and bullets in a crusade that took the lives of innocents but never did manage to snare that Cuban leader, who died at 90 in 2016.[75]

At least the last paragraph in the *New York Times*' article provided some honesty through a third voice: "'He was an international terrorist of the first order,' said Peter Kornbluh, the director of the Cuba Documentation Project at the National Security Archive, who spent decades collecting declassified documents on Mr. Posada's ventures."[76] The *New York Times* arbitrarily lowering the standard of terrorism to innocuous sounding "ventures."

Bosch's obituary carried the same misdirection as to what he really was, with *The Guardian* describing him as a "militant Cuban exile."[77] When he died, also peacefully in Miami, the *Washington Post* headline proclaimed rather proudly that: "Orlando Bosch, Who Battled Castro with Bazookas and Sabotage, Dies at 84."[78]

The article portrayed Bosch as something as a romantic figure while softening the deadly activities he was involved with. Exceptionally, the article at least mentioned the word terrorist, even though throwing the description onto the responsibility of others:

> Orlando Bosch, 84, a Cuban pediatrician turned bazooka-toting militant who plotted to assassinate Fidel Castro and was linked to the 1976 bombing of a Cuban airliner, died April 27 at a hospital in Miami. No cause of death was reported. To some, Dr. Bosch was a Cuban patriot with a justified cause against Castro's tyranny. To others, including officials at the U.S. Justice Department, he was a terrorist responsible for the deaths of scores of innocents.[79]

There should be no moral comparative where "some" think he was a patriot. The *Washington Post* would never write about Osama Bin Laden with such equivalency—it should be clear to any major newspaper who is a terrorist and should be described as such. But when it comes to Cuba, reality is muddled in the never-ending quest to create sympathy even for those who would take the lives of innocent civilians for the sake of political differences.

The lack of authentic coverage of this covert war against Cuban civilians remains a great stain against the media in its treatment of the island nation. In an effort to prevent further acts of terrorism, the Cuban government sent agents to Southern Florida to infiltrate extremist Cuban-American exile organizations involved in attacks. Five agents were arrested in 1998, kicking off one of the most blatant examples of the abrogation of journalist integrity in the history of the United States.[80]

Before the Cuban Five became a cause célèbre, the media had a field day when the Soviet Union collapsed in 1989, throwing their Cuban dependent into economic ruin. That's when the experts in the press boldly predicted the end of the revolution.

Andres Oppenheimer led the way with his widely off the mark book, *Castro's Final Hour*.[81] Oppenheimer, Pulitzer Prize winning reporter with the *Miami Herald*, is generally credited as a national authority on the Cuban Revolution and its leadership. His consistently anti-Cuba bias was no more in evidence in the volume, completely misreading the reality of the population's continued commitment to its socialist society following the collapse of the Soviet Union. Published in 1993, the work predicted the end of the revolution based on misinformation, mistruths and ignoring the majority who wanted to maintain and improve the system despite the economic hardships. The book remains a remarkable achievement in how little it discussed the impact of America's embargo and historical hostility, focusing almost entirely on those experiencing disgruntlement with a government struggling to survive economically. One would not expect finding complaints in a country that just lost 35 percent of its GDP to be a difficult journalistic endeavor. Its fatally defective assumption was that the revolution was structured solely on Soviet economic assistance, and that Cuba's commitment to self-determination would simply collapse like a house of cards.

The title only came physically true with the death of Fidel Castro in 2016. However, the revolution continues with its reforms and advances, with the participation of a large majority of the population. After 60 years, Oppenheimer and the vast preponderance of other Cuba "experts" peering from their US centric view have yet to comprehend how Cubans could still support the revolution, despite certain social and civil restrictions, economic depravations and material limitations. The Cuban sense of independence and sovereignty continues to elude the experts' assessments—as does an honest examination of the harm that US policy has exacted on Cuba's development. It is a historic contingency sustained by media and political elites. Since Oppenheimer's dubious Cuban insights, he has for the past few years been directing the same level of exactitude against Venezuela.

While Cuba struggled to survive its great depression after the fall of the Soviet Union, an incident on February 24, 1996 provided the media with another propaganda tool to break against the island nation and pronounce the end of the revolution. For two years prior to that date, a Miami-based organization whose founder had ties to acts of terrorism became involved with humanitarian activities on the Florida Straits. Brothers to the Rescue (BTTR) was established by José Basulto, a well-known anti-revolutionary with CIA connections, who was accused of shooting up a Cuban hotel along with various other violent acts.[82] He led the BTTR pilots in picking up rafters leaving Cuba during the immigration crisis of 1994. When the USA and Cuba came up with a new migration policy that virtually eliminated the rafters, the prime mission of BTTR no longer existed. That's when Basulto decided on a more provocative strategy that ended in a tragic incident costing four lives.

By 1995, the group was filing false flight plans in order to illegally fly over Cuban air space, dropping anti-revolutionary propaganda on Havana citizens. What made the Cuban government particularly nervous was that it had information that Basulto was also training to drop incendiary bombs over Havana.

Ricardo Alarcon, former president of the Cuban National Assembly noted:

> The Cuban government had intelligence agents in Miami, one who infiltrated the BTTR group, and there were specific details that Basulto was going to start dropping bombs during these overflights. Something he had done years before over sugar cane fields.[83]

The intelligence agent Fidel Castro had implanted with the BTTR was Pablo Roque, who fled back to Cuba just prior to the tragedy that provided the mainstream media with such sanctimonious outrage.[84]

Basulto's group conducted approximately 12 illegal overflights into Cuban airspace, each time the revolutionary government protested this incursion, each time the Federal Aviation Authority (FAA) promised to ground the flights. Nothing happened until Castro publicly declared that the next intrusion would result in his air force taking action, which occurred in 1996, when two of the four civilian aircraft were shot down with the loss of four lives. Direct warnings were ignored, with Basulto claiming his right to invade Cuban airspace. Basulto was in one of the other two planes not targeted, flying close to the water to evade Cuban radar.

Immediately following the incident, Havana declared the shoot down occurred in Cuban airspace, while the American side claimed it was over international waters. To this day, satellite imagery, which would conclusively provide evidence where it happened has yet to be released; the information under the control of American authorities.[85] The incident created international condemnation, including by the UN Security Council, while Havana defended the decision claiming the right to protect its national borders.

The mainstream media had no compunction to declare unquestionably the location of the downing, at the same time, ensuring the background, the previous incursions and the warnings, went unreported or were designated as immaterial.

The *New York Times* provided little information as to why the planes were flying over Cuba, implying it was an unproved attack with no justification. It was only at the very end of the article that the *New York Times* mentioned any previous BTTR flights, "A State Department spokesman, Glyn Davies, said United States Government officials had previously repeatedly warned the group that 'flying into Cuban territorial waters or over Cuban territorial waters is a dangerous proposition.'"[86] It was not just a dangerous proposition, but also an illegal one that the US authorities knew of but did nothing to prevent. *CNN* did briefly note Cuba's warnings, but did not connect them to the BTTR illegal overflights, leaving the reader somewhat confused as to the purpose of Havana's protests.[87] It was left to the fringe media to cover the incident in its entirety.

Even 20 years after, the mainstream press still considers it was simply an unprovoked act by the Cuban government. *NBC* went so far as to report the BTTR were still involved in rafter rescues at the time of the shoot down, with the news anchor misinforming that: "Four men died that day on a humanitarian mission." No mention was made that the mission had ended more than a year ago, and that the overflights were one of numerous illegal incursions into Cuban airspace.[88] Soon after the shoot down the FAA revoked the license of BTTR.[89] BTTR head José Basulto, along with fellow anti-revolutionaries Luis Posada Carriles and Orlando Bosch, has long been given deferential treatment in the press. The *South Miami News* was remarkable in its disingenuous coverage of Basulto's violent history in a 2018 article on the naming of a street after him:

> After the revolution, he was trained by the CIA in intelligence, communications, explosives, sabotage, and subversion in Panama, Guatemala, and the U.S. He was later placed back into

> Cuba, posing as a physics student to help prepare the ground for the Bay of Pigs Invasion. In August 1962, he was involved in an expedition of the Directorio Revolucionario Estudantil which took a boat to Cuba and fired a 20mm cannon at a hotel, though nobody was killed in the incident.[90]

The lack of a death is presented as something of a qualifier to the seriousness of the terrorist incident.

One of the most unfortunate fallouts of the BTTR tragedy was then president Clinton passing the Helms–Burton Act, a piece of legislation he had been refusing to sign as it violated a series of international regulations. Speculation persists that the BTTR overflights were purposefully planned to create such a tragedy in order to apply sufficient political pressure for Clinton to sign the Act. "The anti-Cuban groups wanted to do something to make President Clinton pass the Act, they knew he wasn't going to sign it otherwise. So for Cuba defending itself the Americans were able to increase the pressures of the blockade," Roberto Alarcón former president of Cuba's National Assembly commented.[91] The Act made it more difficult for international companies to do business in Cuba and placed the economic embargo under congressional control.[92]

The *New York Times* joined the long line of media speculating on how the Act's increased punishment of Cuba would hasten the end of the revolution:

> Driven largely by the downing of two civilian American planes by the Cuban military, Congressional negotiators and the White House agreed today on a package of sanctions intended to punish Fidel Castro by curbing foreign investment in Cuba ... But the package, the most tangible reaction yet to the downing of the planes last Saturday, also includes more potent provisions that supporters said would deter foreign investment in Cuba and thus hasten the downfall of an ailing regime.[93]

Experts in the press have consistently misconstrued—intentionally or not—the depth of commitment the majority of Cubans have to the revolution and the ideal of self-determination. Independence has come at a great cost in its challenge to American hegemony. The economic embargo measures material loss; the information blockade is a harder price to determine. With the media blackout on the history of terrorism, the average American has no understanding why Cuba shot down the planes, why it would be so paranoid to consider small aircrafts to be a threat. Nor would they know of the incidents of sugar cane and other agricultural crops destroyed by such small planes, diseases such as Dengue 2 introduced intentionally by spray from US civilian aircraft, or the thousands of civilians killed by acts of terrorism. All go unreported in the American press. It is the rationale for Cuba's hypersensitivity to terrorism and the anti-revolutionary extremists who are responsible.

Yet when the subject does come up, as in the case of the Cuban Five, the press coverage has been as extraordinary as it has been revealing.

3
The Case of the Cuban Five

On September 12, 1998, five men were arrested in Miami on charges of spying against the United States. Gerardo Hernández, Antonio Guerrero, Ramón Labañino, Fernando González and René González turned out to be unregistered intelligence agents working for the Cuban government.

While the case electrified the highly charged anti-Cuban political atmosphere in South Florida, the story turned out to be even more compelling when it was revealed that a number of prominent Miami journalists sold their integrity to the US government to ensure the men, known as the Cuban Five, would not receive a fair trial.

The five were convicted in 2001 of conspiracy to commit espionage, conspiracy to commit murder, acting as an agent of a foreign government and other illegal activities in the United States. The controversial trial was held in Miami, with the government refusing to transfer it to any other location. Following the verdict, the United Nations Human Rights Commission called for a new trial, declaring the original, "did not take place in the climate of objectivity and impartiality."[1] The case made its way to the US Supreme Court where the judges refused the hear it.

According to the American position the five were part of a group, known as the Wasp Network, sent to spy on government institutions. The Cuban side countered that they were in the United States to observe and infiltrate violent anti-revolutionary Cuban-American groups including Alpha 66, the F4 Commandos and the Cuban American National Foundation. Another organization under surveillance and infiltration, Brothers to the Rescue (BTTR), had been conducting a series of illegal overflights into Cuban airspace that had resulted in the shoot down of two of their planes in 1996.[2] The incident had a direct impact on the trial and the condemning of Gerardo Hernández to two life sentences for his alleged connection with the incident, a sentencing the Cuban government claimed was just one example of how unjust the proceedings were.

The Cuban Five were sent to the United States in order to prevent further acts of terrorism by anti-revolutionary groups. These organizations had a clear history of committing such acts against civilian targets, including the wave of 1996 hotel bombings in Havana organized by anti-revolutionary terrorist Luis Posada Carriles. The inability of the US government to crack down on the groups led to the sending of intelligent agents. As author and political activist Noam Chomsky noted, press coverage of US terrorism against Cuba has long reflected the government's position as not worthy of serious consideration, "The American attacks are often dismissed in US commentary as silly pranks, CIA shenanigans that got out of hand."[3]

Media misrepresentation of the five's mission helped secure a conviction before the trial got underway. Much of the reporting was later revealed to be part of a campaign that involved a number of South Florida journalists paid by the US government to write prejudicial articles against the five. Additionally, these nationally recognized reporters received thousands of dollars to broadcast biased and false information on the trial through the government's anti-Cuba propaganda outlets Radio Televisión Martí. It became a remarkable illustration of the abrogation of any sense of media trustworthiness in the pursuit of state objectives. Those involved became paid propagandists for the purpose of corrupting a judicial process.

Despite the prosecution not providing any evidence of government documents or secrets being compromised,[4] the five were convicted, given extraordinarily long sentences and held under extreme conditions, including solitary confinement for more than 17 months. All were placed in separate institutions, some for dangerous criminals. Eventually, René González was the first released, on October 7, 2011, having completed 13 years of his sentence, with three years of probation in the USA remaining. He was allowed to return to Cuba for his father's funeral on April 22, 2013, and a federal judge granted him permission to stay provided that he renounced his United States citizenship. The second, Fernando González (no relation) was sent back to Cuba on February 27, 2014. The remaining members were freed on December 17, 2014, in a prisoner swap for an American intelligence officer, identified as Rolando Sarraff Trujillo. The exchange of prisoners also included the release of American Alan Phillip Gross, although the governments characterized it as being unrelated to the prisoner exchange. Gross was charged with bringing in illegal high tech communication equipment in support of American regime change strategies and spent five years in jail.

Much of the credit for the attention of the unjust trial and lengthy imprisonment went to the various Cuban solidarity groups around the world who worked tirelessly to bring the case to the general public. They knew little would come from the mainstream media.

Director of the National Committee to Free the Cuban Five, Gloria LaRiva remembered:

> Our organization worked from the beginning to bring this case to the public, holding meetings and demonstrations. We knew the mainstream media wasn't going to cover it, and when they did it was always anti-Cuban. When we brought out the information about the journalists being paid to write all these terrible stories about the five, there was little attention about the case, but about the journalists being paid. The US news media has never covered the Cuban Five story sufficiently.[5]

Regarding the payment to journalists, LaRiva commented:

> This is the most blatant and outrageous example of government influence destroying the right to a fair trial and the right to appeal. During the pre-trial period, there were hundreds of articles on the Cuban Five and not one was favorable.[6]

With evidence of the payments mounting, *Miami Herald* reporter Oscar Corral broke the story nationally on September 8, 2006. Many of the journalists on the US government payroll were working at the *Miami Herald* and its sister publication *El Nuevo Herald*. When the revelations hit, resulting in the resignation of

Miami Herald publisher Jesus Diaz Jr.,[7] the *New York Times* covered the media scandal far more than why the five were in Florida in the first place. One of the *New York Times*' most significant articles carried a headline that ignored the actual issue in favor of turning it into an ideological dispute: "US Paid 10 Journalists for Anti-Castro Reports."[8] As long as "anti-Castro" was in the headline, the reader was certain to draw all the historical negative inferences required to come to a conclusion entirely unconnected with the facts.

During the trial, various reports written to condemn the five bordered on the incredulous, reflecting the almost entire revocation of editorial integrity that surrounded coverage of the case. Wilfredo Cancio Isla wrote a remarkable article in *El Nuevo Herald* on June 4, 2001, the day the jury began its deliberations on the question of guilt or innocence, implausibly claiming that: "Cuba used hallucinogens to train its spies."[9] The article had no basis in reality, making the unsubstantiated claim from an anonymous Cuban spy deserter—with two pseudonyms—that Cuba gave its agents LSD and other hallucinogens before sending them on missions abroad. The article provided illumination as to how far editors put aside their journalistic judgment in order to publish anti-Cuban propaganda.[10]

Following their return to Cuba, the five were able to comment on the impact the media's negative coverage had on the case.

Gerardo Hernández remarked:

> We really had no chance of a fair trial, we were convicted before it started thanks to the media's reporting—calling us all sorts of terrible things. And there were some articles about how the Cuban government gave us drugs to help perform our missions better. How that was supposed to help I have no idea.[11]

Cancio Isla's article was intended to ensure that the jury, at the moment when they were beginning deliberations, would come to no other conclusion than the evil intent of the Castro government. The story, quoting the same anonymous source, linked the group to a massive infiltration of agents bent on the destruction of the United States:

> At the beginning of this year, motivated by the trial taking place in Miami against five presumed Cuban spies, he [the deserter] decided to break his silence. … "I can assure you that the Wasp Network (broken up in September 1998) is just a part of the espionage work that was conceived to infiltrate the United States on a long term basis."[12]

The article should have been grounds for a mistrial, as Cancio Isla knowingly violated the Court's gag order and courtroom instructions which prohibited the media from informing the public about private discussions of the prosecution, the defense and the judge, while the jury was removed from the Courtroom.

Cancio Isla continued to violate the court order with an article on April 19, 2001. His *El Nuevo Herald* report headlined, "The Prosecution Fears Cuban Control in Spy Trial: Cuba is Preparing a Fabricated Version of the Facts." The story revealed an "ex parte" private debate between the government and defense attorneys that the jury was not supposed to hear. In it was included a claim by US prosecutor Caroline Heck-Miller that Cuba is, "constructing a fabricated version of the facts." Heck-Miller was opposing a request by the defense attorneys for permission to travel to Cuba to obtain more physical evidence related to the Brothers to the Rescue plane shoot down in 1996, the incident in which Gerardo Hernández was convicted for conspiracy to commit murder.[13] While that type of unproven charge from Heck-Miller was not permitted before a jury, Cancio Isla made certain it made headline news to the entire Miami community, including the jury members who had not been sequestered during the trial.

Six days prior to the article, judge Joan Lenard had warned the media not to make public the conversations between the government and defense, noting:

> The Court and the parties have an interest in protecting the jury from matters not presented to it in the open courtroom and that is the reason for the gag order that was entered by the Court with respect to discussion of attorneys and the like.[14]

It was an order often ignored by Cancio Isla and the other reporters paid by the US government.

Cancio Isla received approximately US$22,000 to promote the government message by revealing information about the trial unknown by the jury, according to the investigative report done by the website *Counterpunch*.[15] Although Cancio Isla was fired by the *Miami Herald* for his violation of journalist ethics, he was soon re-hired after elements of the right-wing Cuban-American community organized a boycott of the newspaper.

Another journalist accused of accepting payment for negative reports was Julio Estorino, a radio commentator and news director with extensive broadcast exposure in Miami. He was broadcasting daily morning and evening talk shows at the same time as working for *Radio Martí*, the US government run anti-Cuban propaganda broadcast network. Estorino was also a frequent contributor for *Diario Las Américas*, including during the period of the Cuban Five's prosecution, from September 12, 1998 through their conviction on June 8, 2001. One of the most serious false accusations he made regarding the five came in a column headlined "Espionage and Indifference." His column claimed the men were infiltrating weapons:

> For if the insanity shown in the downing of the airplanes from Brothers to the Rescue over international waters, with cold, malicious calculation, were not enough, now it comes to light that Castro's secret services have been trying to find infiltration points for weapons and explosives on the coastlines of this country, a task that was assigned to some of those implicated in this spy network … the one that has been discovered and is being tried.[16]

At no time did the prosecution bring up any mention or proof regarding that claim. Estorino apparently received $89,000 during the prosecution of the five.[17] Estorino was a member of the ultra-right-wing exile group Junta Patriotica Cubana, an organization that favors the violent overthrow of the Castro government, according to Cuban Exile.com. A fellow member was Ariel Remos, a regular reporter for *Diario Las Américas*. Shortly after the arrest,

Remos began writing a series of articles, most notably one that made an unsubstantiated allegation regarding the five's trial in the January 19, 2001 edition, titled, "Fidel Castro Planned the Assassination of (Anti-Revolutionary Exile) Jesus Cruza Flor in the U.S.A." The report claimed:

> At the trial of the Cuban spies that made up the so-called "Wasp Network," it has been shown that Fidel Castro's regime has openly conspired to undertake terrorist acts in the U.S.A., and that the Cuban exiles have not exaggerated when they denounced the penetration of Castro's agents in this country … Through the trial in question it has not only become known that the Cuban regime planned to disembark arms and explosives on United States territory, but also planned the murder of prominent Cuban exiles because of their opposition to the regime.[18]

No evidence of those charges was ever brought up during the trial. Remos received $10,400 during the prosecution of the intelligent agents.

With the long unknown history of terrorism and the infiltration of weapons into Cuba by anti-revolutionary groups in Florida, the Havana government remains particularly sensitive to assertions such as the ones Remos and Estorino promoted. Those articles in turn exacerbated an already highly charged Miami community predisposed to accept whatever unchallenged accusation supported their anti-revolutionary attitudes. Reports that were available to the jurors fed into a biased climate that left little doubt as to the outcome of the trial. It was a situation that judge Joan Lenard commented on afterwards, lamenting that not even her "most explicit instructions" could shield the jury from the negative influence the media would have on the trial.[19] Her complaints did nothing to mitigate the unfairness of the process or the extraordinarily long sentences.

Throughout the seven-month proceedings, the jury went home every night and had available the prejudiced press articles. As LaRiva noted,

> They were filmed by TV cameras, their images were clearly shown on TV news programs, for co-workers, friends and the broader public to identify them, including many terrorists running free in Miami. The message was clear to the jury: We know who you are, and a verdict of not guilty could result in negative consequences.[20]

Other journalists accused of being paid by the government included *El Nuevo Herald* reporter Pablo Alfonso, who wrote 16 negative articles during the trial. Those reports apparently netted him $58,600. He was paid an additional $175,000 to host shows on Radio Televisión Martí, according to government documents obtained by the *Miami Herald*. And Olga Connor, a freelance reporter who wrote on Cuban culture for *El Nuevo Herald*, received approximately $71,000 from the U.S. Office of Cuba Broadcasting.[21]

Journalists being paid by the US government is not an altogether unique event. However, in previous such cases when reporters were funded to support a particular political perspective, such as when the Bush Administration paid Armstrong Williams $240,000 to promote the No Child Left Behind program, the Government Accountability Office declared the payments illegal.[22] No such statement has ever been made in the Cuban Five case.

Following the revelation of payments, the defense team called for a mistrial, with civil rights lawyer Martin Garbus declaring:

> These U.S. government paid-for stories appeared in newspapers, magazines, radio and TV and influenced public opinion in the community, including jury members and their families, and therefore calls into deep question whether a fair trial in Miami was possible for the five accused men.[23]

The brief further stated: "The U.S. government's successful secret subversion of the Miami print, radio, and television media to pursue a conviction was unprecedented, and violated the integrity of the trial and the Due Process Clause of the Constitution."[24] Garbus finished the report by condemning the process:

> The Government, through millions of dollars of illegal payments and at least a thousand articles published over a six-year period, interfered with the trial and persuaded the jury to convict. The Government's Response to this motion is factually barren and legally incorrect. The conviction must now be vacated.[25]

The trial, and convictions, were upheld. In the aftermath, the *Miami Herald* fired those affected on the grounds they had broken a basic code—taking money from the government to write prejudicial articles. The paper's *mea culpa* stated:

> Thomas Fiedler, the Executive Editor and Vice President of *The Miami Herald*, when talking about the monies paid to his staff members and members of other media entities by the Government, said it was wrongful because it was "to carry out the mission of the U.S. Government, a propaganda mission. It was wrong even if it had not been secret."[26]

At no time during the trial or sentencing did the government admit payments were made to influence the proceedings.

* * *

While the Cuban Five trial attracted substantial media attention in South Florida, the issue generated little national notice. What coverage it did produce showed, along with customary Cuban bias, an unexpected amount of balance that impartially included information as to why the agents were in Florida and recognition of the Cuban government's position. It was a revealing shift in the attitude of a portion in the mainstream media and demonstrated what balanced coverage looked like. Along with the treatment of a famous Cuban boy who washed up on the shores of Florida around the same time as the trial of the five,[27] the media would not exhibit such ostensible attempts at fairness again until President Obama's opening with Cuba in 2014. However, the apparent modification toward less biased coverage often made the standard anti-revolutionary misinformation even more effective as it came with the appearance of even-handedness.

The *New York Times* reporting of the Cuban Five demonstrated both the traditional bias as well as some refreshingly honest coverage. An early article on the shoot down of the Brothers to the Rescue (BTTR) planes in context to the trial started badly by misinforming readers:

> F.B.I. officials said their investigation of Cuban intelligence gathering in South Florida began after Brothers to the Rescue, known for making mercy flights between Florida and Cuba searching for people in boats fleeing Cuba, lost two planes in an attack by Cuban fighter jets in 1996.[28]

The planes were not shot down while rescuing refugees, as readers might assume; instead, by the time of the shoot down, the rafter crisis that precipitated the rescue operations was over by more than a year. The overflights at the time of the incident were consistently and illegally penetrating Cuban airspace in order to incite a military response from Havana.

The *New York Times*, however, became one of the first corporate media outlets to inform its audience that there were two sides to the story:

> Cuba has vigorously defended five of the spies who fought and lost their cases in federal court … insisting that the men sought only to thwart terrorism by radical exiles, like a spate of Havana bombings in 1997 that killed an Italian tourist.[29]

It was an important piece of background information that put Havana's position in context with a specific incident that few in the United States would have known about. Also providing relevant material on the history of terrorism against Cuba was the *Associated Press* during a series of articles on the trial that ran in various newspapers across the country. Included in the reports were arguments from the defense team, who contended that the five were necessary to infiltrate violent anti-revolutionary organizations as the: "United States was either unwilling or unable to prevent them from supporting terrorist attacks in Cuba." The article included quotes from defense attorney Joaquin Mendez, who cited a, "string of eight bombings in Cuba over a four month period in 1997" as "only part of a 40-year history of raids, bombings and arms smuggling missions that justified the agents' undercover work in South Florida." *Associated Press* also described the charges against Gerardo Hernández in relation to the BTTR shoot down, stating that the planes were illegally flying into Cuban territory on "a mission to drop 500,000 political leaflets."[30]

While the *New York Times* and *Associated Press* supplied readership with previously unreported background information, it did little to offset the overwhelming amount of negative coverage conducted by the paid journalists as well other corporate media that remained in the more traditional anti-Cuba mode. During the arrest of the five, the *Washington Post* printed nine articles, two making the front page with most of the rest buried deep in section A. The *Washington Post* articles in general lacked in context and balance, implicating the agents as a gang of spies, including the story published September 15, 1998, quoting US attorney Thomas E. Scott twice, who outrageously misrepresented the case, saying the five were determined, "to strike at the very heart of our national security system."[31]

The *Washington Post* went silent on the issue until June 2001, after the sentencing stage, when an article reported the five as, "a committed band of spies working to infiltrate South Florida's military installations and Cuban exile community." While the *Washington Post* did remark that: "There were no Cuban Americans or anyone with close ties to the large Cuban American community here on the 12-member jury, which deliberated for five days," the piece did not mention the anti-Castro bias prevalent in Miami-Dade County or the payment of the journalists. The jury did not have to be made up of Cuban-Americans to ensure the proper judgment required by the government would be rendered. Despite the *Washington Post*'s traditional anti-Cuba slant, there was one attempt at balance when an article included that the defendants were: "Cuban patriots, trying to protect their country from Cuban American extremists in South Florida" and that their "spying" on military installations did not actually threaten national security.[32]

The *Washington Post* report that presented an unexpected amount of perspective came out a few years after the sentencing.

In a 2006 front page headline: "Cubans Jailed in U.S. as Spies are Hailed at Home as Heroes," the newspaper allowed that:

> American officials tend to paint Cuban agents as infiltrators bent on undermining U.S. national security. But the Cuban government asserts they are men of courage, sent to the U.S. to ferret out terrorism plots by Cuban exile groups waging war against President Fidel Castro.[33]

The story also contained that rarest of information—a quote from an actual Cuban resident, Antonio Lage who expressed anger at their continued incarceration: "'Hypocrites, that's what Bush and the Americans are—hypocrites,' he said. 'They talk about fighting terrorism, but they keep these heroes in prison for trying to stop the terrorists in Miami.'"[34] The *Washington Post* coverage demonstrated a small, but emerging duality where the customary, intractable anti-Cuba coverage was tempered by a developing acknowledgement of the other side's position.

As far as television coverage of the case was concerned, it was virtually non-existent with *CBS* and *CNN* airing brief, short reports. No defense lawyer was interviewed on behalf of the Cuban Five, no opposing viewpoints were presented.[35]

Although the case of the Cuban Five has faded from public memory, the FBI is apparently still diligently working to prevent further Cuban intelligence agents infiltrating South Florida. According to a report in the *Miami Herald* in September 2018, numerous and widely publicized visits by special agents of the Federal Bureau of Investigation have been made to the homes and workplaces of those Cuban émigrés who have been identified as supporting normal relations between the United States and Cuba. The US government seemingly sees those Cuban-Americans who want to end hostilities as somehow being suspicious characters. The *Miami Herald* article quoted the FBI as stating the reason for such warning visits was, "to send to the Cuban government the message that the FBI is looking for and watching Cuban spies who might be infiltrating the United States."[36]

Coverage of the Cuban Five was one of the starkest examples of a segment of the media literally selling its soul to the government.

While not aware of just how influential that sale was, the five were afterwards able to reflect on the inevitability of their conviction and long jail sentences as a result of media corruption.[37]

Speaking in Havana, Gerardo Hernández acknowledged there was little chance of fair coverage from the press, most notably the reporting from South Florida. Hernández was most affected by the prejudiced reporting as he was handed down two life sentences after being convicted of conspiracy to commit murder. This was based on the charge that he had prior knowledge of the Cuban government's shoot down of the Brothers to the Rescue planes, which were conducting illegal overflights into Cuban territory. The prosecution claimed that Hernández as head of the group was aware of Havana's intent to shoot down the planes and so was indirectly responsible.[38]

Hernández speculated that his sentence was so severe partially as a result of the media's ability to misinform the jurors in Miami's highly charged anti-Cuba atmosphere.

> My punishment of two life sentences was based on the prosecution saying that I had previous knowledge of when the shoot down was going to happen, which was not true. I didn't even know the planes were going to be shot down. The Cuban government made the decision the day it happened, I had no way of knowing that. We were aware our government was trying to stop the illegal flights into our airspace, but exactly what they were going to do, I didn't know. But this was the case, the jury and the public would believe anything against us, regardless of the facts. And the media was reporting on so many things that were not true, we had no chance.[39]

Hernández was among the final three to be released following Obama's opening with Cuba in 2014 and the agreement to swap prisoners. "I was shocked when the release came, I thought I would remain in jail for the rest of my life," he admitted. His story had a particularly happy ending when he was able to come home to his wife Adrianna and his first child Gema, who was born thanks to a rare political cooperation between the two adversaries.

> During my final years in jail we were able to arrange with American officials to have my wife artificially inseminated. We didn't think there would be any other way to have a child, and I thank people like (US Senator) Patrick Leahy for working to make it possible. It was an incredible gift.[40]

Hernández smiled. "She has been such a joy, and even more special as to how it happened," he added, "and now since I've been back to Cuba we've been able to have a second child."

Hernández commented on the somewhat surprising evolution of the press coverage during the trial.

> It went through stages. At first they always called us spies, we explained we were not spies, but it didn't matter they always called us spies. So we had no chance right from the start. Then for a long time the mainstream media didn't address the case at all; even though this had everything—terrorism, politics, Cuba–US relations, intelligence agents. But they ignored it because there were too many things the media didn't want the public to know about, the history of terrorism, and why we were there. The only media that covered it constantly was in Miami, and that coverage was awful.
>
> So we had no chance. We found out later that some journalists in Miami, about five, were paid by the US government. The press there would reproduce comments from the prosecutor, who said we were "bent on the destruction of the United States"—can you imagine that? How ridiculous. The corporate media coverage was bad, but it was so much worse in Miami. The radio stations, TV stations, they'd spend 24 hours a day about anti-Cuban things. And then they'd spend 24 hours a day about us, all negative of course. I heard once on the radio that, "give them to us and we'll hang them."[41]

Hernández remarked that it was the way they handled themselves at the trial that resulted in some of the most outlandish articles. "There was so much wrong information when the trial started, we were convicted by the press before the trial even began.

When they saw us facing the trial with dignity, not begging, the press began these crazy stories."[42]

Another of the five, Fernando González, recognized the US media has a long history of one-sided coverage of Cuba.

> The US media has always had a tendency to talk about the time before the revolution, like Cuba had just such a great economic situation, so why did they need a revolution? The press never understood the history of Cuba, there always is the effort to revisionism, to rewrite history in a different way, from the US perspective and nothing else. And that continued when the press covered our trial, and case, there was no coverage about why we had to be there, the history of terrorism. The press, even those journalists not paid by the government, knew they had to write anti-Cuban articles, to convict us before the trial.[43]

He remembered the judge at one point did issue a gag order against coverage of the trial,

> but it was mostly directed at the defense, who were demonstrating that what we were doing was not spying, but trying to stop terrorism. So the gag was mostly to make sure the real information didn't get out; but it didn't stop all the negative articles that convicted us and turned the community against us before the trial started.[44]

Now president of the Instituto Cubano de Amistad con los Pueblos (Cuban friendship institution), González says little has changed, "Even today the US media does not understand that most of the people in Cuba support the revolution, that trying to take us over didn't happen in 1961 at Playa Giron (Bay of Pigs), and won't happen today."[45]

And as far as René González (no relation to Fernando) is concerned, the trial:

> Should have been on the front page of all the papers in the US, if they were really interested in reporting on terrorism. We were there to prevent acts of terrorism, and yet that aspect was rarely

> covered when the case of the Cuban Five was reported. The *New York Times* sent a lady to report on the trial, and after one week she left, she didn't want to report on a case that would do so much damage to the US government. She'd have to report on the history of terrorism against Cuba. And that's a topic the press and government doesn't want anyone to know about.[46]

He understood the trial was already decided before it started, as a result of the press coverage:

> The local press in Miami was just a constant drumbeat against us. And then we find out they were paid by the government, we were convicted before the trial started. The press was used to influence the judges to give us the harshest sentences, it was unprecedented. Because it was in Miami, you can find such a bunch of journalists that will do this. Even to the point of the press identifying who was on the jury, and that was a form of threat to make sure the jury convicted us. But there was no mistrial. The media is simply a reflection of the establishment, and the establishment wanted us punished.[47]

* * *

The release of the final three members of the Cuban Five as part of the prisoner swap under Obama's 2014 opening was partially linked to an American businessman who generated his own mini-industry of misrepresentation in the corporate media.

Alan Gross was a contractor working for the United States Aid for International Development (USAID), an organization with a long history of interfering in the internal affairs of other countries. USAID has no official status in Cuba and the Havana government considers the organization as but one element in America's overarching regime change strategies. USAID operates under the Helms–Burton Act, a major piece of legislation designed to hasten the overthrow of the Cuban government, passed in 1996 as a consequence of the Brothers to the Rescue shoot down.[48]

On its website, USAID has acknowledged its Cuban intentions and the strategy of hiring Americans to interfere in the internal affairs of the island nation, using classic regime change code words.[49] A contractor's proposal submitted and accepted by USAID that led to Gross going to Cuba stated:

> The U.S. government has an "obligation" to "facilitate" democratic change in Cuba. Absent a successful transition, "the United States could face a massive humanitarian catastrophe on its shores." Cuban activists "lack the necessary skills" required to carry out a democratic transition "in a deliberate and strategic manner."[50]

Gross, who had never been to Cuba previously, was hired by USAID to bring in communication equipment ostensibly to help set up internet connectivity to the small Jewish community in Havana. He was reportedly paid $600,000 through a third party over a period of approximately five trips in 2009.[51] Gross's assertion that he was to help Havana's small but active Jewish community was met by denials from spokesperson Adela Dworin, who stated: "We don't need the sophisticated equipment that supposedly Gross brought to Cuba. We have legal Internet." Jewish leaders spoke of a good working relationship with the government, as well as strong international contacts that provide them with whatever technology is required, including computers and cell phones.[52]

USAID, and later corporate media, claimed Gross was simply carrying in low-level communication equipment, similar to cellphones. What he actually had was an illegal high tech Broadband Global Area Network (BGAN) system, designed to create untraceable satellite communication networks, equipment prohibited not only in Cuba but in any country in the world. Once set up, the signal is independent from any regulatory oversight. The small size and big capabilities to potentially connect directly with anti-government organizations or terrorist groups places BGANs as a device most authorities want under their control and knowledge. If a foreigner was caught coming into the United States with such undeclared equipment, he or she would soon find themselves facing charges under the Foreign Agents Relations Act. Cuba is highly sensitive to an American working for a dedicated anti-revolutionary government organization trying to set up an illegal communication system within its territory. It is a situation that unsurprisingly would not end well for anyone attempting to do so.

That's exactly what happened when Gross was arrested in Havana for committing Acts Against the Independence or Territorial Integrity of the State, declared a spy and sentenced to 15 years in prison. He implausibly protested he had no idea of the long animosity between Cuba and the United States, acknowledged he didn't speak a word of Spanish and then later revealed he had friends bring in part of the equipment without their knowledge.[53]

Gross apparently did know his actions were illegal, noting in spring 2009 to his supervisors that the project was "playing with fire." Then adding: "This is a risky business in no uncertain terms." His account concluded, "Detection of satellite signals will be catastrophic."[54] While spending almost five years in jail, Gross went on a hunger strike and became seriously ill. His ordeal finally came to an end when presidents Obama and Raúl Castro announced their agreement to thaw relations, it was accepted that Gross would be included in the exchange with the remaining members of the Cuban Five. Following his release, Gross sued USAID for misleading him on the contract, reaching a settlement reportedly in the amount of US$3.2 million.[55] Washington refused to admit Gross was anything other than a private citizen arrested for carrying in legal communication equipment.

The Gross affair led corporate media to diligently fall in line with the state's spin. Consistently misrepresenting what he was doing in Cuba, the press constructed the issue as a helpless American only trying to bring, "free speech to an oppressed people under the nose of a government that did not want that to happen," according to *CBS* news.[56]

Even with the facts firmly determined, mainstream media spun the story with little regard to the truth. *Miami Herald*'s Andres Oppenheimer led the way with an allegation that anyone who had ever been to Cuba knew was untrue. "Obama did not mention the case of Alan Gross, the US contractor who was sentenced to 15 years in prison this month for taking telephone equipment to Cuba."[57] Bringing telephones, including cell phones, into Cuba presents absolutely no problem, as thousands of visitors will attest to. State of the art military grade BGAN equipment, that's a different story.

The *Washington Post* spewed the same fallacy with an additional twist a few days after his arrest: "The Cuban government has arrested an American citizen working on contract for the US Agency for International Development who was distributing cell phones and laptop computers to Cuban activists."[58] And former Democrat from Florida, Debbie Wasserman Schultz, famous for her anti-Cuban rhetoric, covered the false religious angle when she was reported in the Miami media: "American Alan Gross has languished in a Cuban cell since December without access to medical care, for his crime of distributing cell phones to the Jewish community in Havana."[59]

At the end, it seemed that Gross himself was able to bring more honesty to the situation than the mainstream media. During a hearing on Capitol Hill a year after his arrest, the *New York Times* published an article that covered his written remarks to the House Committee on Foreign Affairs, in which he stated clearly: "As Members of the Committee know, I recently concluded five years of imprisonment in Cuba due to my participation in a USAID-sponsored program authorized and funded pursuant to the Helms–Burton Act."[60]

The *New York Times* then editorialized the issue in a rare display of candor:

> Mr. Gross, by telling the truth, made news and left the State Department rather exposed. This is not their story. From early January 2010, when State began taking questions on his case, it would never concede what Mr. Gross said so plainly today. Instead, its spokespersons told the U.S. public he was arrested for "facilitating Internet access for Cuba's small Jewish community," he was "innocent," his case was a matter "of a sitting government having locked up a human—an assistance worker on no basis whatsoever," and so forth. This was spin they would repeat for five years and it wasn't true. Mr. Gross's testimony corrects the record by clearly stating he was arrested for activities funded by the Helms–Burton law to overthrow Cuba's government.[61]

Although important for setting the record straight, what the editorial failed to address was the media's—including the *New York Times*'—complicity in sustaining the spin. It was, however, a refreshing admission that the truth doesn't always have to be hidden when covering Cuba. Even if the media ignored its part in the concealment.

Alan Gross was not the only unsuspecting individual caught in the cross-hairs of corporate media misinformation about Cuba. It was the personal misfortune of a small child who became the subject of intense scrutiny, the majority of which devolved into applying historical standard criticisms of the Cuban Revolution. However, the coverage also provided an indication of a perceptible shift from certain journalists who saw the matter as it really was, and not simply through an anti-Cuba lens.

Elián González was the six-year-old rescued from certain death at sea after his mother and ten others drowned on a raft leaving Cuba. The November 1999 event garnered instant international attention. When Elián was taken in by his Miami family, the press turned the tragic tale into an ideological struggle with the little boy as a political football. Elián stayed with his relatives in Miami for six months in an increasingly circus-like atmosphere, until the US government stepped in and rescued the boy. The famous photo of an armed INS agent grabbing a scared Elián from the arms of a resisting Donato Dalrymple while the two hid in a closet encapsulated how extremely partisan the issue had become. Dalrymple, who had helped find the child at sea, became a minor celebrity and self-proclaimed Cuban expert who the media turned to in order to support an anti-revolutionary perspective. It was a point of view that had a surprising amount of pushback from certain segments of the press and the pubic, who grew tired of the intransigent behavior of the relatives who used Elián as a pawn for their personal grievances against Fidel Castro. The domestic aspect of the issue, regardless that it had a Cuban element to it, undoubtedly played a role in the division among segments in the media. In large part, it was a reflection of the separation of the public's mood between those who wanted the boy to return to his homeland and those against. It was not strictly an anti-revolutionary topic, and as a result, the press could eventually provide more nuanced coverage.

At the start of the saga, however, it became apparent that because there was a Cuban angle to the story, the treatment would be anything but balanced. An extensive examination by national media watchdog *FAIR* (Fairness and Accuracy in Reporting) of how the media first handled the Elián affair noted:

> The press likes to call it "a complicated story," though it's safe to say that if Elián was from any other country, he would simply be home by now. National and international policies call for the INS to return unaccompanied immigrant children to their biological parents unless the parents are unfit. And, of course, just living in Cuba does not make Juan Miguel González an unfit parent.[62]

Normal immigration policy in a case such as Elián's was not the only information missing in media coverage, facts that should have been self-evident in any other situation. The press created a series of false narratives that merged into characteristic anti-Cuba bias—including a report that Elián wouldn't last six months if he returned to the horrors of Cuba; that his father Juan Miguel really didn't want to have his son back; and that his mother died in a desperate bid to gain freedom on America's shore. All of those charges simply lacked any reasonable assumption of veracity when examined closely. When some of the press pushed back on the false chronicle, one of the most influential conservative publications came down hard on those it perceived to be not anti-Cuban enough.

A story in the *Miami Herald* promoted the misinformation that Elián would face, "a tragic life of deprivation if he returns to Cuba." The article quoted a bystander who was capitalizing on the media circus by selling sun-visors outside Elián's Miami home: "If he goes back, he will starve to death … It would be a crime to send him back."[63]

In one of the initial retorts to that myth and the boy's plight in general, *TIME* magazine's Joshua Cooper Ramo pointed out that if returned to Cuba:

> It won't be a life of Disney World, but it won't be a life of destitution either. Juan Miguel, one of the lucky Cubans to be paid in dollars, is part of the nation's small middle class. At home in Cardenas, Elián has a spacious room to himself, unlike the one he is now sharing with four cousins in Little Havana. He'll also be surrounded by all four of his grandparents.[64]

Another *Miami Herald* article specifically selected a negative example and tried to extrapolate it into an anti-Cuban norm, when a subheading within the story asked: "What Would Elián's Life Be Like in Cuba?" The reporter had never spent any time with Elián's family, but apparently went out of the way to describe a household in a low-standard condition, not completely unusual in Cuba but certainly not indicative of how the majority live. The article described a (supposedly arbitrary) visit to the Havana home of Marielena García, a 31-year-old woman who lived with her husband and three children in a, "tiny, two-story apartment that lacks what many in the United States would consider basic amenities: a kitchen sink, a refrigerator and a stove, among other things. She and her husband Miguel, installed the toilet themselves."[65] The article implied that every Cuban household, including Elián's, faced similar deprivations, when in fact that instance was more the exception that does not prove the norm. Furthermore, the report had nothing to do with Elián's residence in Varadero.

"Go to any Havana house or apartment and you wouldn't find one in 100 that doesn't have a sink or stove, or refrigerator," Havana resident Heriberto Nicolás commented. He added, "You can find homes like that described, but if you use it as some sort of indication as to how everyone lives, that is simply misleading and inaccurate."[66]

The *FAIR* report also looked at how the media attempted to cast negative aspersions on the father–son relationship, commenting that the matter was:

> Raised by *Dateline NBC*'s Mike Taibbi (January 17, 2000) who dubbed the controversy "a choice between his father and freedom." Elian's "freedom" was perceived through incentives most American kids would never have access to, including

being "showered with gifts from relatives and well-wishers" (*AP*, December 24, 1999), receiving "three bicycles" and "a promise of $2 million for staying" (*Washington Post*, December 16, 1999), frequent trips to amusement parks and rubbing shoulders with the likes of magician David Copperfield and Yankees pitcher Orlando Hernández.[67]

Elián became the unwitting poster boy for American crass consumerism, manipulated materially as well as psychologically when he claimed in a video that he didn't want to go back to Cuba. Many described it at the time as a hostage video. When Elián's father, Juan Miguel González, was interviewed, there was skepticism that he actually wanted his son returned. The *New York Times* irresponsibly speculated as to whether Juan Miguel was simply, "a puppet of the Castro government" who "not only would allow his son to stay but would seek asylum himself" if he "had the freedom to speak his mind."[68] The assumption is, of course, that Cubans who want to remain in Cuba must be brainwashed by Castro.

When Elián's real father wasn't the topic of custody, the press moved it up a few notches to then president Fidel Castro. The *New York Times* summed up the case by declaring in a December 13, 1999 article: "Elián is at the center of an international custody fight. President Fidel Castro of Cuba has demanded the boy's return, and thousands of Cubans have marched in the streets waving posters of the boy." As an afterthought, the *New York Times* added, "Elián's father also wants his son back."[69] When a Miami judge awarded temporary custody to Elián's great-uncle, the *New York Daily News* front page screamed, "Not So Fast Fidel!"[70]

The press realized focusing on Fidel Castro was a much easier route to garner support for keeping the child in the USA, regardless of what the real father wanted.

Although the father's intentions were often questioned, Elián's mother Elizabeth Brotons Rodríguez was turned into a near saint. From the very first accounts, she was reported to have, "given her life for her child's freedom"—a commentary that was utilized to justify extreme actions, such as Congress considering granting Elián instant US citizenship.[71] Most reporters never questioned Brotons' judgment in taking her son across the Florida Straits in a rickety, 17-foot aluminum boat with 12 other people. Nor the real reason why she ventured on the dangerous trip in the first place—not for political freedom but for a personal relationship.

One who did challenge the false narrative was *Dateline NBC* correspondent Keith Morrison. He joined a slowly expanding cluster of journalists seemingly almost exasperated with a hysteria they themselves helped to create. Morrison reported that Brotons did not leave Cuba to escape Castro as much as she left to be with her boyfriend Lazaro Munero—the man that orchestrated the journey to Florida. As he noted, "It was an affair that had nothing to do with politics … It's about a woman who followed a man."[72]

When the media did exhibit a modicum of honest reporting over the Elián case, even that was too much for some right-wing publications. The conservative *Weekly Standard* took its brethren to task for not completely upholding the strict anti-Cuban bias, no matter what the justification.[73] Those in the media who challenged the narrative that Elián should be kept in the United States were simply unwilling dupes of the evil Castro government, so the publication chastised.

The *Weekly Standard* criticized journalists who saw the episode for what it was—an unlawful attempt to keep a child away from his sole surviving parent:

> Thomas Friedman, for one, could barely contain himself last week. In fact, he didn't: "Yup, I gotta confess," said the *New York Times* columnist, "that now-famous picture of a U.S. marshal in Miami pointing an automatic weapon toward Donato Dalrymple and ordering him in the name of the U.S. government to turn over Elián González warmed my heart." Cuban-Americans, he said, believed "they could get away with kidnapping Elián. America is a lot better off today because Janet Reno taught them otherwise."[74]

The *Weekly Standard* showed particular concern when it printed the opinion of the *New York Times*' Miami bureau chief Rick Bragg, who confessed to Knoxville's *Metro Pulse*:

> It's the dumbest thing I've ever covered. Some people think hell is a place where you wake up in the morning in a bed of coals. I think it's where you wake up and find out you'll be writing about Elián for the next 643 days.[75]

It was left to the *St Petersburg Times* to encapsulate the frustration of the Elián affair and how the media might finally be able to recognize that just because it had a Cuban angle it didn't have to be reported through an anti-revolutionary viewpoint. In fact, sometimes the perspective from Havana was the correct one:

> If Elián's Miami relatives had cared more about the boy's welfare than in using him as a political trophy in the propaganda war against Fidel Castro, they would have sent him back to his father weeks ago … Elián was manipulated and brainwashed by his Miami relatives. … [They had] abused this child long enough.[76]

After the young boy was finally sent home with his father, the *New York Times* ran an editorial that not only perceptively described the political fallout, but added to the small shift in the media's attitude toward Cuba. The public:

> became more aware of America's outdated policy of isolation toward Cuba. It is perhaps not surprising that just one day before Elián's flight home, the House Republican leaders agreed to end four decades of sanctions on food sales to Cuba. The saga of this Cuban child helped to hasten that shift in policy.[77]

In the final analysis, Elián's tragedy produced a not insignificant amount of coverage that reflected the reality of the issue—the manipulation of a little boy by an increasingly isolated Cuban-American community not supported by the majority of the American public. While a preponderance in the media, particularly in the Florida press, had attempted to shift the story's framework from personal heartbreak into an indictment against the Cuban system, an emerging segment did not subscribe to that narrative—and in fact pushed back.

Elián helped turn a portion of the media away, if not from the reflexive unthinking criticism of the revolution, to at least rise above the anti-Cuba dictum and look at the issues individually with a higher degree of journalistic integrity.

It was not just Elián. The Cuban Five, Alan Gross—these incidents indicated a fragmentation in the media—the overwhelming bias against Cuba remained in place, but there were hints of an ideological modification in coverage. The right-wing press remained steadfastly anti-revolutionary, but the so-called liberal media, while consistent in its criticism of the country's basic social/economic make-up, permitted some space to include Cuba's position when warranted. The mere ability to present Havana's perspective and bring into the public discourse topics such as terrorism against Cuban civilians represented an alteration in editorial attitudes. Anti-revolutionary prejudice and adherence to regime change promotion was still particularly easy to distinguish, but at least in specific cases there appeared to be informational context not usually evident when the mainstream media deals with Cuban issues. The shift in media attitudes could, however, make the anti-Cuban narrative more effective as it came under the guise of journalistic even-handiness.

The seemingly more balanced reporting from some of the most influential newspapers and cable news networks received another boost, within defined limits, when Barack Obama and Raúl Castro decided to make a serious attempt to move beyond decades of hostility.

4
The Media Opens and Closes Against Cuba

For more than 100 years, dating back to the Spanish–American War of 1895, America's establishment media has displayed, with few exceptions, an impressive counter-factual narrative of Cuba. As a reflection of state purposes, the press echoed aspirations to possess the island nation from its Spanish colonial masters. Once achieved, the coverage focused on the supposedly unquestionable benevolence of American hegemony. When those ungrateful revolutionaries imposed their own perceptions of national identity, the media became unrelenting in its approbation against Fidel and his followers—publicly advocating Washington's regime change objectives under cover of ideological incompatibility or self-aggrandized political controversies. The press, owned by capitalists, reinforced by the greatest capitalist nation on earth, could be expected to do no other than create a biased narrative through misinformation and propaganda in order to sustain its own political/economic foundations. This was conveyed regardless of the national ideological bent of individual media outlets—differences in left- or right-wing domestic issues evaporated when it came to presenting a united front of anti-Cuba coverage. "Bipartisanship ends at the water's edge"[1] was apparently meant not only for political consideration, but for the dissemination of misinformation to the masses.

Then along came President Barack Obama, who in December 2014 decided it was time to try a different approach. Instead of the stick, maybe the carrot would be more effective in changing those intransigent socialists in Havana. In a joint announcement with Cuban President Raúl Castro, it was decided that a path to normalization would be attempted to set aside more than 50 years of hostility. It would be based on easing travel restrictions, permitting more Americans to visit Cuba, as well as reducing various barriers for US commercial operations to access the Cuban market. Other considerations included taking Cuba off the list of states that sponsor terrorism. Havana long considered that a particularly galling designation considering the unknown history of terrorism against Cuban civilians by anti-revolutionary organizations based in Florida. Both sides additionally agreed to upgrade their interest sections to full embassies in Havana and Washington, for the first time since before the revolution. A structure was established to hold bilateral conferences to resolve core disputes such as compensation for nationalized properties and the American imposed embargo.

Normalization for the Cuban side was meant to afford an easing of hostilities, if not an end to them. Havana expected it would provide the framework where a path eliminating America's economic punishment was possible, leading to a level of development envisioned since 1959. For the Americans, the new move was foreseen to accomplish the same result—regime change—by using a different route.

Corporate media almost instantaneously bought into Washington's new tack that underlined the normalization process—offering an olive branch with one hand, while keeping regime change strategy firmly hidden inside the other. The press produced a steady stream of coverage in support of Obama's shift in policy, all the while utilizing verbiage that helped obscure—while remaining faithful to—the goal of ending Cuba's revolutionary government. Regime change narratives persisted, only in more subtle form.

Obama acknowledged the move toward reconciliation did not relinquish regime change strategy, only reconfigured it. The *Wall Street Journal* dutifully quoted his intention:

> In the most significant changes in our policy in more than 50 years, we will end an outdated approach that, for decades, has failed to advance our interests, and instead we will begin to normalize relations between our two countries … I do not expect the changes I am announcing today to bring about a transformation of Cuban society overnight.[2]

Clearly articulating that the end of the current government would be the desired outcome, just that no one could tell when.

In his statement, Obama verbalized old regime change code words wrapped in new phraseology: "to help the Cuban people to achieve a better future for themselves." The strategy sought a "prosperous, stable Cuba. It does not serve America's interests, or the Cuban people, to try to push Cuba toward collapse," Obama declared. It was a remarkable comment considering Cuba was already one of the most stable counties in Latin America, despite America's decade-long attempts to undermine it. He even claimed "we will not pursue regime change" or that it ever had—all the while ignoring the realities of the past at the same time acknowledging the flood of US tourists and American capitalist culture would assist in accomplishing that very goal.[3]

It was Obama's national security adviser, Susan Rice, who clarified the president's objective in her widely reported remarks that all those decades-long "democracy programs"—which the Castro government denounced as secret efforts to destabilize the country—now be "transparent." She added: "The United States used to have secret plans for Cuba; now our policy is fully out in the open and online for everyone to see and read."[4]

In other words, it is acceptable for the USA to continue violating the United Nations Charter and international agreements by attempting to force the Cuban people to change their political and economic system—as long as it is done openly. The press responded with seemingly positive articles on Cuba, covering topics of a more non-political nature—sports, culture, economic reforms. On the surface, it seemed balanced, but long-standing media bias was still evident—just more circumspect.

Cuba watcher and journalist Karen Lee Wald speculated that from the beginning of the opening,

> this was just a new strategy to change Cuban socialism. After 50 years they realized hostility wasn't working, and that the United States was becoming isolated within the international community. So a new tactic was announced—with the same regime change objectives.[5]

In absolute deference, media coverage, such as the *New York Times*, "made it clear they don't have any greater love for Cuban socialism than before, and are only upset that methods until now haven't done the trick of producing regime change—costing a lot of money without getting results," Wald said.[6]

Proof that while appearances suggested a new opening, America's work toward regime change remained constant came when it was reported Obama was authorizing millions of dollars in the continuation of anti-Cuban programs. According to Tracey Eaton on his Cuban blog, *Along the Malecón*, a year after the opening:

> The State Department is asking for more than $6 million to convert the U.S. Interests Section in Havana to an embassy and $528,000 for a new program called "Cuba Outreach Initiative," budget documents show. Separately, officials are requesting $15 million for civil society programs and $5 million for rule of law and human rights programs in Cuba for fiscal year 2016.[7]

With the money still flowing to maintain regime change tactics, Obama decided to take a trip to Havana in 2016 with the intent to cement the new relationship. During his visit, the president was treated like a rock star by the locals and a transcendental figure by the press. While the *New York Times* and others called the trip "historic,"[8] *TIME* magazine couldn't resist commenting that Obama's words would have the opportunity to awaken the ill-informed Cubans.

> This is a country where the media is strictly controlled by the government. So when Obama meets with a select group of Cuban entrepreneurs, talks with human rights activists and gives a broad address to the Cuban people, he'll have a rare opportunity to send his message directly to the country's citizens.[9]

The historic narrative, that the locals were unaware of the outside world, continued to display itself in such reporting.

Even more disparaging was an editorial in *USA Today*, which was ostensibly from the side of endorsing the opening, but brought up all the bias and ingrained rationalizations for American hostility against Cuba:

> For nearly 60 years, its government has done two things exceptionally well: repress its own people and make a mockery of U.S. efforts to compel change through economic sanctions … Without question, U.S. economic sanctions have been an exercise in frustration. They have not prompted a popular uprising or compelled the Cuban regime to open up. If anything, they have been counterproductive, allowing the Castro regime to blame its woeful economic performance on vindictive U.S. policies, rather than on its failed communist ideology.[10]

USA Today evoked archetypal narratives that readers would be expected to accept as axiomatic—that the embargo was justified but failed because it didn't do enough harm to the Cuban people for them to overthrow their own government. The idea that American hostility and regime change policy would be a significant dynamic in the creation of a siege mentality preventing Cuba society to 'open up' is beyond examination, as is an honest recounting of the economic damage the American embargo has inflicted upon the citizens. Knowing where the blame should actually be placed is not that difficult to ascertain as the data is within easy grasp of the mass media. All that is needed is a copy of the annual report to the United Nations outlining in both general and specific ways how the embargo continues to act as a restriction to Cuban social and economic development.[11]

In conjunction with the lack of balanced analysis, many in the media brought in anti-revolutionary experts who opined that those Cubans wouldn't be broken even with the president's words of encouragement. As *The Guardian* reported:

> Jorge Domínguez, a Cuban born professor of international relations at Harvard University, agreed that an attempt to broker political reform inside Cuba would be flawed, even if it were Obama's intention. "On the larger question, which every president since Kennedy has faced: how to foster democracy and human rights—quid pro quo has been a perfect failure …

> Whenever it has been framed in that way, the Cuban government shuts down."[12]

The two concepts, democracy and human rights, continued to be used as a specious stick to beat the Cubans with, regardless of how those issues were misconstrued by restrictively imposed US political definitions parroted by the establishment media.

Obama trotted out those denunciations against Cuba, saying the country:

> Has not yet observed basic human rights ... I and the American people will welcome the time when the Cuban people have the freedom to live their lives, choose their leaders, and fully participate in this global economy and international institutions.[13]

The press and political elites have consistently ignored Cuba's political make-up as well as its models in human rights as defined—by any developing country—as the necessity to meet basic food, housing and health care requirements. As well, a cursory investigation would reveal that Cuba is well integrated in the global economy (the USA is one of the few nations it does not have trade relations with) and the country is connected with as many, if not more, international institutions as any other. Cuba is not a member of the International Monetary Fund—part by choice and part from American pressure not to allow them affiliation.

But the media's role is not to examine Cuba's society fairly; it is to validate regime change. In a commentary by Robert Sandels and Nelson P. Valdés, the two concisely described that concept through the establishment of an unchallenged fiction, one that remained unchanged under Obama:

> To justify the long hostility toward Cuba, the United States mainstream media has created a Cuba that never existed; a tropical gulag of indiscriminate terror where hordes of political prisoners rot while a cartoon dictator recites hours of his political poetry to a captive audience.[14]

The column then addressed political and media terminology that has been used as a weapon against the revolution:

> Why is it that regime change is couched in fuzzy terms like "freedom" devoid of any economic, social or cultural content? And why is it that Obama criticizes the old policy because it "failed to advance our interests" without acknowledging what those interests really are? Nothing in Obama's speech corrects the half-century assault on truth. Many of the media commentaries on the Obama speech recite from the fantasies concocted over the years to mask the insanity of the policy.[15]

Counterpunch columnist Matt Peppe also recognized the media's hypocritical control of terminology:

> U.S. calls for "democracy" and "human rights" in Cuba have an important historical connotation, which in reality has nothing to do with representative government nor human rights. The term is nothing more than a propaganda tool, instantly elevating the accuser to a superior moral status and subjecting the accused to an indefensible position regardless of the real facts, history and context. The U.S. is not suggesting that Cuba should be judged by established human rights and international humanitarian laws … It is suggesting Cuba abide by the criteria the U.S. sets out for them and sees fit to interpret itself.[16]

Peppe's article ended with a condemnation of American duplicity:

> The reality is that the United States does not get to serve as judge and jury for other countries' internal affairs, just as they would laugh in the face of anyone who tried to do the same to them. To pretend that your demands are more important than the law that governs the international system is beyond condescending … Obama's sanctimonious remarks about Cuba demonstrate his disregard for the law that applies to both countries equally, and his unwillingness to be held to the same standard that he preaches to others.[17]

That interpretation has long been reflected through the corporate media lens, demonstrating the partiality toward holding Cuba to a higher standard than to US allies committing far worse human rights abuses, as in Saudi Arabia, Egypt, Honduras and elsewhere. A look at that historical hypocrisy would reveal dozens more examples since World War II.[18]

One who recognized the political motivation behind the opening and Obama's trip was media's favorite whipping boy, Fidel Castro, whose critical comments were covered as nothing more than sour grapes from the last Cold War soldier. In an article in Cuba's national newspaper *Granma*, Fidel Castro had the audacity (as far as the US press was concerned) to bring up America's historical hostility and questioned what the nation could learn from US culture. "We don't need the empire to give us anything," he impolitely wrote.[19]

CNN was quick to chastise the Cuban president, criticizing his "acidly critical and rambling article,"[20] implying that Fidel Castro was being quite ungrateful to America's new benevolence and even more ill-mannered as to question the harm US policy has done in attempting to thwart Cuban nationalism. It reflected historical media attitudes by telling the Cubans how they should behave toward their betters. *CNN* then expressed further offense to the article, noting that: "Castro wrote, before listing a litany of what he said were abuses the United States had perpetuated against Cuba."[21] Conveniently, the network did not provide any examples of what that list contained, leaving the consumer to wonder if there were any "abuses" at all, signifying that Fidel Castro was just a rambling, inconsiderate ingrate not to be taken seriously.

An important but rare example of how certain media outlets refused to toe the establishment line against Cuba came when *Slate Magazine* defended his position:

> Pundits portrayed Castro's comments as a sign of supposed ill will and ingratitude. But an objective look at the history shows that his response was not only wholly justified; it was frankly quite mild. For the crimes—and there is no question that they are crimes—the U.S. has repeatedly and continuously committed against its sovereign neighbor over the past five decades include:

a violent invasion that left hundreds dead; more than 600 assassination attempts; myriad covert campaigns dedicated to fomenting "hunger, desperation and overthrow of government" the unilateral imposition of a suffocating embargo; and the harboring of CIA-trained admitted terrorists who murdered Cuban civilians in hopes of toppling the socialist state.[22]

That response, infrequent as it was, demonstrated the continuation within segments of the media of a more honest approach to Cuban coverage, first evidenced during the trial of the Cuban Five and the treatment of Elián González and Alan Gross.[23] It would maintain and expand itself during the attempts to establish normal relations.

* * *

The opening in 2014 made Cuba one of the hottest spots to visit, and not for the weather. Thousands of Americans flocked to the island, mostly to Havana, to see what they had been missing for 50 years. Cuba's socialism was as much the attraction, perceived as being both romantically exotic and hopelessly antiquated. They came to experience first-hand how the system did, and didn't work, as well as to gawk at the old cars and other cultural relics of America's pre-revolution presence.

Although international tourism had been well established in Cuba for the past 20 years, the influx of Americans harkened back to the heydays of the 1950s, both in location and attitude. A portion of those US visitors were able to feel as superior as they had pre-revolution, looking down on the obvious economic difficulties, unpainted walls and challenging tourist infrastructure including iconic places like the Hotel Nacional. Cuba also became the newest destination for celebrities; movie stars such as Vin Diesel filmed *Fast and Furious 8*, the Rolling Stones performed a free concert in front of thousands in Havana, and television stars including Conan O'Brien devoted one of his shows to the humorous idiosyncrasies of Cuban culture. Jay Z and Beyonce made the trip during their 5th wedding anniversary—with the media such as *USA Today* assuring fans the visit was legal.[24] Happily, as it coincided with Obama's decision to ease travel restrictions.

Media also flocked to the island. Much of the coverage would focus on the mistakes and inefficiencies made under a centralized, state-controlled economy—of which there are plenty of examples—while ignoring or diminishing the negative impact the embargo has placed upon Cuba's efforts to develop; or the social advances the country has accomplished under those conditions. The press would consistently turn to descriptions of "crumbling infrastructure"[25] and "failures in the system"[26] to reinforce the storyline of Cuba's disastrous experiment in socialism.

An indignant response to those demeaning designations came from Cuban writer and intellectual Manuel Yepe, who commented,

> We accept the reporting on our problems, we know what they are and are always working to correct them. But not to acknowledge how the embargo hurts our economy, our ability to advance, our people, that's just the media intentionally ignoring the truth. Look at the things we have accomplished under the revolution, in health care, education; so many positive things you never read about.[27]

The reporting, regardless of whether it was on Cuban culture or arts, always retained critical elements against the country's political and economic structure. A *TIME* magazine story reported what it perceived to be the contradiction of Cuban people enjoying life in the streets while signs of economic distress dominating the landscape. It commented disdainfully that after the fall of the Soviet Union, Fidel Castro was forced to open the country to "the very tourists (and prostitutes) he had come to power to scourge."[28] To the Cubans, it was a pragmatic decision; to certain American reporters it was proof of the failure of the system.

So much of the coverage now moved through the prism of tourism with the underlying chauvinism assuming that the influx of direct and supposedly positive American influence would finally bring the political changes that everyone, including the locals, were desperate for. The press was in a positive mood for Obama's carrot, even though the stick was still at hand if needed.

Corporate media became instrumental in promoting the new narrative that the Cuban Revolution was a misguided, mismanaged anachronism. All that was needed was an influx of US tourism, business and capitalism to end the failed experiment and evolve these obsolete socialists into a more appropriate era of economic modernity—under American tutelage. It would be the key to end Cuban socialism once and for all. It became the media's twenty-first-century informational hubris toward the island nation.

Leading the charge was the *New York Times*, running a series of relatively positive articles on Cuba, prior to Obama's announcement. Speculation still exists as to whether the *New York Times* was out in front of state objectives, or worked in conjunction with Washington's roll-out of the new strategy.

One of the first in a series of editorials came out two months prior to the announcement, stating: "For the first time in more than 50 years, shifting politics in the United States and changing policies in Cuba make it politically feasible to re-establish formal diplomatic relations and dismantle the senseless embargo."[29]

The editorial asserted it was now appropriate for an American president to end the embargo imposed on Cuba since 1961, which it argued, "for decades was an utter failure," and to move toward normalization, thereby better positioning Washington "to press the Cubans on democratic reforms" and "create opportunities to empower ordinary Cubans, gradually eroding the government's ability to control their lives."[30] The *New York Times* concisely revealed media's new storyline—end the embargo not for the harm it has done, but that it hasn't been effective in compelling those stubborn Cubans to change their system under American precepts. Obama's opening changed Washington's tack in the direction of reconciliation—with the same end game unmoved. The media aligned right along with the shift, now promoting openness and an end to the punishment in the hope the Cubans would kick out their leaders once they saw the benefits American friendship would bring.

Fernando González, one of the Cuban Five intelligent agents jailed in the United States for trying to prevent terrorist acts,[31] commented on how he perceived a change in media coverage since the opening, and how misguided it was:

> There was a new approach in some sections of the media. The intent to establish relations has helped in better coverage, more balanced but there are still the preconceived attitudes about Cuba—that the new relationship will change Cuba, help bring down the revolution because of American ideas, that the Cubans are desperate for the Americans to come with their culture and economy and democracy, as they define it. That won't happen; the revolution will grow and strengthen once we have normal relations.[32]

As he noted, American media continually promotes the misconception of: "Wanting to bring freedom to Cuba. We already have it. I wasn't a free man till I arrived in Cuba on the day of my release from jail."[33]

The *New York Times* editorial was part of an impressive series of articles on Cuba, close to 50 written from February 2014 to September 2015. Many were authored by Ernesto Londoño,[34] who insisted the national paper was not churning out the pieces in order to prepare the public for Washington's new policies. Londoño addressed the scheduling of the editorials during an extensive *NPR* interview:

> There's been no shortage of speculation and conspiracy theories about the timing of these editorials. And if you look at, you know, how intensely we went after the subject and the timing of the announcement last month, it's certainly a valid question. We began this series, you know, largely by accident. It wasn't designed as a series from the start.[35]

He noted that an international conference was the incentive for the editorials:

> There's going to be a regional summit in Panama. Where, for the first time really since Fidel Castro came to power, there was an expectation that the Cuban president and the American president were going to be at the same table at a diplomatic forum. So this was really forcing some awkward questions for the Obama administration about how to handle this meeting. It

> was the first time when Latin American countries insisted that the United States had to agree to let Cuba attend this meeting. So the impetus for this first editorial that we write is to make a loud call about just how retrograde and ineffective U.S.–Cuba policy appeared to us at the time. And when we thought about this issue, we felt it was pretty much a backwater policy issue in a pretty crowded agenda. We had no real reasonable expectation that this was something that was going to emerge as a priority in the political landscape, but we figured it was worthwhile to give it a shot.[36]

That first editorial, titled "Obama Should End the Embargo,"[37] attracted the attention of Fidel Castro. The editorial was quoted extensively in a column by the former Cuban leader in the state-run newspaper *Granma*, indicating a positive response and desire for the Cuban government to pursue normalization.

The *New York Times* editorial Fidel Castro commented on was enlightening in its recognition of the embargo's true purpose, coincidently revealing the parameters of the mainstream media's truth telling. "Starting in 1961, Washington has imposed sanctions in an effort to oust the Castro regime. Over the decades, it became clear to many American policy makers that the embargo was an utter failure."[38] Mentioning the intent to "oust" the revolutionary government is acceptable; admitting the embargo was primarily designed to hurt the civilian population not so much.

Other editorials in the series addressed Cuba's role in combating the Ebola outbreak and the impediments presented by the embargo and lack of diplomatic ties (October 20, 2014); assessed the shifting politics of the Cuban-American community (October 26, 2014); supported the idea of a prisoner swap (November 3, 2014); critiqued the subterfuge of numerous misadventures that the USA pursued to achieve regime change in Cuba (November 10, 2014); lamented the brain drain effect of US policies to lure skilled Cubans away from the island (November 17, 2014); and advocated facilitation of US business ties to help invigorate Cuba's own tentative economic reforms (December 15, 2014).

Londoño acknowledged the concurrence of state and media narratives, but declared it was nothing official:

> I think it's reasonable to say government has used the media … and journalists, sometimes within reason, are willing to play that game if in the process of doing so they're also doing journalism they find worthwhile. However, in this case, there was really no such collusion or no formal cooperation or collaboration in what they were doing and what we were doing.[39]

Others weren't so convinced, with the *Washington Post* media blogger Erik Wemple grumbling: "That's a hell of a lot of well-timed Cuba editorializing. Perhaps a bit too well-timed? Did the *New York Times* editorial board get a little heads-up from the Obama administration on all this stuff?"[40]

"None," responded Londoño, "we had no visibility on or insight into the secret negotiations. Some administration officials agreed to speak to us about Cuba policy, at our request, but they did not shed light on what was happening behind the scenes."[41]

During the *NPR* interview, Londoño articulated the historical hypocrisy American hostility has been wrapped up in under the guise of noble intent. Addressing the various regime change policies, he blandly admitted punitive legislation such as the 1996 Helms–Burton Act,[42] specifically designed to encourage the overthrow of the Cuban government, was necessary to fulfill US regime change objectives:

> Any reasonable reading of the full bill makes clear that our purpose was to facilitate Cuban Democrats to overthrow their government and to have free elections and a new system of government. So I think our policy, as a legislative matter since 1996, has been for the United States to spend money and take steps to empower ordinary Cubans who wanted a democratic system to replace the government they had, which on principle is something that we might back. We definitely support Cuban Democrats and Cubans who want greater freedoms.[43]

He added that American policies would be successful if, "ordinary Cubans are going to be more inclined and more empowered to ask tough questions of their government and to start having a more meaningful conversation about the way they want to be governed."[44]

It has been the long-standing media narrative, of which Londoño adds his name to, that the average Cuban has no opportunity to influence their own society, nor will the government permit public dialogue as to its construct. It is one of the most egregious prejudices that retain special status within anti-revolutionary mythology promoted by the press. The narrative also reflects the most basic of arrogances; in that the United States, after decades of hostility and now attempts at normalization, unilaterally determines the Cuban people are helpless at defining their own fate—regardless of what the actuality reveals. It is a historical echo reverting back to media portrayals of the inadequate rebels in their fight for independence against the Spanish more than a century ago.

In reality, nationwide dialogues between the government and its citizens on how revolutionary society should advance have been a mainstay of the relationship between the leaders and the people. During the early decades, public rallies and events would gauge the mood of the *vox populi*. Social organizations from youth groups, farmers, students, unions and artistic institutions were formed from the participation and input of the masses. Over the past few years, there have been two major outreaches to the population to address how Cuban socialism would move into the twenty-first century. The first was held in 2011 while the government was formulating new laws for the establishment of economic reforms under President Raúl Castro. Thousands of assemblies were held in working centers and educational facilities across the country to garner the opinions and suggestions from the general public. This feedback was used by the government to finalize the more than 300 *lineamientos* (guidelines) of the economic reforms. The resulting changes included new legalities to buy and sell private homes, cars and the expansion of non-state enterprises and cooperatives. It also began the process of moving 1 million government workers into the private sector.

Cuba's latest referendum was initiated in 2018 with the restructuring of the constitution. The new constitution will expand personal rights and increase economic freedoms including private property as well as incorporating certain elements of a free market and term limits on the president and others in leadership positions.[45] The process was discussed in more than 100,000 workplaces and community meetings. Once the debate wrapped up, the National Assembly approved the constitution before submitting it to a nationwide vote in February 2019 for ratification.[46] According to government results, the new legal framework was approved by 86 percent of those eligible to vote, including Cubans living outside the country. More than 60 percent of the original draft was restructured as a result of proposals from the general public, which also overwhelmingly voted to maintain the country's socialist make-up.[47] The new constitution was passed by an overwhelming majority in April 2019.

Cuban society, including a variety of organizations for women, unions and youth, has always been built on the participation of the masses. It is a concept the media has been either willfully ignorant of or has intentionally disregarded. The only voice usually provided has been from the minority who favor a closer alignment to US-style political/economic structures. The press remains unconvinced the majority want improvements while retaining the socialist system—ignoring all evidence to the contrary.

In certain cases, when the referendum process is acknowledged, it is degraded. The *Miami Herald* published an extensive article interviewing only anti-revolutionaries, who inaccurately claimed that the Cuban people would not have a say in the construction of the new constitution (even while admitting it would go to a full nationwide vote).

The lead paragraph in the story revealed the *Miami Herald*'s viewpoint under the cover of the dissident's opinions: "They call it 'a fraud,' 'a trap' and 'illegitimate.' Those are some of the words Cuban government opposition activists on the island and in Miami use to describe a proposed new constitution endorsed recently by the National Assembly."[48] No one supporting the referendum or providing accurate information was interviewed, as the media has little use for opinions that run counter to well-established anti-Cuban narratives.

In fact, when major social policies are enacted without public input, there is a substantial backlash. This occurred in 2018, following the government's announcement of Decree 349, appearing to censure independent art and cultural expression; artists across the country strongly protested the measure. Shortly after, President Miguel Díaz-Canel apologized and promised to open up the proposal for discussion. He acknowledged that the government had failed to go through the normal process of consulting with the population before enacting any new law or regulation.[49]

President Obama's move to establish normal relations with Cuba has elicited a great amount of media attention. An investigation to determine if the *New York Times* coverage helped lay the groundwork for the public's acceptance for normalization was undertaken by French journalist Marie Sanz.[50] The 2015 report attempted to demonstrate the paper's supposedly historic stance in criticizing Washington's hostility and support for maintaining relations. However, it simply revealed that the *New York Times* advocacy for engagement was a recognition that antagonism was counter-productive as it had not resulted in regime change. The *New York Times* has been as critical, if not more critical, of Cuban socialism as any other establishment press in the United States. If there is any revelation in Sanz's study it's that the *New York Times*' position, historic and current, has been that engagement would be the best method to achieve the identical result. This would strengthen America's ability to enforce the regime change policies in place since the revolution. Same ends, different means.

The idea that the *New York Times*—whether by design or coincidence—assisted in the normalization of relations sustains itself to this day. Much of the difficulty to accept that interpretation is based on the characterization of "normal." While the opening created positive developments in bringing the two sides together (almost all of which has been squandered by the Trump administration), the foundations for America's hostility and regime change have remained in place. However, "normal" is not applicable terminology for this relationship. Not as long as the embargo continues, certain travel restrictions remain in place, or if the extra-territorial aspects of US legislation against the island nation, including millions of dollars in fines against international banks doing business with Cuba, are still enforced. The perception and practice of the USA needing to impose change to Cuba's political/economic system has been a constant. Obama set a new tone, a new tactic, but the end goal was the same—regime change. That can be considered as normal relations since 1959. What Obama and Raúl Castro were trying to accomplish could be measured as abnormal.

Although the *New York Times* and other mainstream media supported at least the concept of normalization, not everyone was on board. The *Washington Post* did not approve, instead preferring the old hardline approach. In a patronizing editorial on October 20, 2014, the *Washington Post*'s headline contained one of the most frequently used code words for regime change: "Cuba Should Not be Rewarded for Denying Freedom to its People."[51] The editorial focused in on the death of dissident Oswaldo Payá, who lost his life in a car crash. No proof was offered that it was something other than an accident, although that didn't stop the establishment media from blaming the Castro government of nefarious action. It ended with the customary demand that the embargo should continue until the Cuban leadership accede to US arbitrarily defined standards: "A concession such as ending the trade embargo should not be exchanged for nothing. It should be made when Cuba grants genuine freedom to its people, the goal cherished by Mr. Payá."[52]

In its response to the opening, the *Miami Herald* followed the *Washington Post* by pleading with the government not to abandon the punishment until the Cubans give something in return: "U.S. lawmakers who harbor doubts about the wisdom of the White House's decision should demand that the Cuban government put something substantial on the table before agreeing to drop what's left of the Cuban embargo."[53]

That disingenuous ultimatum was called out by Max Castro, a high-profile journalist and academic based in Miami. Castro, a Cuban exile who was stanchly anti-revolutionary before reconciling with the government, retorted in an article that:

> There is not much difference between such a demand and the policy in place for more than five decades. In other words, it's a non-starter, a guaranteed dead end. The same old failed policy. If there is one thing the Cuban government has systematically demonstrated over the years is that it will not yield to blackmail or trade sovereignty for economic gain.[54]

He enunciated the unspoken hubris of the United States in its relationship with the revolutionary government in Cuba, recognizing how the media never allows it to be expressed or challenged:

> The unstated and unquestionable assumption underlying the *Herald*'s take is that the United States holds the moral high ground in the relation between the two states. For that to be the case, over the last five decades Cuba would have had to arm a brigade of Black Panthers and other American revolutionaries to invade this country, organize repeated attempts to assassinate a U.S. president, try to economically strangle the United States (including interfering with American dealings with other countries), and attempt to isolate it diplomatically. In fact, it was the other way around.[55]

The *New York Times*' support and *Washington Post*'s opposition would appear to demonstrate a clearer demarcation of media coverage. In fact, the division was over how to achieve long-standing state goals—not over the objective itself. The *New York Times* saw the opening as a new avenue for regime change, in accordance with Washington's updated perspective. The *Washington Post* and *Miami Herald* conversely called for the maintenance of the old strategies. Both sides were speaking for the achievement of the same end—the removal of the revolution and the re-imposition of American interests. Neither questioned the legality of those policies, the effectiveness or the harm caused to the Cuban population.

But even the *New York Times* found itself reverting back to the decades-long tradition of cataloguing the conditions Cuba had to accede to before the United States fulfilled its offer at reconciliation. In an article covering the raising of the Cuban flag at the embassy opening in Washington on July 20, 2015, the *New York Times* sternly declared: "The full normalization of relations between the United States and Cuba will take years and will be an arduous process," mentioning, among other issues,

> the disposition of American property the Cuban government seized in the 1960s, and the fate of the United States Navy base in Guantánamo Bay ... It would be naïve to expect that the

> Cuban government, a dynastic police state, will take big steps in the near future to liberalize its centrally planned economy, encourage private enterprise or embrace pluralistic political reform.[56]

There is no Castro leading the country today, putting lie to any charge of a dynasty, and anyone who has ever visited an actual police state such as Myanmar or Honduras would realize how ludicrous that charge is. The *New York Times* also must have missed out on the extensive amount of economic reforms focusing on private businesses that have taken place in the country since 2011—or did not want to disrupt its editorial partiality by acknowledging them. The *New York Times* represents the twenty-first-century equivalent of the same story—Cuba must change to conform to American standards, nothing more, nothing less. The media's new-found open-minded Cuban coverage could be construed as being more insidious as it is publicly perceived to be fair and balanced. The continued backing for regime change is obscured by the editorials and articles promoting the positive aspects of the new relationship, while ignoring the continuation of America's unaltered objectives. Cuba's insistence of requiring an end to the embargo and hostility before true normalization would be achieved can therefore be portrayed as evidence of the system's intransigence—or simply ignored. The media is then able to carry on with its alignment to Washington's restructured approach against the legitimacy of Cuba's revolution, under the appearance of presenting less biased reporting. The bias has not been removed, it is just blurred through duplicitous distraction.

President Obama's new tactic, however, did not last long. Things reverted back to the bad old days of confrontation when Donald Trump took over the White House in 2016. It was easy for the new administration to turn back the clock. Would the press follow?

* * *

Before Trump announced his intention to roll back Obama's new opening with Cuba, the media demonstrated some of the most one-sided, malicious and ill-informed reporting on an event that marked the end of an era.

The death of Fidel Castro at the age of 90 on November 25, 2016 unleashed a tirade of vitriol in the press, degenerating back to the most distorted and propagandized coverage of the past century. It was a shocking example of just how negative and disrespectful the mainstream media could be, based on lies and the imposition of its own historical fantasies.

Corporate media came out against the memory of Fidel Castro in all its glorious sanctimony, releasing the pent-up frustration it had harbored over the decades. In life, Fidel Castro could have answered back against the slurs, in death, the press had carte blanche to create whatever absurd defamations it wanted. And it did want to. As the slanders piled on relentlessly, it was with little doubt state authorities looked on approvingly at these attacks against the leader of a small country who for so long defied American authority and imperial dictates.

A few of the worst examples came from the supposedly liberal press, including an obituary in *The Guardian* that needlessly dredged up the long-disputed narrative of how the worst elements of the Batista regime were treated in the early post-revolutionary days:

> The newly victorious rebels executed hundreds—some say thousands—after seizing power in 1959. Debate still rages over whether this was a legitimate settling of accounts with Fulgencio Batista's henchmen or kangaroo court-sanctioned atrocities … The revolution's defenders called the oppression (of the dissidents) a survival strategy for a small Caribbean island besieged by a hostile superpower which deployed spooks, stooges and would-be assassins. Detractors called it tyranny.[57]

The executions after Batista's fall have been examined extensively, with considerable controversy as to the number, ranging from a few dozen to no more than a few hundred.[58] A journalist who throws in the pusillanimously lazy "some say" tautology immediately betrays his bias. The only "debate" as to the executions remains in the minds of anti-revolutionaries. It also must take a considerable amount of willful denial to describe terrorists as "spooks" or "stooges."

Iliana García Giraldino, head of media relations for ICAP (Instituto Cubano de Amistad con los Pueblos),[59] directly addressed the long-standing myth:

> Fidel was a visionary, this is a prime example of how media distorted truth against Cuba. Right after the triumph of the revolution, in late January 1959, when the trials of the murderers, torturers and criminals under Batista regime began the media started saying Fidel and the revolutionaries were bloodthirsty killers. They never reported the trials were to punish the worst elements of the Batista dictatorship, to bring justice to the thousands of Cubans who suffered under the regime.[60]

She remembered that:

> Fidel summoned 400 journalists, worldwide and from the US, so they could see that was not true, there was no blood running in the streets—only the punishment of the Batista criminals. He went to the people directly asking if they wanted to punish these criminals, and the people said "yes." That's when the trials began, with the support of the people. But the American media simply did not report the truth and they still use that as anti-revolutionary propaganda.[61]

Regarding the dissidents, in the past Cuba has imprisoned those who opposed the revolution, an undeniable civil rights restriction. However, Havana currently makes a clear distinction when it comes to dissidents who find themselves facing jail or other state authorized punishments. Cuba asserts that the dissidents arrested, including those in 2003 that caused great international condemnation, are being paid by the United States to ferment opposition to their own government. There is ample proof of this charge, including from many of the dissidents.[62] Few countries in the world, including the United States, permit nationals to accept financial or material aid from a foreign entity in pursuit of anti-government activities. It is considered giving aid and comfort to the enemy, the definition of treason. Not surprisingly, that context is consistently missing in the media reports.

A *Counterpunch* article outlined the details usually omitted in mainstream media regarding the treatment of dissidents:

> Seventy-five Cubans dissidents were arrested in April 2003 in what is called the Black Spring. Ever since then they have been referred to as political prisoners or freedom fighters. Actually, they were tried and convicted in a Cuban court for operating as paid agents of the pretend dissident movement funded by the United States. Roger Noriega, former assistant secretary of state for Western Hemisphere Affairs, conspired with James Cason, then head of the U.S. Interest Section in Havana, to openly encourage local dissidents hoping that the Cuban government would kick Cason out and give George W. Bush an excuse for closing the Cuban Interest Section in Washington and worsening bilateral relations. The scheme is what got the 75 arrested ... Among the 75 were journalists, few of whom ever practiced journalism. There also were pretend independent librarians paid by the United States to pose as part of a pretend grassroots defiance of a pretend Cuban control of what people could read.[63]

The article went on to dispute the claim the Cuban government shut down the libraries, quoting one woman who maintained: "No books had ever been confiscated [and] that she was not being intimidated or threatened by the government as a result of having this collection. She said she was asked to operate the library because she is a dissident."[64]

What the media has done so effectively is to amplify Cuba's well-documented and serious problems while making sure America's role is diminished, ignored or brushed off by using meaningless euphemisms like the ones *The Guardian* employed in its jumble of historical convolution of past and present Cuban society. The mainstream media has never permitted serious discussion of Cuba's response to US hostility in terms of the country's sovereign right to defend itself and its citizens.

In a particularly disturbing account on Fidel Castro's passing, *Toronto Star* columnist Rosie DiManno spared nothing in her approbation of the man. She additionally had no compunction to insult the majority of Cubans, who genuinely mourned the loss of their leader, arrogantly attempting to speak for everyone on the island from her jaundiced, ill-informed point of view. The headline, "Castro Took a Country Hostage—His Own: DiManno," made clear the intent of the article. It began by deriding how the Cuban government conducted the memorial for Fidel Castro, then included a superfluous condemnation from one of his relatives:

> There will be no other memorializing of the man who ruled this island-nation with an iron fist for a half-century, Raul Castro declared, in keeping with his sibling's wishes. No cameras were permitted to record the event—stills were released afterwards by the government—and it's unclear who attended; whether any of his children (believed to be nine in number, but possibly more) born to at least four women. Castro obsessively guarded the details of his private life such that the public didn't even know where he lived in Havana, though it was said he roamed from house to house. One daughter, at least, was not in Cuba for her father's rite of departure—Alina, who fled Cuba years ago and worked later at a Miami radio station where she frequently excoriated the old man: "When people tell me he's a dictator, I tell them that's not the right words," she once told the *Miami Herald*. "Strictly speaking, Fidel is a tyrant."[65]

The column contained no mention of the thousands of private ceremonies held across the nation, nor any quote from a Cuban who mourned.

Following the usual recitation of all the supposed ills of Fidel Castro, the column ended by denigrating the gains of the revolution, sarcastically describing them as unworthy in a self-imposed value judgment that paid insult to an entire society and those who supported it:

> But, good man, he provided free education and free health care, sent hundreds of physicians to war zones and disaster zones. His scientists invented vaccines for African diseases. Such a humanitarian!

> It doesn't balance out, hardly.
>
> Instead, I'll drink to his demise. A Cuba Libre—Free Cuba—the rum-and-cola concoction that actually pre-dates the Castro era.
>
> And damn his eternal soul.[66]

As usual, there could be no recognition on how American policies of regime change affected Cuban society, no mention of Fidel Castro's commitment to internationalism, his assistance to bringing an end to apartheid in South Africa[67] or support for the African nations she sneered at. And certainly no examination of why he was mourned by so many around the world, including such respected leaders as Nelson Mandela.

DiManno's piece was consistent with how the mainstream media treated Castro's death. A superficial reiteration of the perceived evils with no attempt at context or perspective of how this small island has survived under the non-stop threats of the world's most powerful nation. Cuba's social gains and international solidarity have come despite America's economic punishment and regime change programs. Journalists like DiManno mention the benefits only to dismiss them as a civil price too high to pay. As if it was her role to judge, instead of the Cuban people. Most disturbingly, she finishes with a condemnation that not only disrespects the man but also the millions who were genuinely saddened by his death—even those Cuban nationals who did not agree with him.

Havana resident Manuel Alberto García commented:

> He did a lot of things that had to be done, many you can criticize and were wrong, and he stayed in power too long. But he was respected, I respected him even though I didn't like him. He gave our country a place in the world, gave us a real national identity. That's how he should be remembered.[68]

The coverage of Fidel Castro's death was so intensely one-sided that it elicited pushback from media critics and other journalists. Stephen Kimber, author and academic at King's College in Halifax, examined the media coverage in a column for *Huffington Post*:

> Castro's body was still cooling when *CNN* announced his death, barely managing to say his name before taking it in vain: "Fidel Castro, the Cuban despot ..." *The New York Times* couldn't get through its first paragraph without blaming the Cuban leader for "bringing the Cold War to the Western Hemisphere," and for "pushing the world to the brink of nuclear war" during the Cuban missile crisis. The *Washington Post* "One of the most brutal dictators in modern history has just died." [69]

Kimber scrutinized the media's predictable rationale for the coverage, and did what few writers commit to when it comes to Cuba—offered balance and context:

> And so it has gone. The media is one great echo chamber of conventional American mass media un-wisdom: about Castro, his life, his death, his legacy; about Cuba's past, its present, its future. None of this is to suggest Fidel Castro was a saint, nor that Cuba is a paradise. Far from it. When it comes to individual human rights and press freedoms, for example, Castro's record is less than stellar. We can explain it—start with the more than $1 billion the United States government spent trying to assassinate Castro and foment a Cuban counter-revolution, and you begin to understand why the Cuban government might doubt dissidents' sincerity—but we shouldn't excuse it, or ignore it. The problem is that, by monochromatically portraying Fidel Castro simply as a brutal dictator—full stop—the western media has had to do pretzel-twists to explain away the reality of why so many people in Cuba, Latin America and, indeed, much of the developing world do see him as an heroic, larger than life figure, whose passing is a cause for sadness while his legacy is reason for celebration. History may indeed absolve Fidel Castro; we shouldn't so easily excuse the media's abysmally one-sided, post-passing portrayal of him.[70]

Kimber's voice was but a small whisper against the cacophony of righteous bleating falling from the avalanche of mainstream media misinformation.

An illuminating comparison of how corporate media handles the death of an acceptable statesman occurred when former president George Bush passed away in late 2018. Under the flood of gushing memorials, there was not even a murmur mentioned of some of his many controversial actions when heading the CIA, including his support for the terrorist program known as Operation Condor[71] and the right-wing dictatorships in Latin America in the 1970s and 1980s. There was also scant mention of the illegal invasion of Panama or his efforts to cover up the Iran–Contra scandal—including the role Cuban-American terrorist Luis Posada Carriles had in the affair. The acceptable limit of press criticism was on display with the *New York Times*' mild rebuke over his, "Seeming inattention to domestic affairs."[72] Speaking ill of the dead is the strictly controlled purvey of the corporate media.[73]

* * *

With Fidel Castro gone and the media having taken its pound of flesh, the corporate press turned its attention to the shocking presidential election of Donald Trump. It wasn't long, however, before Cuba came back into the news when the new man in the White House declared his intention to turn back the clock.

After signally his support for normal relations between Cuba and the United States during the campaign, Trump flipped his position and decided it would be more politically expedient to reverse Obama's openings. This despite the positive effects the rapprochement was having for the Cuban economy and relations between the two adversaries—or maybe because of it. Trump's roll-back was a craven submission to the hard-right Cuban-American politicians in Florida, foremost Republican Senator Marco Rubio who has consistently opposed any engagement with his family homeland. Trump's endorsement of Rubio's position came despite the strong animosity between the two. During the presidential nomination process, Trump constantly denigrated Rubio to the delight of mainstream media, calling him "Little Marco,"[74] decried "oh he lies" and even insulted his wife and father. Still, politics trump personality when it comes to Cuba policy.

Trump announced a return to the punishment at a June 2017 Florida rally in front of a large group of anti-revolutionaries, with the *Miami Herald* lauding the reversal. As the paper described: "Casting it as a 'great day' for Cubans, Trump powered into East Little Havana and announced a sweeping change in relations intended to rebuke his predecessor's opening toward the island."[75]

A majority in the establishment press took a generally negative perspective on Trump's return to normal hostility, including the *New Yorker*, *CNN* and *USA Today*,[76] positioning the roll-back as harmful to tourists and business, with little attention on the adverse economic impact it would have on the Cuban population. The media's continued support for the opening remained grounded in the expectation that Obama's policy would finally bring about regime change. Trump was jeopardizing that new strategy by returning to the old strategy.

That position was expressed in a *New Yorker* article written by Jon Lee Anderson, who presented a jumble of pro- and anti-revolutionary qualifiers while seeming to come out against Trump's decision:

> Yet Trump's use of the bully pulpit to upbraid the island for its failings seems as hypocritical as it is counterproductive. Cuba still lacks some of the basic civil liberties that Americans take for granted, such as a free press and free elections. However, compared with many countries in the Western Hemisphere, most of which espouse some variant of democracy and a free-market economy, Cuba is a secure society with some enviable social indicators. Its murder rates are among the region's lowest; its infant-mortality rates are lower than those in the United States; and its citizens are guaranteed state-subsidized education and free health care. Yet, while the Trump Administration has tangled with some Latin American nations, Cuba is the only one under sweeping U.S. trade sanctions.[77]

The piece ended with a pragmatic point of view that revealed the fatal flaw in Trump's decision as counter-productive to the new regime change strategy:

> Trump's bullying only makes it more likely that the Cubans, with or without a Castro, will do what they have done for the past fifty-nine years: exhibit stubborn pride and, if necessary, forge tactical alliances with any of America's geostrategic foes who might be willing to watch their back.[78]

The New Yorker and others recognized the return to hostility represented a challenge to the updated narrative of disguising regime change through the process of normalization, a viewpoint that was found to be easier to present and far more difficult to challenge.

Trump's retrograde policy included re-instituting restrictions on individual American citizens traveling to Cuba, as well as prohibiting business negotiations with tourist facilities connected with the Cuban military. It was meant to put a damper on direct interactions between US citizens and Cubans. As with most things Trump, the bluster turned out to be a great deal more than the actuality. Although proclaiming, "I am canceling the last administration's completely one-sided deal with Cuba,"[79] he did nothing of the sort.

Trump did not end the airlines coming to Cuba, nor did he shut down American management companies running Havana hotels—even though US citizens couldn't visit them.[80] Cuba remained (at the time of this writing) off the list of States that Sponsor Terrorism and Obama's ending of the "wet-foot; dry-foot" immigration policy that gave Cubans special entry benefits was left unchanged.

Trump's most significant aggression against Cuba came in April 2019 with his decision to no longer suspend Title III of the 1996 Helms–Burton Act;[81] allowing American individuals to sue international companies under allegations of using "confiscated property" in Cuba. Permission to sue has also been granted to Cubans now living in the USA but who were not American citizens at the time of nationalization. Every president since Bill Clinton had refused to implement Title III as it would open up a flood of controversial lawsuits not only with Cuba, but also international claims of confiscated property including against America going back to its revolution. It would also defy long-standing norms of sovereignty rights regarding nationalizing properties. Carnival Cruise Lines was one of the first to be sued under Title III,[82] although experts predict it will difficult to obtain judgments against American businesses that have the legal right to operate in Cuba.

The decision elicited considerable media attention, most usually ignoring long-standing international law permitting any sovereign nation to expropriate property.[83] Also missing was any mention that Cuba has repeatedly offered to negotiate compensation with US entities, as it successfully did with investors from other countries following the revolution. The American government has consistently refused to engage in any serious discussions to resolve the matter.

Along with the suspension of Title III, Trump also threatened to roll back the amount of remittances individuals living in the USA could send to Cuba, as well as increasing some travel restrictions,[84] all for the purpose of inflicting more economic punishment on those intransigent Cubans in the hope that they will finally overthrow their government. In June 2019 he banned cruise ships from stopping in Cuba.

One economic aspect the roll-back has affected is individual travel, after the president eliminated the popular People to People designation that permitted Americans to visit the island under US government permission. It was one of 12 categories that allowed legal travel under the restrictions that have been in place since the 1960s.[85] It was the most popular and easiest to conform to, as American visitors could book air, hotel and other aspects of their trip on the Internet with just the minimum amount of documentation need to qualify, circumventing the more expensive and restrictive group tours. Americans came by the thousands, on their own, to interact on a personal, uncontrolled level to meet and talk with Cubans one-on-one; to see the good, the bad and the indifferent—often to challenge with first-hand experiences the historically biased media narratives. Most came to Havana, the city that had been off limits for decades. An estimated 200,000 Americans visited Cuba in 2017, with the number dropping by more than 50 percent following Trump's announcement, according to a *Washington Post* story that examined the numbers pre- and post-Trump.[86]

While the corporate media came out strongly against the roll-back, coverage was usually framed within the paradigm that

Obama's strategy would be the one to bring about regime change. Going back to the bad old days would complicate American attempts to bring about the desired downfall of the revolution. There was little comment on how the Cubans still might not be in favor of a foreign country dictating how it should structure its social/economic system.

A 2017 column in the *New York Times* by former head of the US Interest Section in Havana, Vicki Huddleston, faithfully promoted the continued right of the United States to influence change in Cuba as the reason Trump's roll-back should be criticized. "The result is a return to a Cold War mentality and a set of failed policies that will do little to improve human rights in Cuba or to hasten the end of the Castro regime."[87]

She condescendingly complained that the roll-back, which included reducing staff at the US embassy in Havana affecting the process of travel visas,

> means that tens of thousands of Cubans are no longer able to visit family in the United States and bring home items like televisions, radios, cellphones and video players—products that for the first time in decades were putting them in close contact with the rest of the world.[88]

As Cuba expert and journalist Karen Lee Wald retorted:

> As anyone who has spent any time in Cuba, read, seen and heard its media, is well aware, Cubans are far more in touch with "the rest of the world" than people in the United States were. What Huddleston means, of course, is that those who wish to remake Cuba in US image would like Cubans to be more inundated with US media.[89]

Trump's attempt to restrict individual American travel to the island was for the most part reported inaccurately in the media. Of the 12 categories American citizens can legally travel to Cuba under, two pertain to general individual travel—People to People and Support for the Cuban People licenses. The rest were structured for group tours. The two individual categories were designed to lawfully allow Americans to travel for non-specific religious, professional or educational exchange purposes. Visits to the beach were still off limits (considered too touristy) but anyone with an interest in Cuban cigars, dance or just talking to its citizens could easily fill out the documentation required and fly into Cuba from a number of direct locations in the USA. Documentation to obtain the license was self-controlled, with the People to People category requiring a little less paperwork. Trump eliminated People to People, while the Support for the Cuban People grouping remained in place. It was somewhat confusing, but should not have been beyond the scope of any quality journalism.

The misunderstanding might have been Trump's intent, but it was the media that played the most important part in spreading the misperception. As the *Washington Post* did when it reported:

> By reinstating restrictions on independent travelers, the Trump administration's new policy will hurt Cuba's emerging private sector that caters to American visitors, critics insist. Instead, the new rules will herd Americans back toward the kind of prepackaged, predictable group tourism that the Cuban government actually prefers—and earns more revenue from.[90]

Newsweek also demonstrated the ability to misinform by reporting on just part of the truth: "Americans are no longer able to go on 'people-to-people' trips, which was previously the easiest category of authorized travel to qualify for. People-to-people allowed travel to the country if visitors engaged in a full-time schedule of educational activities."[91] There was no mention of the ability for individuals to continue traveling to Cuba under the Support for Cuban People license.

Intentionally or not, mainstream media created a level of confusion through misinformation that reported individual Americans could no longer travel to the island. As two US citizens from Washington DC proved, that was simply not the case.

> We went online, booked airfare, two days at the Hotel Nacional and after we're going to the beach in Varadero for three days. It was very easy, all the paperwork and documents needed to fall under the legal requirements we did all online. Very easy.[92]

Some did get it right, but with little effect in stopping the damage that the distortion had already done. One publication that did cover the situation accurately was *Forbes* magazine, stating that: "However, according to experts, not much has changed for Americans interested in Cuba travel. Individual travelers are still able to visit the country for the purpose of supporting the Cuban people."[93] The expert used was John McAuliff,

> who has been working to create more ties between Cuba and the U.S. through travel for over twenty years says that although individual "people-to-people" trips were eliminated in June, Americans can visit the country without a tour operator under support of the Cuban people.[94]

Even more direct was coverage in *Travel Market Report*, taking the media to task for its errors:

> For those in the know, individual travel to Cuba by Americans is still permitted, if the traveler closely adheres to U.S. Treasury Department rules and regulations, and compiles and maintains the required documentation. But the nuanced nature of the Treasury Department rules, and the ambiguous language in public documents published and promoted in early November 2017 have left many Americans confused; and have led some prominent travel publications to insinuate that group travel and cruise lines are the only permissible kinds of Cuba tourism.[95]

Mainstream media has never been overly concerned with accuracy when reporting on Cuban issues. The new standard, while not as blatant as previously, continues to utilize obfuscation and inaccuracy as acceptable journalistic devices against the island nation.

Possibly the most damaging aspect of Trump's return to hostility occurred when he shut down half the staff at the US embassy in Havana. The decision was based on the controversial "sonic attack" incident, providing the media with another opportunity to display its predilection for assuming the worst when covering Cuba.

The political storm was based on information that two dozen American diplomats or their family members in Havana were affected by a variety of mysterious ailments in late 2016. The cause was blamed on a series of disturbing high-pitched sounds heard by embassy staff, apparently targeting them at work and home. Illnesses ranged from dizziness, vomiting and potential permanent brain damage. A number of Canadian officials were reported to have suffered similar difficulties.

As a result, Trump recalled half the embassy staff, while expelling an equal number of Cuban envoys from Washington.[96] The reduction in personnel at the embassy in Havana has meant a halt to processing visas for Cubans seeking to travel to the United States.[97] A travel warning was then issued, resulting in a further drop of American visitors. The Trump administration has held Cuba responsible for the sonic attacks, while Havana has denied any involvement. As of this date, no definitive cause for the ailments has been found in more than two years of investigation by the FBI and other US and Cuban authorities.[98]

The latest information suggests everything from mass hallucination[99] to the conditions resulting from stress, to natural sounds including lovelorn crickets.[100] Some scientists have suggested electromagnetic-pulse technology, or pulse radiofrequency or lasers as possible causes. Others have argued that ultrasound or infrasound could have been the "mechanism of injury." But holes have been poked in all those theories, officials said, because the physical circumstances of the Havana incidents would have made those technologies difficult to deploy. In a still-classified report prepared late last year, the FBI discounted the possibility that a sonic weapon had been used, according to those with knowledge of the account.[101] No tourist or Cuban national has ever been affected.

One hypothesis suggested the medical team that inspected the 21 diplomats believe that the unusual reports of loud, painful sounds experienced by the victims may be attributed to the Frey effect—a phenomenon in which the brain is tricked into perceiving non-existent noises by microwaves. The source and motive behind the attacks is still unknown.[102]

Coverage revealed the mainstream press was most interested in exploring the science fiction possibilities of a high-tech sonic weapon with the ability to specifically target the diplomats and their movements. International experts quickly dismissed the likelihood, citing no proof such an instrument exists. That didn't stop media reports blaming the Cubans, the Russians, the Chinese and a host of other potential government agents or rogue elements for the attacks.

Vicki Huddleston's opinion piece in the *New York Times* reached deep into conspiracy theory, then threw in traditional language against Cuba and standard concepts the government was against "freedom"—as she and the press saw it:

> It is possible that attacks were carried out by a breakaway group of hard-liners in the government. Some conservatives who had been aligned with Fidel Castro are unhappy with the thaw in relations between the United States and Cuba and may be working to outmaneuver more reform-minded competitors.[103]

The former chief at the US Interest Section in Havana added archetypal misinformation long accepted by mainstream media:

> The Trump administration's reaction to the diplomats' ailments—suggesting the Cuban government is responsible and further rolling back Obama administration efforts toward normalization—has only strengthened the position of the Cuban hard-liners who reject internal reform and greater freedom for the Cuban people.[104]

A misleading front page article in the *Toronto Star* apparently tied the sonic attacks controversy to the feet of the Cubans.[105] The story was from Canadian ex-envoy Alex Ballingall, who worked in Cuba in the 1980s and recalled some attempts to compromise his position through sex and blackmail. His experiences, headlined as "Dog Poisonings, Sex Propositions: Canada's Man in Havana Remembers the Cold War Weirdness," were conflated with the sonic incidents as some sort of continuation of Cuban chicanery. However, when Ballingall was in Havana, it was the height of the Cold War with both sides attempting any method to gain the upper hand. What those experiences had to do with the sonic controversy was never explained in the lengthy article that offered no proof that the Cubans had anything to do with the attacks on Canadian diplomats. But the reader would easily connect the two stories and assume it was the Cubans at fault. Intentionally or not, the media solidified a connection that had no basis in fact and one totally unrelated to the 30-year span the report focused on.

The champion of nebulous reporting on the sonic incident went to the *Washington Post*, posting a convoluted hypothesis: "It's impossible to disprove the existence of invisible agents ... the agent is a theoretical weapon wielded by unidentified assailants that leaves no trace."[106] Not the greatest example of responsible journalism attempting to clarify the issue.

The closest the media came to a balanced report that recognized the Cuban side was found in an *Associated Press* piece that quoted a US senator, who admitted there was no evidence of "sonic attacks" in Cuba:

> Republican Sen. Jeff Flake says the U.S. has found no evidence that American diplomats in Havana were the victims of attacks with an unknown weapon ... The Cubans told Flake the FBI has told them that, after four trips to Cuba, its agents have found no evidence that mysterious illnesses suffered by U.S. diplomats were the result of attacks. Flake told the *Associated Press* on Saturday morning that classified briefings from U.S. officials have left him with no reason to doubt the Cuban account, although he declined to discuss the contents of those briefings.[107]

As Cuba became more frustrated with the deteriorations of relations over a matter it claimed it was not responsible for, government officials such as Cuba's foreign minister, Bruno Rodríguez Parrilla reacted, "There is no evidence whatsoever" of the "alleged incidents or the cause or origin of these ailments reported by U.S. diplomats." Mariela Castro, daughter of former president Raúl Castro, mocked the illnesses, claiming that: "even 'Star Wars' didn't contain such fantasies."[108] According to a report in *The Guardian*, some neurologists suspect that the ailments may be some form of "mass hysteria."[109]

Revealingly, when US diplomats in China came down with similar symptoms, the Trump administration response was entirely different. There were no accusations of Chinese wrongdoing, no travel warning, no media outrage. It was simply another study in how Cuba is held to a higher, duplicitous set of standards by the government and the media.[110]

This was again on display as corporate media focused on the revolutionary government's election of its first president not named Castro.

5
Future Coverage

Since the triumph of the Cuban Revolution more than 60 years ago, the American government and mainstream media have converged far more often than not in constructing an overwhelmingly negative judgment of the island nation's political/economic arrangement. Much of it has been grounded on a biased misrepresentation of the revolution's goals and achievements and the denial of the impact regime change policies have had on the country's development.

That verdict was established as soon as Fidel Castro and his followers became "official enemies." A designation that created the symbiotic justification for the US government's hostility and the media's advocacy for every form of punishment the state was prepared to inflict upon the Cuban people.

Both media and government antagonism against the revolution became settled law. An important element in regime change strategy was to ensure Cuba would not represent the threat of a good example that other developing nations in Latin America might follow. To that end, it was necessary to create the narrative that the revolution represented a "disease" or "cancer" that had to be isolated and eradicated. As the *New York Times* commented, Cuba was "a point of infection by the Communist virus for the whole hemisphere."[1] However, it was the revolution's challenge to what author Louis Pérez described as America's "moral authority to presume power over Cuba" that was most unforgiveable.[2] When Fidel succeeded in establishing true national sovereignty, the media's historical revisionism claimed US hegemony had been benign and beneficial, that the only requirement was the removal of the Batista dictatorship while maintaining the hegemonic status quo. To this day, the press attempts to frame the revolutionaries as ungrateful extremists who, without justification, turned against all the good things the USA was providing—and that everything the revolution has accomplished since is of no value. Examination of neo-colonialism harm, or the right to self-determination, became subjects intentionally ignored.

Cuban historian Herbert Perez, who won the country's National History Medal in 2017, articulated long-standing American objectives:

> The United States understood quite well that the Revolution opened up possibilities that didn't exist before and still don't in many other countries, and that fact determined part of their strategy: to establish an economic embargo that was like a full military blockade during war, to undermine support for this process by making people suffer, have a very hard life, in the hope they would then blame their government and turn against it. That has always been Washington's goal and it still is.[3]

In 2016, the *Financial Post* trotted out all the stock pre-revolutionary myths in an article apparently upset with the increased amount of tourists traveling to the island. The commentary disingenuously compared certain social data in the 1950s to selected European countries, using favorable Havana-centric indices with no consideration to the utter poverty found in the majority of Cuba's countryside.[4] At the same time, diminishing the current impact of the embargo with the preposterous attempt to deflect the extra-territorial aspects by claiming Cuba can trade with other countries. Apparently, the *Financial Post* was—conveniently—ignorant of the US law prohibiting American subsidiaries in other countries to trade with Havana. The subheading suggested with little proof that the nation before Fidel Castro was known for genius in "arts, industry and athletics."[5] Author Patrick Luciani cited entertainer Desi Arnaz as an example, leaving out the fact that he left Cuba in the 1930s to escape the dictatorship of Gerardo Machado. Arnaz became famous in the United States by representing the racially tinged formulaic Cuban—a white singer/dancer performing clichéd Latin music the Americans were socially comfortable with. He was immensely popular with Lucille Ball in the 1950s television show *I Love Lucy*, playing a hot-tempered, somewhat scatter-brained but harmlessly apolitical character—perfect for what most Americans wanted their Latin men to be. But then, maybe Luciani meant someone else, as he misspelled Desi's last name—as Arnazes.

The *Financial Post* article exemplified how the press has long misinformed its readers about Cuba. In actuality, pre-revolutionary Cuban arts were characterized by stereotypical actors such as Arnaz, industry was nothing more than sugar production and athletic success internationally was virtually non-existent.

A more honest report would reveal that the revolution has created artistic expression beyond ideological pinning (except for the period in the 1970s, where art was an uncreative reflection of Communist orthodoxy) including world-class ballet, music forms ranging from reggaeton to the *Buena Vista Social Club* and Silvio Rodríguez. Films such as *Fraise y Chocolate* explore sensitive social themes, while *Temas* magazine directly criticizes government inefficiencies and shortcomings. Industry has diversified, often not successfully, but Cuba is known worldwide for scientific and medical breakthroughs including treatments for diabetes,[6] meningitis and cancer.

Even such apparently positive news doesn't escape media spin. An *NBC* news report on the successful results achieved from Cuba's biotech research couldn't resist sticking in a gratuitous and disingenuous paragraph,

> Some U.S. officials have questioned the industry's real purpose, alleging that it's a façade for military research to manufacture biological weapons such as like anthrax and bubonic plague. Cuban scientists dismiss the charges, stating that their work is rooted in finding cures for many diseases.[7]

This totally contrived assertion was considered for no other reason than to make sure that whenever there's something positive about Cuba, the media must follow its credo of injecting negative misinformation, no matter how preposterous the claim. It is but one example of the latest style of Cuban coverage among corporate media since Obama's opening—maintaining the core of anti-revolutionary bias under a thin cover of apparent positive reporting. Adding that paragraph was a conscious decision on the part of the author or editor, in order to artificially create a damaging counterpoint that would supplant any constructive aspect of the article. This was based on the abrogation of any sort of journalist integrity through the discredited use of unnamed and unchallengeable "some U.S. officials." It was intended to ensure the consumer maintains a negative opinion about Cuba, despite reading of its accomplishments.

Regarding achievements in sports, Cuba has punched far above its weight class since 1959. Internationally renowned athletes such as boxer Teofilo Stevenson and runner Alberto Juantorena are but a few who have succeeded under the revolution's determination to provide athletic opportunities for the whole nation. Current Cuban baseball players are recognized as some of the best in the major leagues, and the women's volleyball side has consistently ranked among the top teams worldwide. In the three Olympics before the revolution, in 1948, 1952 and 1956, the Cubans won a total of one silver medal. By the 1992 games in Barcelona, the country ranked fifth overall with a medal haul of 31 including 14 gold. Thanks to the *Financial Post*'s seemingly calculated decision to misinform, the reader would be completely unaware of the vastly greater artistic, industrial and athletic achievements Cuba has accomplished under the revolution as compared to before—areas where the *Financial Post* author has either failed to research or has deliberately ignored in order to propagate yet another anti-revolutionary myth.

The *Financial Post* article, as have so many other similar reports, occurred under the foundational truth riveted in the American psyche—that there is a free press that operates without prejudice and with an honest reliability to tell the truth. Acceptance of that doctrine is the assignment of an almost blind trust between media and consumers in matters of foreign affairs. While battles rage between government officials and the media over charges of "fake news" when it comes to domestic issues, the controversies most often fade away when the press and state inform the general public of whom are the international good and bad guys. There is also little confrontation as to how the media manipulates information to reinforce those designations. Or as FAIR program director Janine Jackson described the relationship, the press willingly accepts the concepts of "US exceptionalism, and the rights of empire, are the price of admission to the elite media's foreign policy conversation."[8]

The concept of what is a free press has come under increased scrutiny, with a greater appreciation that the free press is often permitted to say what it likes—as long as the ruling class likes what it says. When it comes to Cuba, reporting anything negative is fine, any derogatory comment about the revolution is also an acceptable default position, but reporting truthfully on the shortcomings and accomplishments, as well as the historical roots of the revolution—not so much. Despite recent events such as Obama's opening and Trump's roll-back, that baseline has not altered. It has become more nuanced, less vitriolic and interspersed with the appearance of balance. What remains, however, is the foundational assumption that the Cuban system must change under American benevolence.

The other definition of mainstream media is more an expression of American capitalist society in that, "freedom of the press belongs to those who own one." As that "freedom" is becoming concentrated in fewer hands, an unfortunate consequence is that ownership is falling under the control of hedge fund scavengers such as *Digital First* and *GateHouse*.

According to an article in *Truthdig*, these corporations:

> Know nothing about journalism and care less, for they're ruthless Wall Street profiteers out to grab big bucks fast by slashing the journalistic and production staffs of each paper, voiding all employee benefits (from pensions to free coffee in the breakroom), shriveling the paper's size and news content, selling the presses and other assets, tripling the price of their inferior product—then declaring bankruptcy, shutting down the paper, and auctioning off the bones before moving on to plunder another town's paper.[9]

Although certain segments of the press find themselves under threat by vulture capitalism, those pressures have done little to ameliorate mainstream media's unrelenting criticisms of Cuba's socialist society. It narrows the parameters of accepted discourse in the media, while conforming almost entirely to Washington's foreign policy objectives.[10]

So freedom of the press becomes another concept with two distinct perspectives on either side of the Florida Strait. America defines it as a private institution, where Cuba sees it as part of the social commons. Both say the other's interpretation leads to a corrupt media beholden to state dictates. While the US press rarely acknowledges its adherence to government objectives, it is quick to criticize Cuban media for being nothing more than a propaganda arm of the state.

There is little doubt that Cuban media has often been guilty of extremely anti-American propaganda. Misinformation throughout the past 50 years have portrayed US society as composed of nothing more than drug-riddled, crime-infested, racist capitalists. As the American mainstream media usually finds little of value in Cuban society, so have their counterparts in Havana. It is a reflection that, without regard to ideological bent, media regularly creates conditions where it is far easier to criticize others than it is to focus on one's own problems. For the anti-revolutionary politicians and commentators, Cuban media is nothing more than the direct propaganda arm of the government. That feeling is reflected on the other side.[11]

Arlin Albergy Loforte is a subdirector for *Granma International*, the primary newspaper in Cuba. It is found in both traditional and internet forms, and whenever *Granma* is referred to in US corporate media, the derogatory designation "state-run" is consistently utilized. As far as Albergy Loforte is concerned, the purpose of *Granma*, "is to tell the truth about Cuba, to combat the media lies as best we can with our resources available."[12] While recognizing *Granma* is the official voice of the government, she rejected the criticism from her northern neighbor.

> The American media says the press in Cuba is not free—because we don't publish what they want us to publish. The international media is dominated by US media and its anti-Cuba propaganda. One of the lies they say is that the Cuban press doesn't publish complaints or cover the problems we have, only positive things about the revolution. That's not true at all, we publish critical articles, we publish complaints from the public, there is great

> discussion as to how to improve what we have. But we don't publish support for a foreign power to tell us how we should be forced to change our system.[13]

Within that system, Cuba's electoral structure has additionally come under misrepresentation by American media.

Havana translator and editor Heriberto Nicolás complained that the press outside Cuba has little understanding of how his country's democratic process operates:

> We have democracy, just not narrowly defined by the United States. People at every constituency propose and then vote their delegates for the municipal government. Once municipal government is formed, they propose and vote their delegates, among their members, for the provincial government. The provincial government once formed propose and vote their delegates (deputies) for national parliament among their members. National parliament elects the president of the country and members of the government (ministers, council of state members, etc.) among its own members. All this means, from the president to every single member of the government, everyone had to be nominated in the first place at the community where he lives that knows him well.[14]

He then challenged the press to report honestly on Cuba's system.

> Does the US mainstream media talk about this? Have they made a sincere comparison between both electoral systems? I'm sure not. So the central question is, perhaps, is the US electoral more democratic, as many claim, just because their "more than one party system" elects the president nominated by their parties; that responds, as everyone knows to special corporate interests and not to the people. There is simply not just one democratic system. And we have chosen the one that guarantees unity and thus security. Cuba has the right to choose the electoral system that best protects this small more-than-50-years besieged nation.[15]

Institutions, such as politics and media, reflect fundamental national social constructs. Albergy Loforte recognizes that similarities exist within media requirements regardless of ideology forms.

> Some media respond to capitalism—some media respond to other systems. Our media covers the system which has been selected and approved by the Cuban people. We are not so arrogant to tell other countries how they should live or under what system. One of the principals is to reveal the truth—but it is a truth that the owners of media in the United States don't like to hear. You never see in their mainstream media talking about the blockade, the support for our system, the reality of Cuba. So why doesn't the media in the US cover these things? They only report the negative, and that is in alignment with government objectives of regime change.[16]

The bottom line, she commented, is that each media performs basically the same function.

> The media in the US supports the American system—the media in Cuba supports the socialist system. But if we don't want change (the US media) claims we're not free; but those are not the same standards applied to US media.[17]

* * *

Freedom of the press remains an issue that creates divisions in this contentious relationship between Cuba and the United States. Both media reflect state desires; Havana wants normal relations and the end of regime change strategies and expects the press to support those goals. Washington has received similar fealty from corporate media in regards to its Cuban policy. However, it is the American press that maintains a stricter ideological antagonism in cohesion with political objectives. Both sides lob verbal abuse, but only one side narrates regime change strategies, which are still firmly in place, despite what can often be perceived as a softening, even a balance of coverage when examining specific incidents, such as Elián González, the Cuban Five and even the Alan Gross affair. A more current example occurred in 2018 with the generally neutral reporting on the agreement between Major League Baseball (MLB) and the Cuban Baseball Federation (FCB) permitting Cuban players a safe and legal path to play in the big leagues. However, the press couldn't resist including criticism of Cuba's system by providing extensive coverage to Florida Senator Marco Rubio's gratuitous condemnations. Rubio, a stanch opponent of any engagement with Havana, was allowed to misinform when stating he considered the agreement, "shameful" that MLB "would consider joining with the Cuban regime to exploit Cuban baseball players."[18] This ignored the fact that the arrangement is the same MLB has with other international federations including Japan, Taiwan and Korea. Unfortunately, Trump arbitrarily decided to cancel the agreement in April 2019, ignoring requests from both MLB and the Cuban Baseball Federation to maintain it.[19]

While fair, even positive press reporting can be cited over the past few years, there is always the underlying perspective that Cuban society is inferior and must be altered to US standards. No coverage can be provided without a negative qualifier. The dictum has been a consistent since the beginning of the revolution, even before. And when events such as the death of Fidel Castro happen, any pretense of corporate media's appearance of balance falls quickly to the wayside in an orgy of biased and misinformed vitriol.

Author Nato Green addressed the conundrum in a 2018 article titled: "What If the American Media Covered Cuba Like a Normal Place?" He examined how media partiality can be well hidden not by what it reports, but by what it doesn't:

> Remember ye olde adage, "media most reveals its bias, not in its quotes, but in what it presents under cover of journalistic objectivity as true without the hassle of context or evidence." If that's not a ye olde adage, it should be. Or a more articulate version of the sentiment. The coverage revealed more about the US than Cuba or, something truly subversive, what Cubans wish for themselves.[20]

Green's column focused on mainstream media's coverage during the end of the Castro era in spring 2018. Raúl Castro was stepping down and the new president Miguel Díaz-Canel was taking over. Green observed the press was presenting the change as a momentous event, with coverage such as the *Washington Post* declaring, "Castro Rule in Cuba Ends." "Raúl Castro Prepares to Resign as Cuba's President, Closing a Dynasty" said the *New York Times*, and "With End of Castro Era in Sight, Cuba Prepares to Pass Power to New Generation," declared *NPR*.

As Green wrote:

> It was a big deal for the media, for the average Cuban not so much as they just got on with life. Cubans actively ignoring the news media perfectly summed up the transition of the presidency from Raúl Castro to Miguel Díaz-Canel. On the island, if you didn't watch state television, there was no indication anything happened. While the passing of the Cuban presidency wasn't dramatic in Cuba, it provided US media with a golden opportunity to spin Cold War-era oldies but goodies that have been around longer than the oldest Che Guevara keychains. I believe the press corps was playing a drinking game where everyone had to write "apparatchik" and "iron grip" into stories about Cuba.[21]

His argument demonstrated that the media faithfully follows the precepts of how the Cuban Revolution should be covered. This is not based on what was actually happening in the country but one that reinforces misconceptions rooted in the fiction that any major event is a means to promote social change, ignoring the fact the locals don't see it the same way.

As a counterpoint, Green speculated what it would look like if:

> Our press covered America the way they cover Cuba: The United States, a nation defined by its legacy of genocide and slavery, has allowed a mentally-unstable rapist billionaire to seize power through manipulation of the electoral process and collusion with a foreign power. The government encouraged a climate crisis that threatens the future of human civilization. Despite polls showing growing disillusionment with capital-

ism and expert warnings that soaring inequality destabilizes democracy, politicians feel obligated to pay lip service to illusory American virtues for fear of being branded unpatriotic. And repeat nonstop for 60 years.[22]

In regards to the new president, Miguel Díaz-Canel, media experts were only interested in repeating age-old criticisms, and not in providing context to American's unrelenting attempts to prevent Cuba from solving those shortcomings, Green noted. He provided a number of examples:

- "They expect Raúl's successor to launch reforms to spur the economy, which is growing at its slowest pace in two decades, according to World Bank figures." —*Bloomberg*
- "It will now be up to Díaz-Canel to balance two realities: the need to respond to Cubans' growing frustration over economic stagnation, and the reluctance of the Communist Party to embrace faster reforms." —*Washington Post*
- "Raúl Castro is stepping down as president in an effort to guarantee that new leaders can maintain the government's grip on power in the face of economic stagnation, an aging population and increasing disenchantment among younger generations." —*Associated Press*
- "... an economically distressed country that is perennially in crisis." —*New York Times*[23]

As author Green questioned:

If you seek neoliberal consensus in action, you have found it. As a thought experiment, is it possible even to imagine American media covering successes in a socialist country? Are Americans employed by capitalist media companies capable of admitting that socialism works in the slightest?[24]

A somewhat confounding reproach of Díaz-Canel came from the *New York Times* that seemed to conflate legitimacy to lead with being an actual participant in the historical event. "Mr. Díaz-Canel, who became Cuba's new president on Thursday, the day before his

58th birthday, has spent his entire life in the service of a revolution he did not fight."[25] It takes considerable effort to come up with a criticism so tortured and convoluted in its construct—particularly one with absolutely no relevancy. But when it comes to Cuba, there seemingly is no limit to stretching credibility or setting different standards. As there are no current US leaders who fought in the 1776 revolution, the *New York Times* certainly would not be giving any consideration to make a similar value judgment.

Such false narratives have consequences, not only to the credibility of the mainstream media, but more important, to societies and cultures that endure such hostilities and biases.

While Cuba remains a prime example of media manipulation in support of foreign policy perspectives, others have also had the misfortune of experiencing similar bias.

One international topic that has long been delineated by corporate press value judgments is the Israel–Palestine conflict. Media studies professor Gregory Shupak sees similarities in the coverage of both issues. Author of *The Wrong Story—Palestine, Israel and the Media*,[26] Shupak points to the media's ability to erase history as important factors in the coverage of Palestine and Cuba:

> Media should provide some sort of historical context, which it does not. History is exorcised; the media coverage of the Palestine–Israel issue has only focused on the present, since 2014[27] till now but there is never talk about how it got that point. In regards to Cuba there is the same erasure of the historical reasons behind the Cuban revolution, and why the Cubans might be suspicious of the United States.[28]

Teaching out of the University of Guelph-Humber College in Toronto, Shupak outlined what he said was media bias against Palestine:

> Based on the notion that Palestine–Israel can be understood as "both sides" doing the same to each other. The other narratives include the problem with Palestine is that the "extremists" have

too much power and the "moderates" have too little. And that violence against Palestine is understood as Israel's right to exist.[29]

Shupak states these views have no basis in fact.

There is a massive power difference, which is obscured when you say "both sides"—pretending there is symmetry between what Palestine–Israel have done to each other. It is not the Palestinian ethnic cleaning, nor settling on Israel lands, nor instigating the violence. I'm suggesting that the notion of presenting it in a balanced way—to do so you have to cover the colonization, the occupation and the resistance to that. And imperialism, as well as the US role in the bloodshed.[30]

His research for the book focused in on the so-called liberal media, noting they were often at the forefront of maintaining the misinformation bias.

I looked at the *New York Times*, the *Guardian*, these types of outlets. I wanted to show they conformed to the misconceptions as much as the right wing media, where you would expect it. People see the *Times* as being more balanced, more trustworthy as opposed to hard right media. And the *Times* will criticize Israel to a limited degree, so it seems more balanced. But they have the same bias, the same one-sided coverage in favor of Israel, with not the same consideration to Palestine. Things like blaming the Palestinians for getting killed.[31]

In both Palestine and Cuba, press coverage is a reflection of the political/economic aspirations of the United Sates, he noted. "Coverage of these topics are based on the interests as envisioned by the ruling class," Shupak said.

There are so many media conglomerates, so much media is owned by a few. For the motivation of profits the corporations are deeply interested in US hegemony in the Middle East, and Israel is the proxy. There is no similar investment in Palestine liberation. So the narrative reflects that. The media has been

> deeply opposed to the Cuban revolution for the same similarities of profits for the ruling class.[32]

Controlling the message is key to shaping the narrative, as is who the media allows to speak. "The notion that the Palestinians or Cubans have the right to defend themselves is outside the realm of normal discourse," Shupak said.

> If Cuba has a reasonably strong military for a country its size, and creates civil programs to defend itself—the media portrays it as a dictatorship. In fact, it is the rational response as to what has been done to them. The media's role is also to make sure the other side is not heard. It is hard to think of an instance in the *New York Times* op-ed defending the Cuban revolution and to tell their side of the story. And if there are any instances of articles with a pro-Cuban angle, there is always information included to create an opposite negative view. With anti-Cuba articles that doesn't happen.[33]

Shupak acknowledged the negative impact biased media coverage can have on societies:

> Media coverage informs how our public reacts to our government policies towards Palestine–Israel as well as Cuba. If you have the idea that Israel needs to defend itself above all else, then you are not going to object to the government of the US giving military aid to Israel. The media creates the narrative and the public supports this type of solidarity with Israel without examining any other options.
>
> With Cuba the aggression from the US is accepted, the embargo and the other hostile policies because the media allows people to tolerate those policies. If the information is only one sided that is the result. And the media has created the image of totalitarianism, of absence of democracy, all the negative narratives that have shaped public perceptions of Cuba since the revolution. There is only that side, no reporting on the Cuba side, their reaction to US aggression and right to defend itself. And no serious examination of Cuban society and how it really

> functions. All that is a result of media coverage. This is the public demonization of another government by the media.[34]

Shupak concludes that in both cases, those societies can easily develop a siege mentality,

> that leads to over-reaction and restrictions, it can be a factor in delaying the development of society, and it gets back to extremists and moderates. When a society is under attack, either directly or the sense through regime change polices, and the unrelenting negative media, it has a negative effect.[35]

In Cuba, American corporate media is the informational enabler of Washington's regime change strategy. As such it's an important component in the closing in of Cuban society as a result of those polices, leading to the government's justification for civil rights restrictions, intolerance to dissidents and hypersensitivity to criticism.

Legitimate criticism of the errors and mistakes Cuba has made since 1959 is not debatable. Raúl Castro addressed many of the social problems including corruption, low salaries, vandalism and a host of other difficult issues in a 2013 speech that received wide national attention.[36] Mainstream media has more than enough honest meat to chew on that bone.

What moves this from the realm of journalistic integrity into the depths of biased propaganda is when those criticisms are presented with no balance, with no context as to Cuba's efforts to repair those shortcomings, or America's unrelenting determination to exacerbate the country's missteps—or by ignoring the concrete achievements that have occurred under the revolution. It's not difficult to include that information, and not merely in passing, as some media do. But media has rarely made an effort of placing a modicum of journalistic balance when covering Cuba. Fairness is promoted to be the hallmark of proper journalism. The fact the press doesn't bother, implies either laziness or intent. As it occurs throughout corporate media, in alignment with state objectives, with a consistently bordering on orthodoxy, then the latter option seems more accurate.

It appears the American government will not retrench from regime change strategies, nor will the media end its support. In late 2018, the US State Department released a mission statement on Cuba[37] and one assumes it was taken directly from the 1960s. The report recounted the decades long condemnations of the revolution, then outlined in unambiguous detail exactly how the USA would continue to interfere in Cuban society with the aim of imposing change. This includes increased aid to develop opposition organizations that Havana justifiably considers to be nothing more than artificially created dissidents who promote the policies of a foreign government—something no government would tolerate. Unsurprisingly, there was an absolute lack of recognition of the embargo or the influence these punishments exert on the Cuban citizenry.

No greater hypocrisy was found in the report than the description of Cuba's well-recognized universal health care system:

> Cuba's medical institutions are aging, and there is a growing scarcity of essential drugs and medicine. Shortages of medicines and medical products are significant and medical equipment is not up to world standards. At the same time, the government's long-standing attention to health care and a high doctor-to-patient ratio and focus on preventive medicine is considered the reason behind high life expectancy in Cuba.[38]

Under the embargo, the Cuban government experiences great difficulties in purchasing modern medical equipment and products—the vast majority are still under patent control by US companies. And yet, despite this, the nation continues to exceed most international health standards for developing nations. Revealingly, the State Department report adroitly criticizes without recognizing the limitations the embargo imposes, at the same time giving a backhanded compliment in the condescending description "considered the reason." There is no consideration; high life expectancy under the socialist government has been accomplished in spite of America's non-stop attempts to degrade the system.[39]

The mission statement is nothing more than the latest rulebook for an unsuccessful game that has been played for more than 50 years. Despite Obama's opening and Trump's roll-back, it is the same old regime change strategy. And the mainstream media will utilize the mission statement as accepted truth, maintaining the fiction that US action has no impact on Cuban society or economy. The report outlines in detail how the USA will continue to foster discontent and hardship in order to induce the Cuban people to overthrow their own government, making it clear that regime change will always be the goal, regardless of appearances of normalization. The more things change, the more they will stay the same and the media is vital in sustaining the informational status quo.

One of the most current media criticisms of Cuba is the apparent restrictions to the internet and social media as a way for Havana to keep the outside world away from its citizens, or as it was distorted: "The information revolution is woefully behind in Cuba, as outside news only reaches the elites."[40] If that is the case, it is a nation of elites, as anyone who has ever been to the island will realize, Cubans are well informed on international matters and know much more about America than the other way around.[41]

Putting lie to the myth of internet restriction was demonstrated in late 2018 with the announcement that anyone with a 3G cell phone would be able to connect.[42] It was the latest in a committed effort by the government to increase availability to the informational age. While Cuba remains well below international standards, there is no policy to restrict internet use; the limitations are based on resources and technology, including the continued restriction preventing Cuba from using the fiber optic cable running off its shoreline, owned by the USA. Hundreds of free to use Internet cafés in public locations and educational facilities provide access for the greatest number of people, and private home Internet will soon be introduced. Cell phone use has increased from less than 10 percent of the population five years ago to more than 60 percent in 2018.[43]

With no surprise, mainstream media could not report on the news without injecting superfluous criticism. *CNN*'s story blared with: "Cubans get Internet on Cellphones, But How Many Can Afford It?"[44] Notwithstanding the fact that Cuba is a developing nation under embargo, any country consistently grapples with the balance between technology and the price the individual pays.

When Apple announces its latest cellphone iteration, the question of how many Americans can afford it would never be mentioned, let alone be addressed in the headline. The article then contrived a remarkable conglomeration that managed to denigrate three disparate social programs. "For all its purported strides in health care and education, communist Cuba's level of internet connectivity was among the lowest in the world."[45] What the attempt to disparage health care and education (there are no "purported strides" but real advances) has to do with access to the Internet can only be explained by someone desperate to present negative modifiers. And *CNN* just couldn't resist sticking in the descriptive "communist" label to ensure the viewer understood all the adverse implications.

That is the definition of fake news, a concept the Cuban nation has dealt with since the early days of the revolution. It is, as a *Granma* report explained, "a new name for old practices."[46] The article utilized the example of when in 2016 Spanish news agency *EFE*, "informed the world of the confiscation of 401 kilograms of cocaine in Panama's Colón port, arriving in a container from the Cuban port of Mariel, that had Belgium as its final destination."[47]

A quick investigation showed that instead of cocaine, the container in question was full of honey. While *EFE* made the correction, the truth was ignored by the majority of mainstream media, leaving the lingering falsehood in the minds and attitudes of the readers. *Granma*'s article pointed out the difficulties in establishing the truth when the lie has been reported first. In this day of instantaneous communications and short attention spans, it becomes an even more arduous task. When you add in the latest modes of internet-based communiqué, the mission becomes harder still.

Social media has exploded over the past decade, where more and more individuals are turning to Twitter, Facebook and dozens of other Internet sites for their primary source of information. It is estimated that a majority of the news now circulating on social media is fake, regardless of where it's coming from.[48] Traditional media is losing control, and while aspects of that may be positive, it can exacerbate the dissemination of misinformation.

This misrepresentation may have already had a major political impact. The 2016 American presidential election was seemingly influenced in favor of Donald Trump thanks to the efforts of a couple of teenagers living in Macedonia, according to an investigative piece in *WIRED*.[49] The article examined how hundreds of pro-Trump articles were sent to various right-wing sites, as well as Facebook, flooding the information world with lies, helping to convince thousands of gullible readers to vote for Trump. The story noted,

> fortunately for him [Trump], the election summoned forth the energies of countless alt-right websites in the US, which manufactured white-label falsehoods disguised as news on an industrial scale. Across the spectrum of right-wing media—from Trump's own concise lies on Twitter to the organized prevarication of *Breitbart News* and *NationalReport.net*—ideology beat back the truth.[50]

Apparently, the teenagers had no ideological motivation; they just did it for the money—which they made a considerable amount of from advertisers.

Social media has become the latest weapon in the anti-Cuban propaganda war. Fake news videos are not uncommon, including those purporting to show Cuba as a police state.[51] The Trump administration embraced the modern media platforms with an announcement in 2018 of an Internet Task Force designed to subvert Cuba's internal order.[52]

One of the most blatant examples is CiberCuba, a website supposedly offering balanced reporting but is predominantly anti-revolutionary. As journalist Karen Lee Wald observed,

> If CiberCuba is the prime example of the Trump administration's attempt to sabotage the Cuban revolution via the Internet, the Cubans have little to worry about. It appears to be a poor online approximation of the ultra-anti-Castro Miami newspaper *El Nuevo Herald* which is apparently meant for, and only read by, extremist right-wingers born and bred in hatred for Fidel Castro and anything even mildly progressive.[53]

Although that website might not be successful, other social media efforts have had an impact. Twitter has been weaponized against Cuba, with an attempt to establish a social network built on texts. Named ZunZuneo, slang for a Cuban hummingbird's tweet, the hope was it could be used to organize "smart mobs" to trigger a Cuban spring in 2014. What few realized was the funding and operation for ZunZuneo came from USAID—the State Department organization that had been for years trying to undermine Cuban society.

At its peak, ZunZuneo drew in more than 40,000 Cubans to share news and exchange opinions. But its subscribers were never aware that it was created by the US government, or that American contractors were gathering their private data in the hope that it might be used for political purposes.

An *Associated Press* investigation revealed the US government planned to build a subscriber base through "non-controversial content" including news messages on soccer, music and hurricane updates.[54] Later when the network reached a critical mass of subscribers, perhaps hundreds of thousands, operators would introduce political content aimed at inspiring Cubans to organize "smart mobs"—mass gatherings called at a moment's notice that might trigger a Cuban spring, or, as one USAID document put it, "renegotiate the balance of power between the state and society."[55] For a clearer interpretation—the intent to promote an opposition funded and organized by a foreign power through social media—not unlike what the Russians were attempting in the 2016 presidential election and the cause of so much outrage in the United States to this day. While USAID made it clear: "There will be absolutely no mention of United States government involvement," spokesman Matt Herrick said the agency is proud of its Cuba programs and noted that congressional investigators reviewed them and found them to be consistent with US law.[56]

It appears Cuba will now be fighting another front in the war on misinformation. However, the greatest threat remains with establishment media and its historical disposition to denigrate the revolution. Its effectiveness is based on the concept that propaganda works primarily through repetition. The vilification of Cuba's government in the Western media has been relentless for the past 60 years, effectively, as the overwhelmingly one-sided bias has become almost impenetrable.

One who has experienced US media bias on a direct basis is Josefina Vidal, former head of the Cuban delegation during the bilateral discussions after Obama's opening. Now Cuba's ambassador in Canada, Vidal was uniquely positioned to recognize how corporate press coverage reflects state objectives,

> During the time I was the Head of the US Directorate at the Cuban Foreign Ministry, I could realize that, in general, US mainstream media has supported the interests of US foreign policy towards Cuba, and has served as a sounding board of the official opinions coming from the White House, the State Department, and other government agencies in order to justify certain decisions. There have even been some instances where traditional media have spearheaded US and other countries' public opinion—provided the global outreach of US media—to support the government's opinion. This has been the pattern of mainstream media coverage during the decades of hardline policy against Cuba and also during the few moments of some détente, including the last two years of the Obama administration, when diplomatic ties were restored and both countries tried to move forward to the normalization of bilateral relations, a process rolled back by president Trump.[57]

Media partiality against Cuba is a conditioned reflex, acquired in the nineteenth century when the USA longed to control the country from its Spanish overlords, then refined following the revolution's rejection of that control. While the reasons for the misrepresentations have shifted, the perspective remains. Currently, it is based on media-imposed definitions of human rights and freedoms—terminology utilized to bludgeon the Cubans with.

Even to the present day, with a new leader guiding the socialist nation into the twenty-first century, with a new generation of Cubans who are pressing for economic reforms and less strident political controls, the corporate media will not relinquish the right to frame the same old narratives. When it comes to the revolution, the more things change in Cuba the less they change in the press.

While cracks in that partiality have appeared and hopefully will continue, it will be a remarkable achievement indeed if the media starts to cover Cuba in a consistently fair and balanced way.

How Cuba will respond to press and state pressures will be of interest over the next few years. No doubt the mass media will champion one path to the future and the Cuban people will simply decide what's in their interest, not what's best for the misperceptions of a foreign press. It will be the continuation of a long struggle to maintain Cuban self-determination, a concept corporate media has sought to undermine. With the new tack of less overt bias, with still underlying criticism of the social foundations in support of regime change policies, the battle of pen, paper and ideas continues.

Notes

Introduction

1. While Cuba has not had an incident of terrorism since the 1990s, the American embargo (blockade as the Cubans call it), remains in effect, despite President Obama's lessening of certain aspects. Trump rolled back some of Obama's openings related to travel and business opportunities. American law still prevents US subsidiaries from other countries from doing business in Cuba. A current article addressed the embargo's effects, see Joy Gordon, "El Bloqueo: The Cuban Embargo Continues," *Harper's Magazine*, July 2016.
2. From a March 2018 press conference, in regards to Trump calling Vladimir Putin for winning the presidential election in Russia.
3. US policy did its best to drive Cuba into the arms of the soviets, see Alan H. Luxenberg, "Did Eisenhower Push Castro into the Arms of the Soviets?" *Journal of Interamerican Studies and World Affairs* 30(1) (Spring 1988): 37–72.
4. "Half of Cuban Men's Field Hockey Team 'Defect to United States': Eight Players from Pan American Games Squad Desert Teammates in Toronto," *The Daily Mail*, July 27, 2015, www.dailymail.co.uk/news/article-3175487/Half-Cuban-men-s-field-hockey-team-defect-United-States-Eight-players-Pan-American-games-squad-desert-teammates-Toronto.html.
5. Richard E. Feinberg, "Cuba's Economy after Raúl Castro: A Tale of Three Worlds," *Brookings*, February 2018, www.brookings.edu/research/cubas-economy-after-raul-castro-a-tale-of-three-worlds/. These reports are often quoted by mainstream media in articles about Cuba; the Institute is considered one of the leading experts on Cuba.
6. Editorial Board, "Cuba Should not be Rewarded for Denying Freedom to its People," *Washington Post*, October 20, 2014.
7. For Cuba's electoral process, see Arnold August, *Cuba and Its Neighbors: Democracy in Motion* (Halifax: Fernwood Publishing, 2013).
8. All other nations accepted compensation for nationalized property, not just farmland—all except the USA. To this day, there has been no resolution, see Keith Bolender, *Cuba Under Siege: American Policy, the Revolution and Its People* (Basingstoke: Palgrave Macmillan, 2013).
9. Leon Neyfakh, "Cuba, You Owe Us $7 Billion," *Boston Globe*, April 18, 2014, www.bostonglobe.com/ideas/2014/04/18/cuba-you-owe-billions.
10. Jane Franklin, *Cuba and the United States: A Chronological History* (Melbourne: Ocean Press 1997).
11. Barbara Crossette, "U.S. Says Cubans Knew They Fired on Civilian Planes," *New York Times*, February 28, 1996, www.nyTimes.

com/1996/02/28/world/us-says-cubans-knew-they-fired-on-civilian-planes.html.

12. Saul Landau, "A Double Standard on Terrorism," *In These Times*, March 4, 2002.
13. Abby Goodnough, "US PAID 10 Journalists for Anti-Castro Reports," *New York Times*, September 9, 2006, www.nyTimes.com/2006/09/09/washington/09cuba; see also Party for Socialism and Liberation, www.pslweb.org/reporters-for-hire.
14. Steven Greenhouse, "Radio Marti Whistle-Blowers at Center of Debate in Congress," *New York Times*, September 6, 1995, www.*nyTimes*.com/1995/09/06/world/radio-marti-whistle-blowers-at-center-of-debate-in-congress.html. See also Tracey Eaton's blog *Along the Malecón* for various reports on the cost of Radio Televisión Martí, such as "Cuba Broadcasting: Plenty of String," *Along the Malecón*,May 1, 2014, https://alongthemalecon.blogspot.ca/2014/05/cuba-broadcasting-plenty-of-string.html.
15. Interview with author, March 15, 2018. For more on how media manipulated coverage of the case, see Jeffrey Huling, "Corporate Media Bias & the Case of the Cuban Five," *Project Censored*, May 2, 2010, http://projectcensored.org/corporate-media-bias-the-case-of-the-cuban-five/.
16. See Abby Goodnough, "US PAID 10 Journalists for Anti-Castro Reports," *New York Times*, September 9, 2006.
17. Aaron Weiner, "US Government-Funded News Network Ran a Hit Piece on Soros That Called Him a 'Multimillionaire Jew,'" *Mother Jones*, October 26, 2018, www.motherjones.com/politics/2018/10/us-government-funded-news-network-ran-a-hit-piece-on-soros-that-called-him-a-multimillionaire-jew/.
18. Joel Whitney, "The CIA's Masterful Use of Fake News," *Truthdig*, January 31, 2019, www.truthdig.com/articles/the-cias-masterful-use-of-fake-news/.
19. Keith Bolender, *Voices From the Other Side: An Oral History of Terrorism Against Cuba* (London: Pluto Press 2010).
20. As relayed in email correspondence with Karen Ann Wald.
21. Adam Johnson, "Fox, Daily Beast Stories on Cubans in Syria Lack One Thing: Evidence of Cubans in Syria," *FAIR*, October 21, 2015, https://fair.org/home/fox-daily-beast-stories-on-cubans-in-syria-lack-one-thing-evidence-of-cubans-in-syria/.
22. Ibid.
23. Matt Peppe, "The Imaginary Cuban Troops in Syria," *Common Dreams*, October 18, 2015, www.commondreams.org/views/2015/10/18/imaginary-cuban-troops-syria.
24. Ibid.
25. Peter Slevin, "Cuba Seeks Bioweapons, U.S. Says," *Washington Post*, May 7, 2002, www.washingtonpost.com/archive/politics/2002/05/07/cuba-seeks-bioweapons-us-says.
26. Email correspondence with author, January 2019.

27. "Watch Out, Costco: First Bulk Store Opens in Communist Cuba," *Fox News*, July 12, 2016, www.foxnews.com/world/2016/07/12/watch-out-costco-first-bulk-store-opens-in-communist-cuba.html.
28. Susana Antón, "Funciona en el país primer mercado mayorista de alimentos," *Granma*, March 16, 2018, www.granma.cu/cuba/2018-03-16/funciona-en-el-pais-primer-mercado-mayorista-de-alimentos-16-03-2018-22-03-02; translated from original in Spanish.
29. Email interview with author, March 22, 2018.
30. "Saudi Arabia: Facts and Photos You Should See," *Horizon Times*, April 13, 2019, www.horizonTimes.com/facts/saudi-arabia?utm_medium=outbrain&utm_source=outbrainjk&utm_campaign=ht-saudi-arabia-1402&utm_term=Fox+News+%28FoxNews%29.
31. Email interview of Karen Lee Wald with author, March 2018.
32. CounterSpin, "Karen Hobert Flynn on Census & Citizenship, Jeff Cohen on Cable News Hawks," *FAIR*, March 30, 2018, https://fair.org/home/karen-hobert-flynn-on-census-citizenship-jeff-cohen-on-cable-news-hawks/.
33. "Mr. Maduro's Drive to Dictatorship," *New York Times*, August 3, 2017, www.nyTimes.com/2017/08/03/opinion/nicolas-maduro-sanctions.html.
34. Alan Macleod, "Dictator: Media Code for 'Government We Don't Like,'" *FAIR*, April 11, 2019. Declan Walsh, "El-Sisi May Rule Egypt Until 2034 Under Parliamentary Plan", February 14, 2019, www.nytimes.com/2019/02/14/world/middleeast/egypt-sisi.html.
35. Email interview of Karen Lee Wald with author, March 2018.
36. Nicholas Kristof, "Why Infants May Be More Likely to Die in America Than Cuba," *New York Times*, January 18, 2019, www.nyTimes.com/2019/01/18/opinion/sunday/cuba-healthcare-medicare.html?action=click&module=Opinion&pgtype=Homepage.
37. See Chapter 4.
38. Email interview of Karen Lee Wald with author, March 22, 2018.
39. Ibid.
40. Justin Sink and Jennifer Jacobs, "Trump Rolls Back Obama-led Cuba Opening with Limits on New Deals," *Bloomberg*, June 16, 2017, www.bloomberg.com/news/articles/2017-06-16/trump-rolls-back-obama-led-cuba-opening-with-new-limits-on-deals. This will be covered in Chapter 4. The result has been a substantial drop in visitors.
41. The roll-back has had an impact on the number of Americans visiting Cuba, with estimates of thousands fewer since 2015; see Carmen Sesin and Orlando Matos, "Trump Administration's Tougher Stance is Hitting Ordinary Cubans, Cuban-Americans," *NBC News*, December 23, 2017, www.nbcnews.com/news/latino/trump-administration-s-tougher-stance-hitting-ordinary-cubans-cuban-americans-n828231.
42. Peter Kornbluh, "What the US Government Is Not Telling You About Those 'Sonic Attacks' in Cuba," *The Nation*, March 7, 2018, www.thenation.com/article/what-the-us-government-is-not-telling-you-about-those-sonic-attacks-in-cuba/.
43. Carol Morello, "16 Americans Suffered Injuries While Associated with U.S. Embassy in Havana," *Washington Post*, August 24, 2017, www.

washingtonpost.com/world/national-security/16-americans-suffered-injuries-while-stationed-at-us-embassy-in-havana/2017/08/24/. For more on the subject, see Chapter 4.

44. Louis A. Pérez Jr., *Cuba in the American Imagination: Metaphor and the Imperial Ethos* (Chapel Hill, NC: University of North Carolina Press, 2008).
45. The new Cuban President Miguel Díaz-Canel took over in April 2018.
46. Commission for Assistance to a Free Cuba Report, May 6, 2004, U.S. Department of State, https://2001-2009.state.gov/p/wha/rt/cuba/.
47. Renaud Lambert, "Cuba on the Verge of Inequality," *Le Monde Diplomatique*, November 2017, https://mondediplo.com/2017/11/03cuba.
48. Edward S. Herman and Noam Chomsky, *Manufacturing Consent* (New York: Pantheon Books, 1988).
49. Bernie Sanders, "How Corporate Media Threatens Our Democracy," *In These Times*, January 26, 2017, http://inthesetimes.com/features/bernie-sanders-corporate-media-threatens-our-democracy.html.
50. "U.S. and Cuban companies reach agreement on Heberprot-p," *Granma*, March 21, 2018, http://en.granma.cu/cuba/2018-03-21/us-and-cuban-companies-reach-agreement-on-heberprot-p. A search on a number of web engines as of March 2018 failed to provide any examples of coverage in the mainstream media. Any stories were restricted to low-level independent press.
51. The six are: GE, Newscorp, Disney, Viacom, Time Warner and CBS; Ashley Lutz, "The 6 Corporations Control 90% of the Media in America," *Business Insider*, June 14, 2012, www.businessinsider.com/these-6-corporations-control-90-of-the-media-in-america-2012-6.
52. Even European countries are denigrated as "socialist," see Lars Christensen, "European Socialism: Why America Doesn't Want it," *Forbes*, October 25, 2012, www.forbes.com/forbes/2012/10/25/european-socialism-why-america-doesnt-want-it/.
53. Peter Phillips, "How Mainstream Media Evolved into Corporate Media: A Project Censored History," *Project Censored*, February 7, 2019, www.projectcensored.org/how-mainstream-media-evolved-into-corporate-media-a-project-censored-history/?mc_cid=3bocc707c2&mc_eid=9d66fc6554.
54. Lars Schoultz, *That Infernal Little Cuban Republic: The United States and the Cuban Revolution* (Chapel Hill, NC: University of North Carolina Press, 2009).
55. Paul Street, "Trump, Corporate Media are Both Enemies of the People," *Truthdig*, August 23, 2018, www.truthdig.com/articles/trump-and-the-corporate-media-are-both-enemies-of-the-people/. All sorts of books have been written on how mainstream media serves the elite, and is not free unless in terms of promoting corporate capitalism. See Herbert Schiller, *The Mind Managers* (Boston, MA: Beacon Press, 1973); Michael Parenti, *Inventing Reality: The Politics of the News Media* (Belmont, CA: Wadsworth Publishing 1986); Edward S. Herman and Noam Chomsky, *Manufacturing Consent* (New York: Pantheon Books,

1988); Robert W. McChesney, *Corporate Media and the Threat to Democracy* (New York: Seven Stories, 1997); and also McChesney, *Rich Media, Poor Democracy: Communication Politics in Dubious Times* (New York: The New Press, 2000).

56. "Iraq and the Media: A Critical Timeline," *FAIR*, March 19, 2007, https://fair.org/take-action/media-advisories/iraq-and-the-media/. *New York Times* reporter Judith Miller is the most infamous of those who turned into stenographers for the government's justifications. Some exceptions were questioning the reasons for invasion, notably Knight Ridder, but they were voices drowned out by majority media in favor of invasion.
57. Howard Kurtz, "Media's Failure on Iraq Still Stings," *CNN*, March 11, 2013, www.cnn.com/2013/03/11/opinion/kurtz-iraq-media-failure/index.htm.
58. Judith Miller, the most infamous reporter, who basically recycled what the government wanted to put out. Erik Wemple, "Judith Miller Tries, and Ultimately Fails, to Defend her Flawed Iraq Reporting," *Washington Post*, April 9, 2015, www.washingtonpost.com/opinions/a-reporters-defense-of-her-flawed-reporting/2015/04/09/5bf93f14-de15-11e4-a500-1c5bb1d8ff6a_story.html?utm_term=.87e5f43c3772.
59. Beenish Ahmed, "Here are All the Things the Media Calls Torture Instead of 'Torture,'" *Think Progress*, December 12, 2014, https://thinkprogress.org/here-are-all-the-things-the-media-calls-torture-instead-of-torture-9f167f43e33e/.
60. For an in-depth look at how the press is not free, see Chris Hedges, "The Myth of the Free Press," *Truthdig*, October 26, 2014, www.truthdig.com/report/item/the_myth_of_the_free_press_20141026/.
61. James Risen, "The Biggest Secret: My Life as a *New York Times* Reporter in the Shadow of the War on Terror," *The Intercept*, January 3, 2018, https://theintercept.com/2018/01/03/my-life-as-a-new-york-*Times*-reporter-in-the-shadow-of-the-war-on-terror/.
62. News networks Gothamist and DNAInfo, along with their local affiliates from Washington DC to Chicago to Los Angeles, were shut down by their owner, the Trump-donor, Joe Ricketts. With no notice and apparently no regard for their years of hard work, over 100 journalists found themselves unemployed and, in the short term, unable to even access their own work as their stories disappeared from the web. Ricketts justified this as an economically necessary decision—but many believe the real reason was the New York newsrooms' vote to unionize. These closures are part of a broader environment which has become deeply hostile to the practice of critical journalism. Another wealthy Trump donor successfully funded a lawsuit to bankrupt Gawker. Trump's Department of Justice has charged journalists with felonies for covering protests at his inauguration. Hamilton Nolan, "A Billionaire Destroyed His Newsrooms Out of Spite," *New York Times*, November 3, 2017, www.nyTimes.com/2017/11/03/opinion/dnainfo-gothamist-ricketts-union.html.
63. Commented on Thom Hartmann program on May 29, 2018.

64. From the 2016 documentary film, *The Brainwashing of My Dad*, directed by Jen Senko. www.thebrainwashingofmydad.com/.
65. The five filters are: 1. corporate ownership; 2. advertising; 3. state manipulation of media information; 4. control of journalists; 5. and creating a common enemy; see www.youtube.com/watch?v=34LGPIX vU5M.
66. Ibid.
67. Erik Wemple, "CNN's Jeffrey Toobin: 'I Regret my Role' in Hillary Clinton False Equivalence," *Washington Post*, January 29, 2018, www.washingtonpost.com/amphtml/blogs/erik-wemple/wp/2018/01/29/cnns-jeffrey-toobin-i-regret-my-role-in-hillary-clinton-false-equivalence/?__twitter_impression=true.
68. Erik Wemple, "Studies Agree: Media Gorged on Hillary Clinton Email Coverage," *Washington Post*, August 25, 2017, www.washingtonpost.com/blogs/erik-wemple/wp/2017/08/25/studies-agree-media-gorged-on-hillary-clinton-email-coverage/?utm_term=.26c06d94dbod.
69. Juan Cole, "Let's Call Bolton What He Is, a War Criminal with Terrorist Ties, Not Just 'Hawkish,'" *Informed Comment*, March 23, 2018, www.juancole.com/2018/03/criminal-terrorist-hawkish.html.
70. For more on Fox News' Sean Hannity actually advising Donald Trump with regard to policy and how to handle media—Nunes report, etc., see David, "Eric Boehlert Rips Nunes Memo Hype: 'They Coordinate With Fox News and Russian Bots … And It's Still a Dud,'" *Crooks and Liars*, February 5, 2018, https://crooksandliars.com/2018/02/eric-boehlert-rips-nunes-memo-hype-they.
71. Sinclair media directs its outlets regarding fake news, but its right-wing slant implies fake news is anything they perceive to be against Trump policies. In March 2018, *CNN*'s Brian Stelter broke the news that Sinclair Broadcast Group, owner or operator of nearly 200 television stations in the USA, would be forcing its news anchors to record a promo about "the troubling trend of irresponsible, one sided news stories plaguing our country." The script, which parrots Donald Trump's oft-declarations of developments negative to his presidency as "fake news," brought upheaval to newsrooms already dismayed with Sinclair's consistent interference to bring right-wing propaganda to local television broadcasts. See Scarce, "Sinclair Broadcasting Enlists Journalists to Wage Trump's War on 'Fake News,'" *Crooks and Liars*, March 31, 2018, https://crooksandliars.com/2018/03/sinclair-broadcasting-enlists-journalists.
72. Chris Hedges, "The Empty Piety of the American Press," *Truthdig*, March 11, 2018, www.truthdig.com/articles/empty-piety-american-press/.
73. Adam Johnson, "Ignoring Washington's Role in Yemen Carnage, 60 Minutes Paints US as Savior," *FAIR*, November 20, 2017, http://fair.org/home/ignoring-washingtons-role-in-yemen-carnage-60-minutes-paints-us-as-savior/.
74. Adam Johnson, "In Run-Up to Vote to End Yemen War, MSNBC Remains Totally Silent," *FAIR*, March 20, 2018, https://fair.org/home/in-run-up-to-vote-to-end-yemen-war-msnbc-remains-totally-silent/;

Adam Johnson, "WaPo Editors: We Have to Help Destroy Yemen to Save It," *FAIR*, May 31, 2018, https://fair.org/home/wapo-editors-we-have-to-help-destroy-yemen-to-save-it/.

75. Adam Johnson, "Think Tank-Addicted Media Turn to Regime Change Enthusiasts for Iran Protest Commentary," *FAIR*, January 5, 2018, https://fair.org/home/think-tank-addicted-media-turn-to-regime-change-enthusiasts-for-iran-protest-commentary/.
76. "Rights for Women in Saudi Arabia," *BBC News*, www.bbc.com/news/av/world-middle-east-32579989/rights-for-women-in-saudi-arabia-progressing.
77. "Saudi Arabia Women Drive," *New York Times*, September 26, 2017, www.nyTimes.com/2017/09/26/world/middleeast/saudi-arabia-women-drive.html.
78. Adam Johnson, "Promoters of Saudi Prince as Feminist Reformer are Silent on His Crackdown on Women," *FAIR*, May 23, 2018, https://fair.org/home/promoters-of-saudi-prince-as-feminist-reformer-are-silent-on-his-crackdown-on-women/.
79. A.Z. Mohamed, "Washington Ignores Saudi 'Involvement in Supporting Terrorism and Terrorist Groups,'" Gatestone Institute, June 19, 2017, www.gatestoneinstitute.org/10542/saudi-arabia-terrorism.
80. Those media Trump supporters were far less critical; see more on this in Chapter 5.
81. Joanna Chiu, "My Friend Michael Kovrig was Arrested in China: Please, Pay Attention," *Toronto Star*, December 11, 2018, www.thestar.com/opinion/2018/12/11/my-friend-michael-kovrig-was-arrested-in-china-i-beg-you-to-pay-attention.html.
82. *FAIR* has consistently cataloged misreporting of enemy states, such as Iran, August 9, 2015 and July 25, 2017; North Korea, May 9, 2017 and March 22, 2017; Venezuela, May 16, 2017 and March 2, 2007; Cuba or Syria, October 25, 2015, where their supposed threat to the world or their human rights violations are ramped up, while downplaying crimes of friendly states, January 2, 2009.
83. Greg Palast, "In Venezuela, White Supremacy Is a Key Driver of the Coup," *Venezuela Analysis*, February 12, 2019, https://venezuela nalysis.com/analysis/14318. An extensive look at how corporate media lies have framed the Venezuelan coverage can be found at Mark Cook, "Venezuela Coverage Takes Us Back to Golden Age of Lying About Latin America," *FAIR*, February 22, 2019, https://fair.org/home/venezuela-coverage-takes-us-back-to-golden-age-of-lying-about-latin-america.
84. Eric Draitser, "US Corporate Media Seek to Undermine Venezuelan Democracy with Lies and Distortions," *Counterpunch*, December 4, 2015, www.counterpunch.org/2015/12/04/us-corporate-media-seek-to-undermine-venezuelan-democracy-with-lies-and-distortions.
85. "Hugo Chávez Departs," *New York Times*, April 13, 2002, www.nyTimes.com/2002/04/13/opinion/hugo-chavez-departs.html.
86. See Alan MacLeod, *Bad News From Venezuela: Twenty Years of Fake News and Misreporting* (New York: Routledge, 2018).

87. Counterspin, "Joe Emersberger on Venezuelan Elections, Dahr Jamail on Antarctic Ice," *FAIR*, April 27, 2018, https://fair.org/home/joe-emersberger-on-venezuelan-elections-dahr-jamail-on-antarctic-ice/; Joe Emersberger, "Western Media Shorthand on Venezuela Conveys and Conceals So Much," *FAIR*, April 23, 2018, https://fair.org/home/western-media-shorthand-on-venezuela-conveys-and-conceals-so-much/.
88. Girish Gupta and Mircely Guanipa, "Some Poor Venezuelan Parents Give Away Children Amid Deep Crisis," *Reuters*, December 15, 2016, www.reuters.com/article/us-venezuela-children/some-poor-venezuelan-parents-give-away-children-amid-deep-crisis-idUSKBN1441TB.
89. Kevin Zeese and Margaret Flowers, "Is a Military Coup or Even a U.S. Invasion Next for Venezuela?" *Truthdig*, February 14, 2018, www.truthdig.com/articles/military-coup-invasion-venezuela-next/.
90. Mark Weisbrot, "Trump Doubles Down on Sanctions and Regime Change for Venezuela," *Progreso Weekly*, November 15, 2017, http://progresoweekly.us/trump-doubles-sanctions-regime-change-venezuela/.
91. José R. Cárdenas, "It's Time for a Coup in Venezuela,: *Foreign Policy*, June 5, 2018, https://foreignpolicy.com/2018/06/05/its-time-for-a-coup-in-venezuela-trump/.
92. Linda McQuaig, "Canada on wrong side of Venezuelan conflict," *Toronto Star*, March 15, 2018, www.thestar.com/opinion/star-columnists/2018/03/15/canada-on-wrong-side-of-venezuelan-conflict.html. The possibility of a coup increased with the announcement in early 2019 of Juan Guaidó as president, an illegal act recognized by the USA and other Western democracies. A full analysis of the misinformation about Venezuela can be found at Kevin Zeese and Margaret Flowers, "Venezuela: What Activists Need to Know About the US-Led Coup," *Popular Resistance*, January 27, 2019, https://popularresistance.org/venezuela-what-activists-need-to-know-about-the-us-led-coup/.
93. Adam Johnson, "ACTION ALERT: MSNBC's 'Resistance' to Trump's Venezuela Coup Ranges from Silence to Support," *FAIR*, February 13, 2019, https://fair.org/home/action-alert-msnbcs-resistance-to-trumps-venezuela-coup-ranges-from-silence-to-support/?awt_l=LEAyG&awt_m=go6LodmIA2R._TQ.
94. Alan MacLeod, "The 'Venezuelan People' are Whoever Agrees With Donald Trump," *FAIR*, January 31, 2019, https://fair.org/home/the-venezuelan-people-are-whoever-agrees-with-donald-trump/?awt_l=LEAyG&awt_m=haoNDCqYi2R._TQ.
95. Nicolas Casey, "'It is Unspeakable': How Maduro Used Cuban Doctors to Coerce Venezuelan Voters," *New York Times*, March 19, 2019, www.nytimes.com/2019/03/17/world/americas/venezuela-cuban-doctors.html.
96. Lucas Koemer and Ricardo Vaz, "Pathological Deceit: The NYT Inverts Reality on Venezuela's Cuban Doctors," *FAIR*, March 26, 2019, https://fair.org/home/pathological-deceit-the-nyt-inverts-reality-on-

venezuelas-cuban-doctors/?awt_l=LEAyG&awt_m=hEMYaW7IF2R._TQ.

97. Ewan Robertson, "Former US President Carter: Venezuela's Electoral System 'Best in the World,'" *Global Research*, February 25, 2019, www.globalresearch.ca/former-us-president-carter-venezuelan-electoral-system-best-in-the-world/5305779.
98. Sandra Cuffe, "Hondurans Protest US-Backed Government as Thousands Flee," *Truthout*, January 31, 2019, https://truthout.org/articles/hondurans-protest-us-backed-government-as-thousands-flee/.
99. Max Blumenthal, "How an American Anthropologist Tied to US Regime-Change Proxies Became the MSM's Man in Nicaragua," *MPN News*, September 26, 2018, www.mintpressnews.com/how-an-american-anthropologist-tied-to-us-regime-change-proxies-became-the-msms-man-in-nicaragua/.
100. Ibid.
101. Lord Fairfax lost millions of acres with no compensation during the American Revolution, and Japanese landholders were subject to severe losses after World War II, based on US imposed reforms.
102. "Embargo Must Go," *Washington Post*, September 8, 1994, A19.
103. These issues will be covered in depth in later chapters.
104. Phillip Knightley, *The First Casualty: From the Crimea to Vietnam: War Correspondent as Hero, Propagandist and Mythmaker* (London: Pan Books, 1989).
105. Liam Hoare, "Let's Please Stop Crediting Ronald Reagan for the Fall of the Berlin Wall," *The Atlantic*, September 20, 2012, www.theatlantic.com/international/archive/2012/09/lets-please-stop-crediting-ronald-reagan-for-the-fall-of-the-berlin-wall/262647/.
106. Jeff Cohen and Norman Soloman, "30-Year Anniversary: Tonkin Gulf Lie Launched Vietnam War," *FAIR*, July 27, 1994, https://fair.org/media-beat-column/30-year-anniversary-tonkin-gulf-lie-launched-vietnam-war/.
107. See above Note 70.
108. Patrick Cockburn, "Embedded Journalism: A Distorted View of War," *The Independent*, November 23, 2010, www.independent.co.uk/news/media/opinion/embedded-journalism-a-distorted-view-of-war-2141072.html.
109. Edward S. Herman, "Fake News on Russia and Other Official Enemies: The *New York Times*, 1917–2017," *Monthly Review*, July 1, 2017, https://monthlyreview.org/2017/07/01/fake-news-on-russia-and-other-official-enemies/.
110. See Note 70. Also see Edward S. Herman and Noam Chomsky, *Manufacturing Consent*.
111. Janet Reitman, "Did the Mainstream Media Fail Bradley Manning?" *Rolling Stone*, March 1, 2013, www.rollingstone.com/politics/news/did-the-mainstream-media-fail-bradley-manning-20130301. Manning was interviewed on Amy Goodman's *Democracy Now!* on March 27, 2018, where she confirmed the information was offered to both papers with no reply; see "We Cannot Wait for Change"—Freed Whistleblower Chelsea Manning on Iraq, Prison & Running for Senate," *Democracy*

Now!, March 27, 2018, www.democracynow.org/2018/3/27/we_cannot_wait_for_change_freed?fbclid=IwAR2-beMsX6Qqvr_UxJIkpNRfx6nFgXOVYP5E_77C69NPIgqXfjpuWEVc7sk.

112. Steven R. Weisman, "President Calls Nicaragua Rebels Freedom Fighters; News Session Transcript, Page D22," *New York Times*, May 5, 1983, www.ny*Times*.com/1983/05/05/world/president-calls-nicaragua-rebels-freedom-fighters-session-transcript-page-d22.html.
113. "Scott Armstrong on the Media & Contragate," *FAIR*, July 1, 1987, https://fair.org/extra/scott-armstrong-on-the-media-contragate/; and "The Iran–Contra Affair 30 Years Later: A Milestone in Post-Truth Politics," *National Security Archive*, November 25, 2016, https://nsarchive.gwu.edu/briefing-book/iran/2016-11-25/iran-contra-affair-30-years-later-milestone-post-truth-politics.
114. Chris Hedges, "The Myth of the Free Press," *Truthdig*, October 26, 2014, www.truthdig.com/articles/the-myth-of-the-free-press/.
115. Camilio E. Mejía, "Open Letter to Amnesty International by a Former Amnesty International Prisoner of Conscience," *ALAI: Latin America in Movement*, June 13, 2018, www.alainet.org/en/articulo/193467.
116. "Saudi Arabia 2017/2018," *Amnesty International*, www.amnesty.org/en/countries/middle-east-and-north-africa/saudi-arabia/report-saudi-arabia/.
117. Jason Lemon, "Saudi Arabia Just Took 4 Major Steps to Improve Women's Rights," *Step Feed*, August 16, 2017, https://stepfeed.com/saudi-arabia-just-took-4-major-steps-to-improve-women-s-rights-7985.
118. Quote Investigator, https://quoteinvestigator.com/2016/12/03/mis informed/.
119. Knoll's Law of Media Accuracy. Knoll had first-hand knowledge of government control of media when US federal court ordered him not to print an article in the *Progressive Magazine* on how America developed H bomb.
120. "'My' Media Versus 'The' Media: Trust in News Depends on Which News Media You Mean," *American Press Institute*, May 24, 2017, www.americanpressinstitute.org/publications/reports/survey-research/my-media-vs-the-media/.
121. Jennifer Harper, "How Americans Really Feel About the Mainstream Media," *Washington Post*, September 12, 2018, www.washington Times.com/news/2018/sep/12/how-americans-really-feel-about-mainstream-media/.
122. Richard C. Auxier, "Global View on Castro and Cuba," *Pew Research Centre*, February 19, 2008, www.pewglobal.org/2008/02/19/global-views-on-castro-and-cuba/.
123. One of the absolute worst articles on Fidel Castro's death was in Rosie DiManno, "Castro Took a Country Hostage—His Own: DiManno," *Toronto Star*, December 4, 2016, www.thestar.com/news/gta/2016/12/04/castro-took-a-country-hostage-his-own-dimanno.html. This will be examined further in Chapter 4.

124. Mark Milke, "Cuba: From Economic Take Off to COLLAPSE UNDER Castro," *Toronto Globe and Mail*, November 2016, www.transactionpub.com/title/Cuba-978-1-4128-5670-6.html.
125. Keith Bolender, *Cuba Under Siege: American Policy, the Revolution and Its People* (Basingstoke: Palgrave Macmillan, 2013), 66.
126. Ibid.
127. Alan Luxenberg, "Did Eisenhower push Castro into the arms of the Soviets?" *Journal of Inter American Studies and World Affairs* 30(1) (Spring 1988): 37–72.
128. T.J. English, *Havana Nocturne: How the Mob Owned Cuba ... and then Lost it to the Revolution* (New York: William Morrow, 2009).
129. Milke, "Cuba."
130. So said a Cuban Minister of Education. Luis E. Aguilar, *Cuba 1933: Prologue to Revolution* (Ithaca, NY: Cornell University Press, 1972).
131. Milke, "Cuba."
132. The figures cited in the text and below come from United Nations and international agency reports, cited in Marifeli Perez-Stable, *The Cuban Revolution Origins, Course and Legacy* (New York: Oxford University Press, 1999); and Andrés Zaldívar Diéguez, *Blockade: The Longest Economic Siege in History* (Havana: Capitán San Luis, 2007). Of the 19 Latin American countries, only Argentina and Uruguay surpass the present Cuban figure. How important public health is to socialist Cuba can be gauged by the budget figures allocated to health—from 21 million pesos before the Revolution to 180 million in 1967, that is, almost a ninefold increase.
133. Sujatha Fernandes, "Freedom Through a Pencil: The 1961 Literacy Campaign in Cuba," *Nacla*, December 16, 2011, https://nacla.org/news/2011/12/16/freedom-through-pencil-1961-literacy-campaign-cuba.
134. These figures from United Nations and international agency reports were cited in Marifeli Perez-Stable, *The Cuban Revolution Origins, Course and Legacy* (New York: Oxford University Press, 1999) and Andrés Zaldívar Diéguez, *Blockade: The Longest Economic Siege in History* (Havana: Capitán San Luis, 2007).
135. Ibid.
136. Author interview with Carlos Andrés Escalante Gómez, Boca de Samá, Cuba 2008.
137. This data was published by the International Labour Organization in Geneva, Switzerland, in 1960. In 1958, Cuba had a labor force of 2,204,000.
138. Manuel E. Yepe, "Cuba was Neither a Paradise nor an Exception," October 6, 2011, http://cpcml.ca/Tmlw2011/W410148.HTM.
139. Catholic University Association 1957 report, from the personal files of the Cuban historian and author, Ramón Torreira Crespo.
140. Hadley Heath Manning, "Think the Cuban Healthcare System is Ideal? No Cigar. Not Even Close," *Washington Examiner*, November 29, 2016, www.washingtonexaminer.com/think-the-cuban-healthcare-system-is-ideal-no-cigar-not-even-close.
141. James Barrood, "Awaiting Cuba's Thriving Tech Industry to Boom," *Newark Star-Ledger*, April 25, 2015, www.michaelmunk.com.

142. Ibid.
143. Silvio Canto Jr., "Cubans Going Hungry so Tourists Can Eat Well?" *American Thinker*, December 11, 2016, www.americanthinker.com/blog/2016/12/cubans_going_hungry_so_tourists_can_eat_well.html; based on "Cuba's Surge In Tourism Keep Food Off Residents' Plates," *New York Times*, December 8, 2016, www.nyTimes.com/2016/12/08/world/americas/cuba-fidel-castro-food-tourism.html.
144. "Over 140 Cuban Cooperatives Selling Products Directly to Hotels," *Radio Cadena Agramonte*, January 23, 2012, www.cadenagramonte.cu/english/show/articles/9158:over-140-cuban-cooperatives-selling-products-directly-to-hotels.
145. Patrick Mazzei, "Rubio: 'Bureaucrats' to Blame for Softening Trump Cuba Policy," *Miami Herald*, November 8, 2017, www.miamiherald.com/news/nation-world/world/americas/cuba/article183486726.html.
146. "Let's Make a 'Better Deal,'" *Cuba Central*, November 10, 2017, https://cubacentral.wordpress.com/.
147. Mourid Barghouti, *I Saw Ramallah*, translated by Ahdaf Soueif (New York: Anchor, 2003).
148. Gregory Shupak, "Slapping an Israeli Soldier More Newsworthy Than Shooting a Palestinian Child in the Face," *FAIR*, January 17, 2018, fair.org/home/slapping-an-israeli-soldier-more-newsworthy-than-shooting-a-palestinian-child-in-the-face/.
149. Salim Lamrani, "Cuba and the Number of 'Political Prisoners,'" *Cuba Solidarity Campaign*, Autumn, 2010, https://cuba-solidarity.org.uk/cubasi/article/125/cuba-and-the-number-of-ldquopolitical-prisonersrdquo.
150. Ian Shapira, "'It was Terrible': Alan Gross Gives First Interview After Being Released from a Cuban Prison," *Washington Post*, November 30, 2015, www.washingtonpost.com/news/local/wp/2015/11/30/it-was-terrible-alan-gross-gives-first-interview-after-being-released-from-a-cuban-prison/?utm_term=.c39081206bc6; "USAID Contractor: Duty to Intervene in Cuba," *Along the Malecón*, October 4, 2014, https://alongthemalecon.blogspot.ca/2014/10/usaid-contractor-duty-to-intervene-in.html.
151. "Alan P. Gross Gains Freedom From Cuba He Thought Would Never Come," *New York Times*, December 18, 2014, www.nyTimes.com/2014/12/18/world/americas/alan-p-gross-gains-the-freedom-from-cuba-he-thought-would-never-come.html. More on Gross in Chapter 3.
152. See the CIA's country by country estimate of the difference between those leaving and moving to each country, based on 2017 figures: "Net migration rate compares the difference between the number of persons entering and leaving a country during the year per 1,000 persons (based on midyear population)," www.cia.gov/library/publications/the-world-factbook/rankorder/2112rank.html.
153. Tom Phillips, "'Breathtaking Homicidal Violence': Latin America in Grip of Murder Crisis," *The Guardian*, April 26, 2018, www.theguardian.com/world/2018/apr/26/latin-america-murder-crisis-violence-homicide-report.

154. Renaud Lambert, "Cuba on the Verge of Inequality," *Le Monde Diplomatique*, November 2017, https://mondediplo.com/2017/11/03cuba.
155. "Misinformation: 2018 Word of the Year," www.dictionary.com/e/s/word-of-the-year-list/?param=tcomserp-mid1#misinformation.
156. Melissa Dykes, "CIA Admits to Congress the Agency Uses Mainstream Media to Distribute Disinformation: 1975 Video," *Global Research*, March 6, 2018, www.globalresearch.ca/1975-video-cia-admits-to-congress-the-agency-uses-mainstream-media-to-distribute-disinformation/5424860.
157. Charles H. Brown, *The Correspondents' War: Journalists in the Spanish–American War* (New York: Charles Scribner's Sons, 1967), 24.

1. Media Control of Cuban History

1. The USS *Maine* was discovered in 2000 by divers who determined the explosion was internal, most likely caused by a boiler exploding.
2. Louis A. Pérez Jr., *The War of 1898: The United States and Cuba in History and Historiography* (Chapel Hill, NC: University of North Carolina Press, 1998), 58.
3. Maj. Danny Sjursen, "American History for Truthdiggers: Tragic Dawn of Overseas Imperialism," *Truthdig*, November 10, 2018, www.truthdig.com/articles/american-history-for-truthdiggers-tragic-dawn-of-overseas-imperialism/.
4. It is recognized that the *New York World* first used the expression in the weeks after the explosion, but it was soon expressed by most national newspapers during the lead up to US intervention. The full sentiment is "Remember the *Maine*! To hell with Spain!"
5. Charles H. Brown, *The Correspondents' War: Journalists in the Spanish–American War* (New York: Charles Scribner's Sons, 1967), 122.
6. Ibid., 123.
7. Ibid., 124.
8. Ibid., 123.
9. Ibid., 126–127.
10. Pérez Jr., *The War of 1898*, 72.
11. Ibid.
12. Ibid.
13. Louis A. Pérez Jr., *Cuba in the American Imagination: Metaphor and the Imperial Ethos* (Chapel Hill, NC: University of North Carolina Press, 2008), 210.
14. Brown, *The Correspondents' War.*
15. Martí lived in the USA for years, "in the belly of the beast" as he called it, and wrote extensively of America's desire to take over his island nation.
16. Pérez Jr., *Cuba in the American Imagination*, 69.
17. Ibid., 55.
18. Ibid., 67.
19. Ibid., 85.

20. Ibid., 87.
21. Washington Gladden, "The Issues of the War," *Outlook*, July 16, 1898.
22. Pérez Jr., *Cuba in the American Imagination*, 112.
23. The Monroe Doctrine was the basic foundation for the United States' imperial policies within the Americas, see "Monroe Doctrine," *Encyclopaedia Britannica*, lasted update April 3, 2019, www.britannica.com/event/Monroe-Doctrine.
24. John Quincy Adams to Hugh Nelson, April 28, 1823, in US Congress House of Representatives, Island of Cuba, 7.
25. Pérez Jr., *Cuba in the American Imagination*, 30–31.
26. *Puck*, January 13, 1897.
27. *Minneapolis Journal*, September 30, 1906, 8.
28. Much of this chapter is indebted to Louis A. Pérez Jr.'s seminal work *Cuba in the American Imagination: Metaphor and the Imperial Ethos* (Chapel Hill, NC: University of North Carolina Press, 2008), No student of Cuban–US history should be without it.
29. Istvan Ojedo Bello, "Louis A. Pérez Jr.: In Search of the Enigma of Being Cuban," *Progreso Weekly*, May 23, 2018, http://progresoweekly.us/louis-a-perez-jr-in-search-of-the-enigma-of-being-cuban/.
30. Pérez Jr., *The War of 1898*, 8.
31. Ibid., 85.
32. Brown, *The Correspondents' War*.
33. Pérez Jr., *Cuba in the American Imagination*.
34. Ibid.
35. Ibid.
36. Ibid., 132.
37. Ibid., 95.
38. Orville Platt, "The Pacification of Cuba", *Independent*, June 27, 1901, 1401.
39. Pérez Jr., *Cuba in the American Imagination*.
40. Ibid., 100.
41. Pérez Jr., *The War of 1898*, 74.
42. Ibid., 100.
43. Ibid., 103.
44. Ibid., 114.
45. Ibid.
46. One example in the early 1900s reads:

> Fortunes in Cuba. The Cuban Colonization Company. Owns and holds deeds for two large tracts of the best land in Cuba, situated on the north coast in the Province of Puerto Principe, the most fertile and beautiful portion of the island. This region is being rapidly colonized by enterprising Americans, who own and are developing thousands of plantations in the immediate vicinity of our holdings. We are selling this valuable land in small tracts, from five to forty acres each, at low price, payable in monthly installments. The purchaser of land from us will have no taxes to pay for the first three years, and can have a warranty deed as soon as his land is paid for.

Enrique Circules, *Conversacion con el ultimo Norteamericano* (La Habana, Editorial Letras Cubanas, 1988). Testimonio grafico.

47. Jane Franklin, *Cuba and the United States: A Chronological History* (Melbourne: Ocean Press, 1997).
48. Louis A. Pérez Jr., *Cuba under the Platt Amendment 1902–1934* (Pittsburgh, PA: University of Pittsburgh Press, 1986), 71–80.
49. Pérez Jr., *Cuba in the American Imagination*, 198.
50. *New York World*, April 25, 1901.
51. Pérez Jr., *Cuba in the American Imagination*, 129.
52. Ibid., 191.
53. Military Governor Leonard Wood to President Roosevelt on October 28, 1901. Leonard Woods papers, Manuscript Division, Library of Congress.
54. Pérez Jr., *Cuba in the American Imagination*, 247.
55. Ibid., 189.
56. Ibid., 153.
57. Ibid.
58. Ibid., 154.
59. Ibid., 191.
60. Ibid., 199.
61. Ibid., 227.
62. Ibid., 239.
63. Ibid., 240.
64. Ibid., 233.
65. Ibid.
66. Ibid., 206.
67. Ibid.
68. Ibid.
69. *Havana Post*, March 29, 1921, 1.
70. *Havana Post*, May 3, 1916, 4.
71. Fidel Castro was hoping the revolution would be able to come to some accommodation with the USA, but as it became clear the Americans would not allow any loss of control, that became impossible. The media played a predominate role in the perception that Fidel Castro was anti-American right from the start. He was a nationalist and would not let anything stand in his way. This will be explored further in Chapter 2.
72. *Meet the Press* interview, Lawrence Spivak (moderator), "Fidel Castro on MTP in 1959: 'I Am Not Communism,'" *NBC News*, April 19, 1959, www.nbcnews.com/meet-the-press/video/castro-in-1959-i-dont-hate-anybody-including-my-enemies-504767043668.
73. Pérez Jr., *Cuba in the American Imagination*, 248.
74. A book written by anti-Castro extremist Humberto Fontova collected a series of media coverage of Fidel Castro in a favorable light, but was written to show how media was duped by Fidel Castro. The book mostly proves that media had no idea what the revolution stood for and contains the usual historical revisionism of how beneficial US hegemony was, implying that Cubans had nothing to complain about. Fontova left Cuba as a five-year old and never returned. Humberto Fontova, *The*

Longest Romance: The Mainstream Media and Fidel Castro (New York: Encounter Books, 2013).

75. US Congress, Senate, Committee on Foreign Relations, Study Mission in the Caribbean Area: Report of Senator George D Aiken to the Committee on Foreign Relations, 85th Congress, 2nd session (Washington DC, 1958), 1 and 5.
76. Earl E.T. Smith, *The Fourth Floor: An Account of the Castro Communist Revolution* (New York: Random House, 1962), 158.
77. *New York Times*, February 26, 1957, 13.
78. This was said when Fidel Castro was in New York in April 1959, after President Eisenhower refused to meet him; he sent Vice-President Nixon. This was well before Cuba had any official contact with the Soviet Union.
79. Pérez Jr., *Cuba in the American Imagination*, 249.
80. Ibid.
81. Ibid.
82. Ibid., 251.
83. Ibid., 248.

2. *The Media Versus the Revolution*

1. Louis A. Pérez Jr., *Cuba in the American Imagination: Metaphor and the Imperial Ethos* (Chapel Hill, NC: University of North Carolina Press, 2008), 241.
2. Keith Bolender, *Voices From the Other Side: An Oral History of Terrorism Against Cuba* (London: Pluto Press, 2010), viii.
3. Pérez Jr., *Cuba in the American Imagination*, 249.
4. *New York Times*, April 9, 1960.
5. Keith Bolender, *Cuba Under Siege: American Policy, the Revolution and Its People* (Basingstoke: Palgrave Macmillan, 2013), 47.
6. Van Gosse, *Where the Boys Are: Cuba, Cold War America and the Making of a New Left* (London: Verso, 1993), 109.
7. Pérez Jr., *Cuba in the American Imagination*, 266.
8. "Cuba Democracy or Dictatorship?" *TIME Newsmagazine*, January 26, 1959, 41.
9. Pérez Jr., *Cuba in the American Imagination*, 223.
10. Ruby Hart Phillips, "Cuba: Island of Paradox," *New York Times*, October 29, 1961.
11. Pérez Jr., *Cuba in the American Imagination*, 223.
12. Herbert Matthews, "Old Order in Cuba is Threatened by Forces of an Internal Revolt," *New York Times*, February 26, 1957; also Herbert Matthews, "Castro Aims Reflect Character of Cuba," *New York Times*, January 18, 1959.
13. Anthony DePalma, *The Man who Invented Fidel: Castro, Cuba, and Herbert L. Matthews of the New York Times* (New York: Public Affairs 2007).
14. For more details, see "Fidel Castro: Times Coverage, 1957–1959," *New York Times*, https://archive.nytimes.com/www.nytimes.com/ref/world/

americas/CASTRO_ARCHIVE.html; and Herbert L. Matthews, "Old order in Cuba is Threatened by Forces of an Internal Revolt," *New York Times*, February 26, 1957, https://static01.nyt.com/packages/html/books/matthews/matthews022657.pdf.

15. Pérez Jr., *Cuba in the American Imagination*, 241.
16. Ibid., 241.
17. Ibid., 143.
18. Pensamiento de Fidel Castro, 1:5; Pérez Jr., *Cuba in the American Imagination*, 242.
19. Pérez Jr., *Cuba in the American Imagination*, 242.
20. Ibid., 250.
21. Lars Schoultz, *That Infernal Little Cuban Republic: The United States and the Cuban Revolution* (Chapel Hill, NC: University of North Carolina Press, 2009), 377.
22. Raymond Bonner, "The Agony of El Salvador," *New York Times*, February 22, 1981, www.nytimes.com/1981/02/22/magazine/the-agony-of-el-salvador.html.
23. See Tracey Eaton, Traceyeaton.com.
24. Ben Norton, "US Government Admits It's Making Fake Social Media Accounts to Spread Propaganda in Cuba," *The Real News*, August 27, 2018, https://therealnews.com/columns/us-government-admits-its-making-fake-social-media-accounts-to-spread-propaganda-in-cuba; and Rosa Miriam Elizalde, "US Uses Facebook to Spread Fake News About Cuba," *Walter Lippmann*, August 22, 2018, https://walterlippmann.com/fake-news-about-cuba-via-facebook/.
25. The company imposed the truck system on its workers, where they were forced to spend their earnings in the company run stores. It was a highly exploitive system that the government supported.
26. Aviva Chomsky, *A History of the Cuban Revolution*, (Chichester: Wiley-Blackwell, 2011), 72, note 16.
27. General assembly 626 (Vii) December 21, 1952.
28. Andrés Zaldívar Diéguez, *Blockade: The Longest Economic Siege in History* (Havana: Capitán San Luis, 2007), 38, citing *New York Times*, April 19, 1959.
29. Ibid., 51.
30. "Economic Embargo Timeline," www.historyofcuba.com/history/funfacts/embargo.htm, see 1992.
31. Known officially as the Cuban Liberty and Democratic Solidarity (LIBERTAD) Act of 1966, see www.congress.gov/bill/104th-congress/house-bill/927. That bill and the Torricelli Act were designed to tighten the economic embargo against Cuba after the fall of the Soviet Union, as well as setting out political conditions as to what US imposed changes Cuba had to agree to before ending the embargo.
32. Leon Neyfakh, "Cuba You Owe Us $7 Billion," *Boston Globe*, April 18, 2014, www.bostonglobe.com/ideas/2014/04/18/cuba-you-owe-billion/jHAufRfQJ9Bx24TuzQyBNO/story.html; see also Michael E. Miller, "Cuba Owes U.S. $7 Billion For 'Forgotten' Property Claims, Lawyers Propose 10% User Fee," *Miami New Times*, March 16, 2012, www.

miaminewtimes.com/news/cuba-owes-us-7-billion-for-forgotten-property-claims-lawyers-propose-10-user-fee-6521233.

33. Leon Neyfakh, "Cuba You Owe Us $7 Billion," *Boston Globe*, April 18, 2014.
34. Timothy Ashby, "U.S. Certified Claims Against Cuba: Legal Reality and Likely Settlement Mechanisms," *The University of Miami Inter-American Law Review* 40(3) (2009): 413–431, www.jstor.org/stable/25593625?seq=1#page_scan_tab_contents.
35. T.J. English, *Havana Nocturne: How the Mob Owned Cuba … and then Lost it to the Revolution* (New York: William Morrow, 2009).
36. Patrick Oppmann and Elywn Lopez, "U.S. Mobster's Heirs to Cuba: You Owe Us—So Pay Up," *CNN*, March 21, 2016, www.cnn.com/2016/03/21/americas/cuba-meyer-lansky/index.html.37.
37. "The Break with Cuba," *New York Times*, January 5, 1961.
38. Ibid.
39. See Introduction, for a pre- and post-revolution comparison.
40. Alan H. Luxenberg, "Did Eisenhower Push Castro into the Arms of the Soviets?" *Journal of Interamerican Studies and World Affairs* 30(1) (Spring 1988): 37–72.
41. "The Cuban Charges," *New York Times*, January 3, 1961.
42. Murray Marder, "Bay of Pigs Invasion was No Secret to Many," *Washington Post*, December 23, 1984.
43. David W. Dunlap, "1961 | The C.I.A. Readies a Cuban Invasion, and The Times Blinks," *New York Times*, December 26, 2014, www.nytimes.com/times-insider/2014/12/26/1961-the-c-i-a-readies-a-cuban-invasion-and-the-times-blinks/; the original article ran April 7, 1961.
44. Ibid.
45. *New York Times*, January 10, 1961.
46. Lars Schoultz, *That Infernal Little Cuban Republic: The United States and the Cuban Revolution* (Chapel Hill, NC: University of North Carolina Press), 146.
47. W. Joseph Campbell, "A Fiasco for the Press, Too: Error, Hype Marked Bay Of Pigs Reporting," *Media Myth Alert*, April 15, 2011, https://mediamythalert.wordpress.com/2011/04/15/a-fiasco-for-the-press-too-error-hype-marked-bay-of-pigs-reporting/.
48. Ibid.
49. Ibid.
50. Schoultz, *That Infernal Little Cuban Republic*, 165.
51. Luisa Yanez, "On Saturday, Bay of Pigs Invasion Veterans mark 50 Years Since Their Release," *Miami Herald*, December 20, 2012. Read more at: www.miamiherald.com/news/special-reports/bay-of-pigs/article1945659.html#storylink=cpy.
52. Interview of Manuel Yepe with author, June 2018.
53. Keith Bolender, *Cuba Under Siege: American Policy, the Revolution and Its People* (Basingstoke: Palgrave Macmillan, 2013).
54. Pérez Jr., *Cuba in the American Imagination*, 253.
55. Ibid.

56. Bill Keller, "Papers Show 1962 U.S. Plan Against Castro," *New York Times*, January 27, 1989, www.nytimes.com/1989/01/27/world/papers-show-1962-us-plan-against-castro.html.
57. Keith Bolender, *Cuba Under Siege: American Policy, the Revolution and Its People* (Basingstoke: Palgrave Macmillan, 2013).
58. Benjamin Schwartz, "The Real Cuban Missile Crisis," *The Atlantic*, January–February, 2013, www.theatlantic.com/magazine/archive/2013/01/the-real-cuban-missile-crisis/309190/.
59. Ibid.
60. "Coverage of the Cuban Missile Crisis," *Stallion of the Cimarron*, March 9, 2017, https://smber100.expressions.syr.edu/coverage-of-the-cuban-missile-crisis/.
61. "Document for October 22nd: Radio and Television Report to the American People on the Soviet Arms Buildup in Cuba, President's Reading Copy, October 22, 1962," *National Archives*, www.archives.gov/historical-docs/todays-doc/?dod-date=884.
62. *Washington Post*, Tuesday October 23, 1962.
63. Ed Cony, "If Cuban Invasion is Eventually Launched: Terrain Easy, but Castro Army Well Armed," *The Wall Street Journal*, October 23, 1962, 18.
64. "The Press—The Press and Foreign Policy Crises," *American Foreign Relations*, www.americanforeignrelations.com/O-W/The-Press-The-press-and-foreign-policy-crises.html.
65. Noam Chomsky, "Cuban Missile Crisis: How the US Played Russian Roulette with Nuclear War," *The Guardian*, October 15, 2012, www.theguardian.com/commentisfree/2012/oct/15/cuban-missile-crisis-russian-roulette.
66. "Operation Mongoose," *PBS*, www.pbs.org/wgbh/americanexperience/features/rfk-operation-mongoose.
67. For a complete history, see Bolender, *Voices from the Other Side*.
68. Ann Louise Bardach and Larry Rohter, "A BOMBERS TALE: Taking Aim at Castro; Key Cuba Foe Claims Exiles' Baking," *New York Times*, July 12, 1998, www.nytimes.com/1998/07/12/world/a-bombers-tale-taking-aim-at-castro-key-cuba-foe-claims-exiles-backing.html. The articles also stated that Carriles was being financed by the CANF, one of the most notorious political groups opposed to Castro, established under Reagan administration; see also "Outrage and Double Standards: The Lockerbie and Cubana Airline Bombings," *Council on Hemispheric Affairs*, November 3, 2009, www.coha.org/outrage-double-standards-and-lockerbie-and-cubana-airlines%E2%80%99-bombings/.
69. "Outrage and Double Standards: The Lockerbie and Cubana Airline Bombings," *Council on Hemispheric Affairs*, November 3, 2009.
70. Tim Weiner, "Cuban Exile Could Test U.S. Definition of Terrorist," *New York Times*, May 9, 2005, www.nytimes.com/2005/05/09/us/cuban-exile-could-test-us-definition-of-terrorist.html.
71. Ann Louise Bardach, "Our Man's in Miami: Patriot or Terrorist?" *Washington Post*, www.washingtonpost.com/wp-dyn/articles/A58297-2005Apr16.html?noredirect=on Sunday, April 17, 2005, B03.

72. Michael A. Fletcher, "U.S. Asylum Sought by Cuban Tied to Terror Cases," *Washington Post*, April 13, 2005, A02.
73. Nora Gómez Torres and Glenn Garvin, "Anti-Castro Militant Posada Carriles is Dead at 90," *Miami Herald*, May 23, 2018,www.miamiherald.com/news/nation-world/world/americas/cuba/article211726514.html; "Luis Posada Carriles, Who Waged Quest to Oust Castro Dies at 90," *New York Times*, May 23, 2018, www.nytimes.com/2018/05/23/obituaries/luis-posada-carriles-castro-foe-dies-at-90.html.
74. "Luis Posada Carriles, Who Waged Quest to Oust Castro, Dies at 90," *New York Times*, May 23, 2018.
75. Ibid.
76. Ibid.
77. "Orlando Bosch, Militant Cuban Exile, Dies in Miami Aged 84," *The Guardian*, April 28, 2011, www.theguardian.com/world/2011/apr/28/orlando-bosch-cuban-exile-dies.
78. T. Rees Shapiro, "Orlando Bosch, Who Battled Castro With Bazookas and Sabotage Dies at 84," *Washington Post*, April 30, 2011.
79. "Orlando Bosch, Militant Cuban Exile, Dies in Miami Aged 84," *The Guardian*, April 28, 2011.
80. For the details of the media coverage of Cuban Five, see Chapter 3.
81. Andres Oppenheimer, *Castro's Final Hour: The Secret Story Behind the Coming Downfall of Communist Cuba* (New York: Touchstone, 1993).
82. Saul Landau, "A Double Standard on Terrorism," in *These Times* magazine, March 4, 2002, www.thirdworldtraveler.com/Terrorism/Double_Standard.html.
83. Interview with author, June 2013.
84. "Retired Spy in Brothers to the Rescue Case Lives in Obscurity," *Florida Center for Investigative Reporting*, October 2, 2012, https://fcir.org/2012/10/02/retired-spy-in-brothers-to-the-rescue-case-lives-in-obscurity/.
85. Stephen Kimber, *What Lies Across the Water: The Real Story of the Cuban Five* (Winnipeg: Fernwood Publishing, 2013).
86. "Barbara Crossette, "U.S. Says Cubans Knew They Fired on Civilian Planes," *New York Times*, February 28, 1996, www.nytimes.com/1996/02/28/world/us-says-cubans-knew-they-fired-on-civilian-planes.html.
87. "Civilian U.S. Planes Shot Down Near Cuba," *CNN*, February 24, 1996, www.cnn.com/US/9602/cuba_shootdown/.
88. "Shoot Down of Brothers to the Rescue Aircraft Remembered on 20th Anniversary," February 24, 2016, www.nbcmiami.com/news/local/Shoot-Down-of-Brothers-to-the-Rescue-20th-Anniversary-369957221.html.
89. William Branigin, "FAA Revokes Cuban Exile's Pilot's Permit," *Washington Post*, May 17, 1996, www.washingtonpost.com/archive/politics/1996/05/17/faa-revokes-cuban-exiles-pilots-permit.
90. Bill Kress, "'Brothers to the Rescue' Leader Honored by South Miami Commission with Street-Sign Dedication," *Miami's Community Newspapers*, January 10, 2018, http://communitynewspapers.com/

south-miami-featured/brothers-to-the-rescue-leader-honored-by-south-miami-commission-at-street-sign-dedication/.

91. Interview of Roberto Alarcón with the author, 2012.
92. Previously, the embargo was under presidential authority that could be eliminated by a Presidential order. Now it takes the full support of Congress to end the embargo.
93. Jerry Gray, "President Agrees to Touch New set of Curbs on Cuba," *New York Times*, February 29, 1996, www.nytimes.com/1996/02/29/world/president-agrees-to-tough-new-set-of-curbs-on-cuba.html; and "Civilian U.S. Planes Shot Down Near Cuba," *CNN*, February 24, 1996.

3. *The Case of the Cuban Five*

1. A May 2005 legal analysis of the Cuban Five case conducted by the United Nation's Human Rights Commission proclaimed the original trial "did not take place in the climate of objectivity and impartiality" required for fair trials. The Commission's report called for a new trial. "The Case of the 'Cuban Five'," *Amnesty International*, www.amnesty.org/download/Documents/36000/amr510932010en.pdf.
2. For more on this, see Chapter 2.
3. Noam Chomsky, "Cuban Missile Crisis: How the US Played Russian Roulette with Nuclear War," *The Guardian*, October 15, 2012, www.theguardian.com/commentisfree/2012/oct/15/cuban-missile-crisis-russian-roulette.
4. Stephen Kimber, *What Lies Across the Water: The Real Story of the Cuban Five* (Winnipeg: Fernwood Publishing, 2013).
5. Interview of Gloria LaRiva with the author, May 2016.
6. Linn Washington, jr., "The Federal Government Paid Journalists to Sabotage Trial," *Counterpunch*, June 4, 2010, www.counterpunch.org/2010/06/04/the-federal-government-paid-journalists-to-sabotage-trial/.
7. "Miami Herald Publisher Resigns Over Cuba Scandal," *CBC*, October 4, 2006, www.cbc.ca/news/entertainment/miami-herald-publisher-resigns-over-cuba-scandal-1.570957.
8. Abby Goodnough, "US Paid 10 Journalists for Anti-Castro Reports," *New York Times*, September 9, 2006, www.nytimes.com/2006/09/09/washington/09cuba.
9. "Wilfredo Cancio Isla," *Reporters for Hire*, April 19, 2001, www.reportersforhire.org/reporters/repoter-wilfredo-cancio-isla.html.
10. Ibid.
11. Interview of Gerardo Hernández with the author, May 2015.
12. "Wilfredo Cancio Isla," *Reporters for Hire*.
13. For details on the shoot down, see Chapter 2.
14. Linn Washington, jr., "The Federal Government Paid Journalists to Sabotage Trial," *Counterpunch*, June 4, 2010.
15. Ibid.
16. Julio Estorino, "Espionage and Indifference," *Diario Las Américas*, January 5, 2001.

17. "Wilfredo Cancio Isla," *Reporters for Hire.*
18. Ariel Remos, "Fidel Castro Planned the Assassination of (Anti-Revolutionary Exile) Jesus Cruza Flor in the U.S.A," *Diario Las Américas*, January 19, 2001.
19. Ibid.
20. Ibid.
21. "Journalists Fired for Taking Gov't Money," *The Oklahoman*, September 9, 2006, https://newsok.com/article/2844691/journalists-fired-for-taking-govt-money.
22. Linn Washington, jr., "The Federal Government Paid Journalists to Sabotage Trial," *Counterpunch*, June 4, 2010.
23. "Press Conference with Lawyer Martin Garbus on the New Legal Step in the Case of the Cuban Five," *Antiterroristas*, www.antiterroristas.cu/en/press-conference-lawyer-martin-garbus-new-legal-step-case-cuban-five.
24. Ibid.
25. Ibid.
26. Danny Glover and Saul Landau, "A Move to Free the Cuban Five," Institute for Policy Studies, August 27, 2012, https://ips-dc.org/a_move_to_free_the_cuban_five/.
27. Elián González, more on his case below.
28. Jeffrey Huling, "Corporate Media Bias & the Case of the Cuban Five," *Project Censored*, May 2, 2010, http://projectcensored.org/corporate-media-bias-the-case-of-the-cuban-five/.
29. Ibid.
30. Ibid.
31. Ibid.
32. Ibid.
33. "Cubans Jailed in U.S. as Spies are Hailed at Home as Heroes," *People's World*, June 4, 2006, www.peoplesworld.org/article/cubans-jailed-in-u-s-as-spies-are-hailed-at-home-as-heroes/.
34. Ibid.
35. Jeffrey Huling, "Corporate Media Bias & the Case of the Cuban Five," *Project Censored*, May 2, 2010, https://projectcensored.org/corporate-media-bias-the-case-of-the-cuban-five/.
36. Mimi Whitefield, "If You're a Cuba Activist and the FBI Comes Knocking on Your Door, Here's What They Might Want to Know," *Miami Herald*, September 21, 2018, http://amp.miamiherald.com/latest-news/article218796335.html.
37. Interviews of Gerardo Hernández with the author, 2016 and 2018.
38. See Chapter 2.
39. Interview of Gerardo Hernández with the author, May 2016.
40. Ibid.
41. Ibid.
42. Ibid.
43. Interview of Fernando González with the author, May, 2016.
44. Ibid.
45. Ibid.
46. Interview of René González with the author, May 2016.

47. Ibid.
48. The Cuban Liberty and Democratic Solidarity Act (known as Helms–Burton Act) set up congressional controls for the American government's regime change attempts, setting out who can and cannot become the new Cuban president. It also enacted tougher economic restrictions. "Cuban Liberty and Democratic Solidarity (Libertad) Act of 1996," www.treasury.gov/resource-center/sanctions/documents/libertad.pdf.
49. "About Cuba," USAID, www.usaid.gov/cuba.
50. Reported from: "USAID Contractor: Duty to Intervene in Cuba," *Along the Malecón*, October 4, 2014, https://alongthemalecon.blogspot.com/2014/10/usaid-contractor-duty-to-intervene-in.html.
51. John Stoehr, "The Real Story Behind Alan Gross's Work in Cuba," *The Hill*, January 27, 2015, https://thehill.com/blogs/pundits-blog/international/230794-the-real-story-behind-alan-grosss-work-in-cuba.
52. Keith Bolender, *Cuba Under Siege: American Policy, the Revolution and Its People* (Basingstoke: Palgrave Macmillan, 2013).
53. Ibid.
54. Scott Pelley, "The Last Prisoner of the Cold War," *60 Minutes*, November 29, 2015, www.cbsnews.com/news/last-prisoner-cuba-alan-gross-60-minutes/.
55. Mimi Whitefield, "Settlement Results in $3.2 Million Check for Alan Gross," *Miami Herald*, December 23, 2014, www.miamiherald.com/news/nation-world/world/americas/cuba/article4901220.html.
56. Scott Pelley, "The Last Prisoner of the Cold War," *60 Minutes*, November 29, 2015.
57. Keith Bolender, *Cuba Under Siege: American Policy, the Revolution and Its People* (Basingstoke: Palgrave Macmillan, 2013), 118.
58. Ibid.
59. Ibid
60. Julie Hershfeld Davis, "Alan P. Gross Gains the Freedom From Cuba He Thought Would Never Come," *New York Times*, December 17, 2014, www.nytimes.com/2014/12/18/world/americas/alan-p-gross-gains-the-freedom-from-cuba-he-thought-would-never-come.html. Helms Burton Act tightened the embargo against Cuba in 1996, for more, see Chapter 2.
61. Ibid.
62. Report written by Lisa Tozzi, ran at time of incident. Tozzi is a Manhattan-based freelance writer, who frequently covers politics and immigration issues. Lisa Tozzi, "Castro Wants the Kid Back," *FAIR*, March 1, 2000, http://fair.org/extra/castro-wants-the-kid-back/.
63. Ibid.
64. Joshua Cooper Ramo, *TIME*, January 17, 2000.
65. Staff reporter, "Cuban Moms Tell How Their Kids Grow Up," *Miami Herald*, December 15, 1999.
66. Interview of Heriberto Nicolás with the author, June 2018.
67. Lisa Tozzi, "Castro Wants the Kid Back," *FAIR*, March 1, 2000.
68. Ibid.
69. Ibid.
70. Ibid.

71. Karen DeYoung, "Rare Act of Congress is Planned for Elian," *Washington Post*, January 16, 2000, A03.
72. Lisa Tozzi, "Castro Wants the Kid Back," *FAIR*, March 1, 2000.
73. Victorino Matus, "The Media Mob vs. Cuban-Americans," *The Weekly Standard*, May 8, 2000, www.weeklystandard.com/victorino-matus/the-media-mob-vs-cuban-americans.
74. Ibid.
75. Ibid.
76. Ibid.
77. "Elian Goes Home," *New York Times*, June 29, 2000, www.nytimes.com/2000/06/29/opinion/elian-goes-home.html. There is also the case to be made that Elián helped elect George W. Bush in 2000. Elián's return under President Clinton galvanized the Cuban-American community to vote Republican in even larger numbers, giving Florida to Bush after the vote counting controversy was settled. With Florida, Bush was able to capture the White House.

4. The Media Opens and Closes Against Cuba

1. To paraphrase the more common saying "Politics ends at waters edge." The first recorded incident of this "politics" saying came from Senator Arthur Vandenburg in 1948 during the passing of the Vanderburg Resolution, see https://en.wikipedia.org/wiki/Vandenberg_resolution.
2. Carol E. Lee, Jay Solomon and José de Córdoba, "U.S. Restores Cuba Ties in Historic Deal," *Wall Street Journal*, updated December 17, 2014, www.wsj.com/articles/obama-moves-to-normalize-relations-with-cuba-1418825981; see also "Statement by the President on Cuba Policy Changes," The White House Office of the Press Secretary, December 17, 2014, www.whitehouse.gov/the-press-office/2014/12/17/statement-president-cuba-policy-changes.
3. Philip Peters, "Obama's Cuba Doctrine," *The American Conservative*, January 26, 2017, www.theamericanconservative.com/articles/obamas-cuba-doctrine/.
4. "Cuba Central News Brief: Obama's Imprint on Cuba Policy: Historic. More than Rum & Cigars. More Left to Do," *Democracy in Americas*, October 14, 2016, http://democracyinamericas.org/cuba-central-news-brief-obamas-imprint-on-cuba-policy-historic-more-than-rum-cigars-more-left-to-do/.
5. Email communication with Karen Lee Wald, June 2016.
6. Ibid.
7. Tracey Eaton, "State Department Requests More Cuba Funds," *Along the Malecón*, May 6, 2015, https://alongthemalecon.blogspot.com/2015/05/state-department-requests-more-cuba.html. These programs standardly target those Cubans opposed to the government in the attempt to create an artificial opposition, tactics the USA has conducted in various other countries.
8. Frances Robles, "Obama Visits Cuba: Obama Spends Almost 2 Hours With Cuban Dissidents," *New York Times*, March 22, 2016, www.

nytimes.com/interactive/projects/cp/international/obama-in-cuba; and Dan Roberts, "Obama Lands in Cuba as First US President to Visit in Nearly a Century," *The Guardian*, March 21, 2016, www.theguardian.com/world/2016/mar/20/barack-obama-cuba-visit-us-politics-shift-public-opinion-diplomacy.

9. Maya Rhodan, "President Obama Arrives in Cuba," *TIME*, March 20, 2016, https://time.com/4265383/barack-obama-cuba-visit/.
10. Editorial Board, "Obama's Historic Trip to Cuba: Our View," *USA Today*, March 20, 2016, www.usatoday.com/story/opinion/2016/03/20/cuba-president-obama-fidel-castro-raul-castro-editorials-debates/81938512/.
11. The UN votes every year to call for an end to the embargo, usually with only two opposing votes, the USA and Israel. The Cuban government presents a detailed report outlining the harm, most often completely ignored by mainstream media. See "Necessity of Ending the Economic, Commercial and Financial Embargo Imposed by the United States of America Against Cuba," The General Assembly of the United Nations, www.un.org/en/ga/62/plenary/cuba/bkg.shtml; and "UN General Assembly Renews Long-Standing Call for End to US Embargo Against Cuba," *UN News*, November 1, 2018, https://news.un.org/en/story/2018/11/1024672.
12. Dan Roberts, "Obama Lands in Cuba as First US President to Visit in Nearly a Century," *The Guardian*, March 20, 2016.
13. Matt Peppe, "Obama's Sanctimonious Human Rights Argument Against Cuba," *Counterpunch*, September 23, 2014, www.counterpunch.org/2014/09/23/obamas-sanctimonious-human-rights-argument-against-cuba.
14. Robert Sandels and Nelson P. Valdés, "Cuba Détente," *Counterpunch*, January 28, 2015, www.counterpunch.org/2015/01/28/cuba-detente/.
15. Ibid.
16. Matt Peppe, "Obama's Sanctimonious Human Rights Argument Against Cuba," *Counterpunch*, September 23, 2014, www.counterpunch.org/2014/09/23/obamas-sanctimonious-human-rights-argument-against-cuba/.
17. Ibid.
18. US support for dictators in Central and South America and Indonesia, in the 1960s through the 1980s, overturning democratically elected governments in Iran and Guatemala, and support for the worst regimes around the world has been a hallmark of American foreign policy, supported by the media. Glenn Greenwald, "Trump's Amoral Saudi Statement is a Pure Expression of Decades-Old 'U.S. Values' and Foreign Policy Orthodoxies," *The Intercept*, November 21, 2018, https://theintercept.com/2018/11/21/trumps-amoral-saudi-statement-is-a-pure-and-honest-expression-of-decades-old-u-s-values-and-foreign-policy-orthodoxies.
19. Fidel Castro Ruz, "Brother Obama," *Granma*, March 28, 2016, http://en.granma.cu/cuba/2016-03-28/brother-obama.
20. Patrick Oppmann, "Fidel Castro Blasts Obama's Trip: Cuba Doesn't Need 'Empire' for Anything," *CNN*, March 28, 2016, www.cnn.

com/2016/03/28/politics/cuba-fidel-castro-blasts-obama-trip/index.html.
21. Ibid.
22. Ben Norton, "The U.S. has Terrorized Cuba for Over 50 years—Fidel Castro is Right to be Wary of Obama's Claims," *Salon*, March 30, 2016, www.salon.com/2016/03/30/the_u_s_has_menaced_cuba_for_over_50_years_fidel_castro_is_right_to_be_wary_of_obamas_claims/.
23. See Chapter 5.
24. Maria Puente, "Beyonce and Jay Z Trip to Cuba was Legal, say Feds," *USA Today*, August 20, 2014, www.usatoday.com/story/life/music/2014/.../beyonce...cuba.../14359477/.
25. Ted Francis, "Cuba's Crumbling Infrastructure No Match for Might of Irma," *The Guardian*, September 13, 2017, www.theguardian.com/world/2017/sep/13/hurricane-irma-cuba-havana-flooding-government-response.
26. Editorial Board, "The Shifting Politics of Cuba Policy," *New York Times*, October 25, 2014.
27. Interview of Manuel Yepe with the author, June 2018.
28. "Inside Fidel Castro's Cuba—and his Legacy," *TIME*, November 26, 2016.
29. Editorial Board, "Obama Should End the Embargo on Cuba," *New York Times*, October 14, 2014.
30. Ibid.
31. See Chapter 3.
32. Interview of Fernando González with the author, May 2016.
33. Ibid.
34. Other articles: Ernesto Londoño, "Still Pondering U.S.–Cuba Relations," *New York Times*, October 14, 2014; Editorial Board, "The Shifting Politics of Cuba Policy," *New York Times*, October 25, 2014; and Editorial Board, "A Prisoner Swap With Cuba," *New York Times*, November 2, 2014.
35. "Did Editorials Influence Obama's Decision to Normalize Relations With Cuba?" *Fresh Air*, National Public Radio, January 7, 2015, www.npr.org/2015/01/07/375628523/did-editorials-influence-obamas-decision-to-normalize-relations-with-cuba.
36. Ibid.
37. Editorial Board, "Obama Should End the Embargo on Cuba," *New York Times*, October 11, 2014.
38. Ibid.
39. "Did Editorials Influence Obama's Decision to Normalize Relations With Cuba?" *Fresh Air*, National Public Radio, January 7, 2015.
40. Ibid.
41. Marie Sanz, "The Persistent Advocate: *The New York Times*' Editorials and the Normalization of U.S. Ties with Cuba," Shorenstein Center, December 16, 2015, https://shorensteincenter.org/new-york-times-editorials-us-cuba-relations-marie-sanz/.
42. The Act was designed to tighten the embargo after the shoot down of the Brothers to the Rescue planes. For more details, see Chapter 3.

43. "Did Editorials Influence Obama's Decision to Normalize Relations With Cuba?" *Fresh Air*, National Public Radio, January 7, 2015.
44. Ibid.
45. Marc Frank, "Cuba's Proposed New Constitution: What Will Change," *Reuters*, August 13, 2018, www.reuters.com/article/us-cuba-constitution-explainer/cubas-proposed-new-constitution-what-will-change-idUSKBN1KY1UC.
46. "Constitución de la República de Cuba," *Granma*, www.granma.cu/file/pdf/gaceta/Nueva Constitución 240 KB-1.pdf.
47. Dianet Doimeadios Guerrero, Edilberto Carmona Tamayo and Irene Pérez, "Cuba ratifica la nueva Constitución con el 86.85% de los votos emitidos, según datos preliminares (+ Infografía)," *Cuba Debate*, February 25, 2019, www.cubadebate.cu/noticias/2019/02/25/cuba-constitucion-referendo-resultados.
48. Nora Gómez Torres, "Cuba's Proposed New Constitution is a 'Fraud,' Dissidents Say," *Miami Herald*, July 31, 2018, www.miamiherald.com/news/nation-world/world/americas/cuba/article215832635.html#storylink=cpy.
49. Sarah Marsh, "Cuban Artists Urge Revision of Decree Feared to Hike Censorship," *Reuters*, October 31, 2018, www.reuters.com/article/us-cuba-art/cuban-artists-urge-revision-of-decree-feared-to-hike-censorship-idUSKCN1N51GV.
50. Marie Sanz, "The Persistent Advocate: *The New York Times*' Editorials and the Normalization of U.S. Ties with Cuba," Shorenstein Center, December 16, 2015.
51. "Cuba Should Not be Rewarded for Denying Freedom to its People," *Washington Post*, October 20, 2014, www.washingtonpost.com/opinions/cuba-should-not-be-rewarded-for-denying-freedom-to-its-people/2014/10/20/753b7bd8-588f-11e4-b812-38518ae74c67_story.html?utm_term=.f59e7e01956a.
52. Ibid.
53. "The Agenda in Cuba" editorial, *Miami Herald*, 2014, www.miamiherald.com/opinion/editorials/article8105853.html.
54. Max J. Castro, "Miami Herald Sees U.S.–Cuba Talks Through a Glass Darkly," *Progreso Weekly*, January 27, 2015, http://progresoweekly.us/miami-herald-sees-u-s-cuba-talks-glass-darkly/.
55. Ibid.
56. "The Persistent Advocate: *The New York Times*' Editorials and the Normalization of U.S. Ties with Cuba," Shorenstein Center, December 16, 2015.
57. Rory Carroll, "Fidel Castro's Dark Legacy: Abuses, Draconian Rule and 'Ruthless Suppression,'" *The Guardian*, November 27, 2016, www.theguardian.com/world/2016/nov/27/fidel-castro-dictator-legacy-abuses.
58. NBC, no friend to Castro, calculated no more than 200 of the worst elements were given the death penalty. "Castro Orders Executions of Batista Loyalists," *Universal Newsreel*, January 1, 1959. NBC Learn, January 17, 2015, www.nbclearn.com/portal/site/k-12/flatview?cuecard=1209. Fidel Castro said he had to have public executions,

otherwise there would be riots in the streets with people taking justice in their own hands against Batista henchmen.

59. Cuba Institute for Friendship With the People—an organization to develop positive relationships with support groups internationally.
60. Interview of Iliana García Giraldino with the author, June 2018.
61. Ibid.
62. Salim Lamrani, "Cuba and the Number of 'Political Prisoners,'" *Cuba Solidarity Campaign*, Autumn, 2010, https://cuba-solidarity.org.uk/cubasi/article/125/cuba-and-the-number-of-ldquopolitical-prisonersrdquo.
63. Robert Sandels and Nelson P. Valdés, "Cuba Détente," *Counterpunch*, January 28, 2015, www.counterpunch.org/2015/01/28/cuba-detente/.
64. Ibid.
65. Rosi DiManno, "Castro Took a Country Hostage—His Own: DiManno," *Toronto Star*, December 4, 2016, www.thestar.com/news/gta/2016/12/04/castro-took-a-country-hostage-his-own-dimanno.html.
66. Ibid.
67. For a complete history of Cuba's internationalism in Africa, as well as for an examination of how Cuba chartered a different foreign policy path from the Soviet Union, see Piero Gleijeses, *Visions of Freedom* (Chapel Hill, NC: University of North Carolina Press, 2013).
68. Interview of Manuel Alberto García with the author, 2016.
69. Stephen Kimber, "Media Coverage of Fidel Castro's Death has been Abysmally One-Sided," *Huffington Post*, December 2, 2016, www.huffingtonpost.ca/stephen-kimber/fidel-castro-death_b_13371596.html.
70. Ibid.
71. J. Patrice McSherry, "Operation Condor: Deciphering the U.S. Role," *Global Policy Forum*, July 2001, www.globalpolicy.org/component/content/article/168/28173.html. Operation Condor was a US-backed terror program that was running while Bush was head of the CIA. For a report on how *Newsweek* squashed a story regarding the program and Bush's involvement, see Robert Parry, "George H.W. Bush, the CIA and a Case of State-Sponsored Terrorism," *Consortium News*, December 1, 2018, https://consortiumnews.com/2018/12/01/george-h-w-bush-the-cia-and-a-case-of-state-sponsored-terrorism/.
72. "George Bush, 41st President, Dies at 94," *New York Times*, November 30, 2018, www.nytimes.com/2018/11/30/us/politics/george-hw-bush-dies.html.
73. The independent media was able to present the other side of Bush Sr., including a scathing article by Michael I. Niman, "I Will Not Speak Kindly of the Dead: Bush Was Detestable," *Truthout*, December 4, 2018, https://truthout.org/articles/i-will-not-speak-kindly-of-the-dead-bush-was-detestable/. It has always been up to the non-mainstream media to provide a counterpoint to the corporate propaganda.
74. Rachel Dicker, "Donald Trump's #LittleMarco Is the Internet's New Favorite Thing," *U.S. News*, March 4, 2016, www.usnews.com/news/articles/2016-03-04/donald-trump-called-marco-rubio-little-marco-at-the-gop-debate-and-twitter-went-crazy.

75. Patricia Mazzei, "In Miami, Trump Toughens Obama Cuba Policy 'Like I promised,'" *Miami Herald*, June 16, 2017, www.miamiherald.com/news/nation-world/world/americas/cuba/article156579409.html.
76. Jon Lee Anderson, "As Castro Prepares to Leave Office, Trump's Cuba Policy Is a Road to Nowhere," *The New Yorker*, March 18, 2018, www.newyorker.com/news/daily-comment/reasons-why-trump-should-change-cuba-policy-as-castro-prepares-to-leave-office; Alan Gomez, "Trump Cracks Down on US Business and Travel to Cuba Here's What's Happening," *USA Today*, November 8, 2017, www.usatoday.com/story/news/world/2017/11/08/trump-cracks-down-u-s-business-and-travel-cuba/843419001/; and Dan Merica, "Trump Unviels New restrictions on Travel, Business with Cuba," *CNN*, June 16, 2017, www.cnn.com/2017/06/16/politics/trump-cuba-policy/index.html.
77. Jon Lee Anderson, "As Castro Prepares to Leave Office, Trump's Cuba Policy Is a Road to Nowhere," *The New Yorker*, March 18, 2018.
78. Ibid.
79. Mimi Whitefield, "Trump's New Cuba Policy is Too Much for Some, Not Enough for Others," *Miami Herald*, June 16, 2017, www.miamiherald.com/news/nation-world/world/americas/cuba/article156676309.html.
80. The latest data says that there have been close to 10 percent less American visitors to Cuba since Trump; "Summary of New Restricted Entities and Subentities Associated With Cuba as of November 15, 2018," https://uy.usembassy.gov/state-department-updates-the-cuba-restricted-list/.
81. For more on Helms–Burton Act, see Chapter 3.
82. Frances Robles, "In Cuba, Carnival Cruise Ships Have Been Using Stolen Ports, Original Owners Say," *New York Times*, May 2, 2019, www.nytimes.com/2019/05/02/us/cuba-lawsuit-carnival-cruise-line.html.
83. Joshua Cho, "The Atlantic Illustrates Everything That's Wrong With Media Coverage of Venezuela Sanctions," *FAIR*, May 6, 2009, https://fair.org/home/the-atlantic-illustrates-everything-thats-wrong-with-media-coverage-of-venezuela-sanctions/?awt_l=LEAyG&awt_m=hoeSPn4haIR._TQ.
84. Katherine LaGrave, "All the New Cuba Travel Restrictions Explained," *Conde Naste Traveler*, April 18, 2019, www.cntraveler.com/story/travel-to-cuba-the-new-restrictions-explained.
85. Patricia Mazzei, "In Miami, Trump Toughens Cuba Policy 'Like I Promised,'" *Miami Herald*, June 16, 2017, www.miamiherald.com/news/nation-world/world/americas/cuba/article156579409.html#storylink=cpy.
86. Anthony Faiola, "In Cuba the Great American Tourist Boom Goes Bust," *Washington Post*, May 11, 2018, www.washingtonpost.com/incuba the great American tourist boom goes bust.
87. Vicki Huddleston, "Trump is Returning Cuba Policy to the Cold War," *New York Times*, November 21, 2017.
88. Ibid.
89. Email correspondence with Karen Lee Wald, May 2018.

90. Nick Miroff, "Trump's Cuba Policy Tries to Redefine 'Good' U.S. Tourism. That Includes Putting Visitors Back on Tour Buses," *Washington Post*, June 17, 2017, www.washingtonpost.com/world/trumps-cuba-policy-tries-to-redefine-good-us-tourism-it-might-be-just-what-the-islands-rulers-want-too/2017/06/17/67fab65e-504f-11e7-b74e-0d2785d3083d_story.html?utm_term=.5760f46be78a.
91. Leah Thomas, "Can Americans Still Visit Cuba in 2018?" *Newsweek*, December 16, 2017, www.newsweek.com/can-americans-still-visit-cuba-2018-748696.
92. Interview with author at Hotel Nacional, June 2018. The two did not want their names used "We took time off from work, but I don't want my boss to know where I am."
93. Alexandra Talty, "Yes, Americans Can Still Travel To Cuba," *Forbes*, April 23, 2018, www.forbes.com/sites/alexandratalty/2018/04/23/yes-you-can-still-travel-to-cuba/#79b7731c378d.
94. Ibid.
95. Richard D'Ambrosio, "Some Media Continue to Get Travel to Cuba Wrong," *Travel Market Report*, April 30, 2018, www.travelmarketreport.com/articles/Some-Media-Continue-to-Get-Travel-to-Cuba-Wrong.
96. Many of the diplomats were later revealed to be CIA agents acting as undercover spies in Cuba. Peter Kornbluh, "What the US Government Is Not Telling You About Those 'Sonic Attacks' in Cuba," *The Nation*, March 7, 2018, www.thenation.com/article/what-the-us-government-is-not-telling-you-about-those-sonic-attacks-in-cuba/. The Canadian government also decided to cut back on its embassy staff in Cuba after another incident in early 2019.
97. They now have to travel to developing countries, at considerable expense, to access US embassy services including travel visas. As of May 2019, the Canadian embassy in Havana also temporarily stopped processing visas for Cuban visitors, following the reduction of staff due to the "sonic attack" controversy.
98. Tracy Wilkinson, "A Year After Trump Reversed Obama's Opening to Cuba, the U.S. is Sitting Out Havana's Political Revamp," *LA Times*, June 22, 2018, www.latimes.com/nation/la-na-pol-us-cuba-20180622-story.html.
99. Peter Dockrill, "Those 'Sonic Attack' Victims are Actually Experiencing Mass Hysteria, Expert Claims," *Science Alert*, July 3, 2018, www.sciencealert.com/sonic-attack-victims-actually-experiencing-mass-hysteria-expert-claims-psychogenic-illness-delusions-robert-bartholomew.
100. "The Sounds That Haunted U.S. Diplomats in Cuba? Lovelorn Crickets, Scientists Say," *New York Times*, January 4, 2019, www.nytimes.com/2019/01/04/science/sonic-attack-cuba-crickets.html.
101. Peter Dockrill, "Those 'Sonic Attack' Victims Are Actually Experiencing Mass Hysteria, Expert Claims," *Science Alert*, July 3, 2018.
102. Ibid.
103. Vicki Huddleston, "Trump is Returning Cuba Policy to the Cold War," *New York Times*, November 21, 2017, www.nytimes.com/2017/11/21/opinion/trump-cuba.html.

104. Ibid.
105. Alex Ballingall, "Dog Poisonings, Sex Propositions: Canada's Man in Havana Remembers the Cold War Weirdness," *Toronto Star*, April 20, 2018, www.thestar.com/news/canada/2018/04/20/dog-poisonings-sex-propositions-canadas-man-in-havana-remembers-the-cold-war-weirdness.html.
106. W.T. Whitney Jr., "Sonic Mystery Continues, Trump Administration Heaps More Abuse on Cuba," *People's World*, September 18, 2018, www.peoplesworld.org/article/sonic-mystery-continues-trump-administration-heaps-more-abuse-on-cuba/; see also Peter Dockrill, "Those 'Sonic Attack' Victims Are Actually Experiencing Mass Hysteria, Expert Claims," *Science Alter*, July 3, 2018.
107. Michael Weissenstein, "US Senator Says No Evidence of 'Sonic Attacks' in Cuba," *Associated Press*, updated January 6, 2018, www.apnews.com/ad203770ca5044db8eef17fffb840a91.
108. Vicki Huddleston, "Trump is Returning Cuba Policy to the Cold War," *New York Times*, November 21, 2017.
109. Julian Borger and Philip Jaekl, "Mass Hysteria May Explain 'Sonic Attacks' in Cuba Say Top Neurologists," *The Guardian*, October 12, 2017, www.theguardian.com/world/2017/oct/12/cuba-mass-hysteria-sonic-attacks-neurologists.
110. "Sonic Attacks—Happened Same in China and How did US Respond?" *Cuba Triangle*, May 23, 2018, http://cubantriangle.blogspot.com/.

5. *Future Coverage*

1. Louis A. Pérez Jr., *Cuba in the American Imagination: Metaphor and the Imperial Ethos* (Chapel Hill, NC: University of North Carolina Press, 2008), 253, citing *New York Times*, April 23, 1961.
2. Pérez Jr., *Cuba in the American Imagination*, 245.
3. Karen Lee Wald email blog, January 5, 2019.
4. For a more detailed examination, see the Introduction.
5. Patrick Luciani, "How Cuba was Destroyed," *Financial Post*, March 1, 2016, https://business.financialpost.com/opinion/how-cuba-was-destroyed.
6. Heberprot-P is saving thousands from diabetes-related amputations, see "Cuban Drug Heberprot-P Patented in Over 30 Countries," *Radio Cadena Agramonte*, June 30, 2014, www.cadenagramonte.cu/english/show/articles/18680:cuban-drug-heberprot-p-patented-in-over-30-nations.
7. Mary Murray, "Cubans Developing Therapy for Diabetic Ulcers," *NBC News*, January 11, 2006, www.nbcnews.com/id/10777359/ns/world_news-americas/t/cubans-developing-therapy-diabetic-ulcers/#.XBUqP2l7nIU.
8. Janine Jackson, "'These Sanctions Amount to Collective Punishment Against the Entire Iranian Population,'" *FAIR*, May 2, 2019, https://fair.org/home/these-sanctions-amount-to-collective-punishment-against-the-entire-iranian-population/.

9. Jim Hightower, "The First Amendment is Meaningless if Wall Street Destroys the Press," *Truth Dig*, December 2, 2018, www.truthdig.com/articles/the-first-amendment-is-meaningless-if-wall-street-destroys-our-press/.
10. Jim Hightower, "Free the Free Press from Wall Street Plunderers," *FAIR*, November 30, 2018, https://fair.org/home/free-the-free-press-from-wall-street-plunderers/.
11. Eugene Humberto Pons, "Aggressive and Passive Propaganda: Cuba and the United States," University of Miami, Coral Gables, FL, December, 2008, www.researchgate.net/publication/254697299AggressiveandPassivePropagandaCubaandtheUnitedStates.
12. Interview of Arlin Albergy Loforte with the author, June 18, 2018.
13. Ibid.
14. Email correspondence between Heriberto Nicolás with the author, December 2018.
15. Ibid.
16. Interview of Arlin Albergy Loforte with the author, June 18, 2018.
17. Ibid.
18. Dave Sheinin and Karen DeYoung, "MLB, Cuban Baseball Federation Reach Agreement; Trump Administration Signals it has Issues with Deal," *Washington Post*, December 19, 2018, www.washingtonpost.com/sports/2018/12/19/mlb-cuban-baseball-federation-reach-agreement-that-will-eliminate-need-players-defect/?noredirect=on&utm_term=.68b2ee17c293.
19. Allie Malloy and Patrick Oppmann, "Cuban Baseball group Criticizes Trump Move to Cancel Player Deal," *CNN*, April 9, 2019, www.cnn.com/2019/04/08/politics/white-house-cuba-baseball/index.html.
20. Nato Green, "What If the American Media Covered Cuba Like a Normal Place?" Blog, *Los Angeles Review of Books*, May 13, 2018, http://blog.lareviewofbooks.org/essays/american-media-covered-cuba-like-normal-place/.
21. Ibid.
22. Ibid.
23. Ibid.
24. Ibid.
25. Azham Ahmad and Frances Robles, "Who is Manuel Díaz Canel-Bermuda, Cuba's New President?" *New York Times*, April 19, 2018, www.nytimes.com/2018/04/19/world/americas/miguel-diaz-canel-bermudez-cuba.html.
26. Gregory Shupak, *The Wrong Story—Palestine, Israel, and the Media* (New York: OR Books, 2018).
27. Referring to the seven-week Israel–Gaza conflict resulting in the deaths of thousands, mostly from Gaza.
28. Interview of Gregory Shupak with author, November 2018.
29. Ibid.
30. Ibid.
31. Ibid.
32. Ibid.
33. Ibid.

34. Ibid.
35. Ibid.
36. "The Gloves are Off," *Havana Times*, July 15, 2013, https://havanatimes.org/?p=96265.
37. "Integrated Country Strategy: Cuba," approved November 27, 2018, www.state.gov/documents/organization/284652.pdf.
38. Ibid.
39. For further examination, see Keith Bolender, *Cuba Under Siege: American Policy, the Revolution and Its People* (Basingstoke: Palgrave Macmillan, 2013).
40. "Integrated Country Strategy: Cuba."
41. The internet is expanding but so also is the packette—CDs full of news, sports and music from around the world that are brought from Miami to private Cubans to distribute.
42. Patrick Oppmann, "Cubans get Internet on Cellphones, But How Many Can Afford It?" *CNN*, December 6, 2018, www.cnn.com/2018/12/06/americas/cuba-cellphone-internet/index.html.
43. Ibid.
44. Ibid.
45. Ibid.
46. Alejandra García, "Fake News: A New Name for Old Practices," *Granma*, April 2, 2018, http://en.granma.cu/mundo/2018-04-02/fake-news-a-new-name-for-old-practices.
47. Ibid.
48. Corporate media is doing its share of fake news through the social media. Twitter posts report Trump lies with no clarification or judgment to its veracity. Simply sending it out gives it undeserved credence. Mix these ingredients together and you have a toxic recipe for an antidote to good journalism and truthful reporting. A prime example of how this results in destructive dishonesty is the tweeted headline from *CBS* on November 27, 2016: "Donald Trump: 'Millions' Voted Illegally for Hillary Clinton." No basis in fact, no research done but *CBS* put it out and by doing that gave it instant credibility, see Reed Richardson, "'Trump Says ...': The Journalistic Scourge of Echo-Chamber Headlines," *FAIR*, December 19, 2018, https://fair.org/home/trump-says-the-journalistic-scourge-of-echo-chamber-headlines.
49. Samanth Subramanian, "Inside the Macedonian Fake-News Complex," *Wired*, February 15, 2017, www.wired.com/2017/02/veles-macedonia-fake-news.
50. Ibid.
51. "CIA Presents a New False Video on Cuba, Through the UN Watch NGO," *Cuba-Network in Defense of Humanity: In Defense of the Truth and Plurality Information*, April 17, 2014, http://cuba-networkdefenseofhumanity.blogspot.com/2014/04/cia-presents-new-false-video-on-cuba.html.
52. "State Department's 'Cuba Internet Task Force' Exposed as One More Attack on Cuban Sovereignty," *International Committee*, https://theinternationalcommittee.org/state-departments-cuba-internet-task-force-exposed-as-one-more-attack-on-cuban-sovereignty/.

53. Email to author, March 2018.
54. "Secretly Created 'Cuban Twitter' to Stir Unrest and Undermine Government," *The Guardian*, April 3, 2014, www.theguardian.com/world/2014/apr/03/us-cuban-twitter-zunzuneo-stir-unrest.
55. Ibid.
56. Ibid.
57. Email interview with Josefina Vidal, March 2019.

Bibliography

Aguilar, Luis E. *Cuba 1933: Prologue to Revolution*. Ithaca, NY: Cornell University Press, 1972.

Alarcón de Quesada, Ricardo and Álvarez Sánchez, Miguel. *Blockade The United States Economic War Against Cuba*. Havana: Edítora Política, 2001.

Allard Jean-Guy and Golinger, Eva. *La agresión permanente USAID, NED y CIA*. Caracas: Colección Alfredo Maneiro Serie Testimonios, 2010.

August, Arnold. *Democracy in Cuba, and the 1997–98 Elections*. Havana: Canada-Cuba Distribution, Editorial Jose Marti, 1999.

Benjamin, Jules R. *The United States and the Origins of the Cuban Revolution An Empire of Liberty in an Age of National Liberation*. Princeton, NJ: Princeton University Press, 1990.

Bohning, Don. *The Castro Obsession U.S. Covert Operations Against Cuba 1959–1965*. Washington, DC: Potomac Books, 2005.

Bolender, Keith. *Voices From the Other Side: An Oral History of Terrorism Against Cuba*. London: Pluto Press, 2010.

Bolender, Keith. *Cuba Under Siege: American Policy, the Revolution and Its People*. Basingstoke: Palgrave Macmillan, 2013.

Bravo, Olga Miranda. *Cuba/USA Nacionalizaciones y Bloqueo*. Havana: Editorial de Ciencias Sociales, 1996.

Brown, Charles H. *The Correspondents' War: Journalists in the Spanish-American War*. New York: Charles Scribner's Sons, 1967.

Chomsky, Noam. *Failed States: The Abuse of Power and the Assault on Democracy*. New York: Metropolitan Books, 2006.

Chomsky, Aviva. *A History of the Cuban Revolution*. Malden, MA: Wiley-Blackwell, 2011.

Cluster, Dick and Hernandez, Rafael. *The History of Havana*. New York: Palgrave Macmillan, 2006.

Demanda del Pueblo Cubano Contra el Gobierno de Estados Unidos por los Daños Económicos Ocasionados a Cuba. La Habana: Editora Política, 2000.

DePalma, Anthony. *The Man Who Invented Fidel: Castro, Cuba, and Herbert L. Matthews of the New York Times*. New York: Public Affairs, 2006.

Erikson, Daniel P. *The Cuba Wars Fidel Castro, the United States and the Next Revolution*. New York: Bloomsbury Press, 2008.

Franklin, Jane. *Cuba and the United States: A Chronological History*. Melbourne: Ocean Press, 1997.

Gott, Richard. *Cuba: A New History*. London: Yale University Press, 2004.

Haney, Patrick J. and Vanderbush, Walt. *The Cuban Embargo: The Domestic Politics of an American Foreign Policy*. Pittsburgh, PA: University of Pittsburgh Press, 2005.

Herman, S. Edward and Chomsky, Noam. *Manufacturing Consent*. New York: Pantheon Books, 1988.

Kapcia, Antoni. *Cuba in Revolution: A History Since the Fifties*. London: Reaktion Books, 2008.

Kimber, Stephen. *What Lies Across the Water: The Real Story of the Cuban Five*. Winnipeg, MB: Fernwood Books, 2013.

Knightley, Phillip. *The First Casualty: From the Crimea to Vietnam: War Correspondent as Hero, Propagandist and Mythmaker*. London: Pan Books, 1989.

Lambie, George. *The Cuban Revolution in the 21st Century*. London: Pluto Press, 2010.

Pérez, Louis A. Jr. *Cuba Under the Platt Amendment 1902–1934*. Pittsburgh, PA: University of Pittsburgh Press, 1986.

Pérez, Louis A. Jr. *The War of 1898: The United States & Cuba in History & Historiography*. Chapel Hill, NC: University of North Carolina Press, 1998.

Pérez, Louis A. Jr. *Cuba Between Reform and Revolution*. New York: Oxford University Press, 2006.

Pérez, Louis A. Jr. *Cuba in the American Imagination Metaphor and the Imperial Ethos*. Chapel Hill, NC: University of North Carolina Press, 2008.

Pérez-Stable, Marifeli. *The Cuban Revolution Origins, Course, and Legacy*. New York: Oxford University Press, 1999.

Ramonet, Ignacio. *My Life Fidel Castro*. London: Allen Lane, 2007.

Reid-Henry, Simon. *Fidel and Che: A Revolutionary Friendship*. New York: Walker & Company, 2009.

Roman, Peter. *People's Power: Cuba's Experience with Representative Government*. Lanham, MD: Rowman & Littlefield, 2003.

Saney, Issac. *Cuba: A Revolution in Motion*. Nova Scotia: Fernwood Publishing, 2004.

Schoultz, Lars. *That Infernal Little Cuban Republic: The United States and the Cuban Revolution*. Chapel Hill, NC: University of North Carolina Press, 2009.

Schwab, Peter. *Cuba Confronting the U.S. Embargo*. New York: St. Martin's Griffin, 1999.

Smith, Wayne S. *The Closest of Enemies A Personal and Diplomatic Account of U.S.-Cuban Relations Since 1957*. New York: W.W. Norton & Company, 1987.

Spadoni, Paolo. *Failed Sanctions: Why the U.S. Embargo against Cuba Could Never Work*. Gainesville, FL: University Press of Florida, 2010.

Sweig, Julia A. *Cuba: What Everyone Needs to Know*. New York: Oxford University Press, 2009.

Weiner, Tim. *Legacy of Ashes: The History of the CIA*. New York: Anchor Books, 2007.

Zaldívar Diéguez, Andrés. *Blockade: The Longest Economic Siege in History*. Havana: Capitán San Luis Publishing House, 2007.

Index